Murderous Tommies

The Courts Martial Of Thirteen British Soldiers Executed For Murder During The First World War

Mark Dunning
Julian Putkowski

16

EasyRead Large

RHYW

Copyright Page from the Original Book

First published in Great Britain in 2012 by
Pen & Sword Military
An imprint of
Pen & Sword Books Ltd
47 Church Street
Barnsley
South Yorkshire
S70 2AS

ISBN 978 1 84884 626 5
eISBN 978 1 78337 852 4

A CIP catalogue record for this book is available from the British Library.

Typeset in 11pt Bembo by Mac Style, Beverley, East Yorkshire
Printed and bound in the UK by CPI Group (UK) Ltd, Croydon, CRO 4YY

Pen & Sword Books Ltd incorporates the imprints of Pen & Sword Aviation, Pen & Sword Maritime, Pen & Sword Military, Wharncliffe Local History, Pen & Sword Select, Pen & Sword Military Classics, Leo Cooper, Remember When, Seaforth Publishing and Frontline Publishing

For a complete list of Pen & Sword titles please contact
PEN & SWORD BOOKS LIMITED
47 Church Street, Barnsley, South Yorkshire, S70 2AS, England
E-mail: enquiries@pen-and-sword.co.uk
Website: www.pen-and-sword.co.uk

TABLE OF CONTENTS

Edited studio photo. 2nd Lieutenant John Paterson, wife Alice on his left.

Sources & Notes: Material for this book has been derived from a variety of sources that have been cited in prefatory acknowledgements, textual notes and bibliographical addenda. However, to economise on space and avoid repetition the following readily accessible reference works are unacknowledged in notes about individual personalities, specifically: the General Register Office Roll of Births, Marriages & Deaths; Medal Roll (The National Archives, Kew, series WO 329 Service Medal and Award Roll 1914-1918); *The Order of Battle of Divisions; Who's Who; Kelly's Directories;* British Army Lists and Indian Army Lists.

List of Illustrations

Photographs (2): Scene of Crime, apartment of Henriette Tremereal, No.4 rue Racine (Crown Copyright)

Extract: War Diary, CRE, 38th Division, 17-19 April 1918 (WO95/254, Crown Copyright)

Sketch: Murder of Lieutenant Lloyd, Section on parade (WO 71/640, Crown Copyright)

Sketch plan: Murder of Lieutenant Lloyd, Section on parade (WO 71/640, Crown Copyright)

Extract: War Diary, CRE, 38th Division (WO95/2547, Crown Copyright)

Map: Pont de Cologne/Coulogne; Coulogne; Halte St. Pierre; Duquenoy family house (inset) (WO 297/80, Crown Copyright)

Photograph: Second Lieutenant John Paterson and spouse (WO 339/111890, Crown Copyright)

Imperial No.2 revolver, 1915 model (Rudi, www.american-firearms.com)

Acknowledgements

The authors are grateful to everyone whose intellect, inspiration and understanding have been of assistance during the years it has taken to conduct the historical research and production of this book.

For unstinting support with information and advice the authors are indebted to Piet Chielens, Director of the In Flanders Field Museum; Dominiek Dendooven, Annick Vandenbilcke and colleagues at the Documentation Centre, Ieper. Special thanks are also due to Dr Diane Atkinson for her scholarly insights and editorial advice; Patrick Hughes for his generosity and Donna Smith for her professional brilliance in conjuring useable graphic images from scruffy sketch maps.

During the search for information about personalities, names and places, in alphabetical order, the following individuals have responded with much appreciated generosity and understanding: Geoff Bridger, Gill Crowhurst, Sean Godfrey, Roger Kelsey, Vic and Diane Piuk, Paul Reed, Mary Saunders, Julian Sykes, Mark Thomas and Phil Tomaselli.

For their assistance in resolving knotty medical problems, thanks are due to Dr Katherine Foxhall and Dr Geoffrey Miller. Professor Jean-Marc Berliere, Université de Bourgogne, provided valuable historical data about the French police. Herve Chabannes and colleagues of the Archives Ville, Le Havre assisted with newspaper and photographic research.

In the search for details about service records, William Spencer's patient response to sporadic enquiries and assistance from the ever helpful staff of the National Archives, Kew, has been especially valued. The authors also appreciate the courtesy and assistance with references and published material retrieved from distant shelves by the ill-remunerated staff of the Reading Room of the British Library, Euston, and the Newspaper Library at Colindale.

In assisting the authors to cope with Post-Traumatic Research Disorder and the rewriting of successive drafts, the love and support of Celia Coram and Amy Dunning has been absolutely indispensible. Feline auxiliaries, Blackie and Wisley have each made a contribution, for which they will certainly seek and receive appropriate epicurean reward.

Finally, the authors discreetly acknowledge the help received from descendants and relatives of the men cited in this book.

Copyright

has been made to trace individuals for permission to reproduce copyright material used in this publication but some remain elusive. We extend our apologies to anyone whose copyright this work unintentionally infringes, and request they contact us via the publishers so that we can respond appropriately.

M.D. & J.J.P.

List of Abbreviations

2/Lt: Second Lieutenant

2nd Cpl: Second Corporal (Royal Engineers)

A&SH: Argyll & Sutherland Highlanders

A/: Acting/(rank)

AA & QMG: Assistant Adjutant & Quartermaster General

Acad Inst: Academic Institution

ADC: Aide de Camp

Adjt: Adjutant

ANZAC: Australian and New Zealand Army Corps

APM: Assistant Provost Marshal

Army Cert Educ: Army Certificate of Education

ASC: Army Service Corps

Asst: Assistant

AWL: Absence without leave

b: Born

B.Litt: Bachelor of Literature

BA: Bachelor of Arts

BAO: Bachelor of Obstetrics

BCh: Bachelor of Chemistry

Bde: Brigade

Beds: Bedfordshire

BEF: British Expeditionary Force

Bn: Battalion

Brev: Brevet

Brig Gen: Brigadier General

CO: Commanding Officer

CSM: Company Sergeant Major

Cam: Cameron

Cam Hs: Cameron Highlanders

Capt: Captain

CCS: Casualty Clearing Station

Cem: Cemetery

ChB: Bachelor of Chemistry

CMO: Court/s Martial Officer

Co: County

Col: Colonel

Coll: College

Coy: Company

Cpl: Corporal

CSM: Company Sergeant Major

DAA & QMG: Deputy Assistant Adjutant and Quartermaster General

DAAG: Deputy Assistant Adjutant General

DCM: District Court Martial

Devons: Devonshire (Regiment)

Dir: Director

Disch: discharged

Div: Division/al

DJAG: Deputy Judge Advocate General

DL: Deputy Lieutenant of County

DLI: Durham Light Infantry

DOW: Died of wounds

DPH: Diploma in Public Health

Dvr: Driver

edn: Edition

educ: Educated

encl: Enclosed

enl: Enlisted

Intell: Intelligence

fn: Footnote

FMS: Free Malay States

FP1: Field Punishment No.1

FP2: Field Punishment No.2

FRCSI: Fellow of the Royal College of Surgeons in Ireland

Garr: Garrison

GCM: General Court Martial

Gen: General PM

Glam: Glamorganshire

GOC: General Officer, Commanding

Govt: Government

Hants: Hampshire (Regiment)

HLI: Highland Light Infantry

Hosp: Hospital

HQ: Headquarters

IBD: Infantry Base Depot

ibid: *ibidem,* in the same place

Inf: infantry

JP: Justice of the Peace

KIA: Killed in action

Km: Kilometre

KORL: King's Own Royal Lancaster (Regiment)

KOYLI: King's Own Yorkshire Light Infantry

KSLI: King's Shropshire Light Infantry

KSLI: King's Shropshire Light Infantry

L of C: Lines of Communication

L/Cpl: Lance Corporal

Lancs: Lancashire

LDS: Licentiate in Dental Surgery

Leins: Leinster (Regiment)

LLB: Bachelor of Law

LLM: Master of Law

LM: Licentiate in Medicine

LNL: Loyal North Lancashire Regiment

LRB: London Rifle Brigade

LRCP: Licentiate of the Royal College of Physicians

Lt: Lieutenant

Lt Col: Lieutenant Colonel

Maj: Major

Maj Gen: Major-General

MB: Headquarters

MBBS: Bachelor of Medicine, Bachelor of Surgery

MD: Doctor of Medicine

MFP: Military Foot Police

MG: Machine Gun

Middx: Middlesex

Mil: Military

Mil Att: Military Attaché

Mil Govnr: Military Governor

Mil Miss: Military Mission

Mil Sec: Military Secretary

MML: Manual of Military Law

MMP: Military Mounted Police

MP: Military Police

Ms: Manuscript

Mtd: Mounted

N Fus: Northumberland Fusiliers

NOK: Next of kin

Norfolks: Norfolk (Regiment)

Northants: Northamptonshire (Regiment)

NOT: Newcastle-on-Tyne (Yeomanry)

OC: Officer Commanding

op cit: *opus citatum,* previously cited

Orgn: Organisation

OTC: Officer Training Corps

Ox LI: Oxfordshire Light Infantry

Pa: Pennsylvania

PM: Provost Marshal

Pte: Private

r: resident

R Fus: Royal Fusiliers

R Innis Fus: Royal Inniskilling Fusiliers

R Irish Fus: Royal Irish Fusiliers

R Irish Rifs: Royal Irish Rifles

RA: Royal Artillery

RAMC: Royal Army Medical Corps

RASC: Royal Army Service Corps

RCS: Royal College of Surgeons

RE: Royal Engineers

RM Sch: Royal Military School

RW Kents: Royal West Kent (Regiment)

RWF: Royal Welsh Fusiliers

Regt: Regiment

res: resident, residence

Res of Offs: Reserve of Officers

retd: retired

RFA: Royal Field Artillery

RHA: Royal Horse Artillery

Rifs: Rifles

RM: Royal Marine/s

RND: Royal Naval Division

RNVR: Royal Naval Volunteer Reserve

RNWMP: Royal North West Mounted Police

RQMS: Regimental Quartermaster Sergeant

RUI: Royal University of Ireland

S: South

Sco Rifs: Scottish Rifles

Seaforths: Seaforth Highlanders

sec: Sections(s)

Sig: Signal

Sig: Signals/Signaller

SMLE: Short Magazine Lee-Enfield (rifle)

Spr: Sapper

SR: Special Reserve/Reservist

SWB: South Wales Borderers

T or TA: Territorial Army

T/: Temporary (military rank)

TNA: The National Archives, Kew

Univ: University

Vols: Volunteers

W: West

WAFF: West African Field Force

Warw: Warwickshire

W'land & C'land: Westmorland and Cumberland

WO: War Office

Yeo: Yeomanry

Introduction: Fearful Symmetry

Soldiers murder to order. During the First World War hundreds of thousands of soldiers were urged to slaughter the enemy and got congratulated for their butchery. British soldiers who objected or jibbed at the prospect of discharging their soldierly duties were charged with military crimes and faced being gunned down by a firing squad.

While hostilities were in progress, British Army courts martial condemned hundreds of men to death for various offences. Confirming officers approved the execution of over 300 convicted deserters, cowards, sleepy-eyed sentries, a few men who thumped their NCOs and a couple of dozen murderers. Much has been written about the soldiers executed for military offences but until now very little has been written about the murderers or their victims. The postponement was prolonged by official secrecy and somewhat paradoxically by the campaign to secure posthumous pardons for soldiers executed by the British Army.

The Army condemned soldiers to death in order to intimidate the rank and file 'for the sake of example', to maintain military discipline. The procedure was quite straightforward: after they had been tried and sentenced to death, all the condemned men were executed by firing squad and ritually damned. Their identities, crimes and punishment were communicated to the rest of the Army via Routine Orders; the executed men's next of kin were sent a brutally frank letter from the War Office; payment of dependants' allowances was stopped and the deceased soldiers' military decorations were generally withdrawn.

Thereafter, the executed men were officially 'unpersoned'; the Army and the War Office embargoed disclosure of details about their cases, including written proceedings of the capital courts martial. This was accomplished via official regulations decreeing that copies of the courts martial proceedings could only be disclosed to the accused, and not his family or legal representatives. The papers were kept under lock and key by the Judge Advocate General's office and when transferred to the Public Records Office, affixed to the cover of each case file lodged in official archives was a label stating that the contents had to remain secret for 100 years.

Public interest in the capital courts martial conducted by the British Army during the First World War continued for a good while after the fighting ended but political debate about the wartime executions was stifled by a couple of official committees.

In 1919 Lloyd George's administration responded to persistent criticism about the Army's use of the death penalty by convening a committee of enquiry about the conduct and regulation of courts martial, in both peace and war. Committee members were carefully vetted, with an illusion of balance being created via the inclusion of a token maverick, Horatio Bottomley MP, the bombastic editor of *John Bull,* an ultrapatriotic tabloid magazine. However, Lord Justice Charles Darling, who chaired the enquiry, blocked Bottomley's efforts to examine individual cases and ensured that the majority of the committee members subscribed to an emollient report that broadly endorsed the existing military-judicial process.

Darling's dissimulation was followed in 1920 by Lord Southborough's committee of enquiry, which was charged with reviewing the incidence and treatment of shell shock. When the Southborough committee report was finally published in 1922, it included some palliative observations about shell shock and cowardice but like the Darling committee, Southborough's neglected to examine individual cases of traumatized soldiers who had been executed for cowardice.

Thereafter, debate focussed on abolition. At Westminster, Ernest Thurtle MP repeatedly called for repeal of the death penalty for military offences during the 1920s. By 1929, his dogged campaign attracted sufficient parliamentary support to amend the Annual Army Act. However, the death sentence was retained for soldiers convicted of treachery, mutiny and murder, and no provision was made to lift the embargo on public disclosure of written proceedings of the wartime courts martial. The secret files avoided incineration when a mass of War Office personnel records archived in London were blitzed during 1940 and remained undisturbed until the early 1980s, when their contents were reviewed by Judge Anthony Babington.

As part of the research for a book he intended to write about the British Army's capital courts martial, Anthony Babington became the first person to be granted permission to examine written proceedings of all the capital courts martial cases. However, as a condition of access, he was forbidden to use direct quotations from the papers or name the defendants in his book, and the sheer number of judicial killings precluded exploration in depth of the context in which offences had been committed. Even so, Babington's distinguished war service and legal status lent authority to serious doubts expressed about the unfairness of the military judicial process in his book, *For the Sake of Example.*[1]

The identification of the men who were executed was a project separately undertaken by Julian Sykes, latterly with the assistance of Julian Putkowski. Their research findings were incorporated in *Shot at Dawn,* and prefaced by a demand for the posthumous exoneration of all the soldiers and military labourers who had been executed under the authority of the British Army Act during and immediately after the First World War. *Shot at Dawn* asserted that the condemned men had not deserved their fate and that their relatives should not continue to be burdened by the associated disgrace. Denied access to the still classified written proceedings, the book drew on publicly available sources to support the contention that officers responsible for the military administration and adjudication of capital courts martial were unfair. It maintained that there was evidence of social bias in the composition of the courts and the conduct of the trials revealed officers frequently failed to make due allowance for defendants' ill health, legal inexperience, lack of education and limited powers of self-advocacy. *Shot at Dawn* maintained that confirmation of death sentences was also flawed by the addition of information prejudicial to the defence, including hearsay evidence that could not be independently verified by those to whom confirming officers termed 'worthless men'. Putkowski and Sykes declared that these shortcomings were so common that it damned all the capital courts martial cases – including those in which defendants had been executed for murder.[2]

At first, neither *For the Sake of Example* nor *Shot at Dawn* attracted much controversy because it had been very many decades since the First World War capital courts martial featured in the mass media. While the war had been in progress a combination of state censorship and editorial reticence combined to prevent dissemination of information about the capital cases. After hostilities ceased the Imperial War Graves Commission maintained secrecy about the names of all the executed men and ensured that their gravestones were indistinguishable from those erected for military personnel who had perished from other causes.

As far as the homicide cases were concerned, outside their immediate communities, expressions of sympathy for the murder victims' families were minimal and short-lived, and killers' relatives and friends had little incentive to invite publicity. Other than a few anecdotal references, there was therefore not a big enough stock of readily accessible 'human interest' material to excite the attention of feature editors or publishers.

After 1939, newspaper coverage of British military murder cases was mostly confined to reports about contemporary courts martial. After 1953, no more British soldiers were court-martialled and executed for murder, and the last judicial hanging of a man convicted by a British criminal court was carried out in 1964. During the mid-1970s, William Moore's book *The Thin Yellow Line* and research conducted by Douglas Gill and Gloden Dallas drew attention to the British Army's use of the death penalty during the First World War but eschewed reference to soldiers who had been executed for murder.[3]

However, the naming of names in *Shot at Dawn* nullified official secrecy about the identities of the executed men, including the murderers, and the government agreed to declassify the written proceedings. The declassification permitted independent scrutiny, and open debate ensued about the military-judicial process and the British Army's deployment of firing squads during the First World War.

Many families were incensed about the unfair manner in which their menfolk had been treated and began to demand posthumous pardons for those who had been shot for military offences. Friends and sympathizers established the *Shot at Dawn* support campaign and Andrew Mackinlay MP persistently sought to persuade Conservative and Labour governments to review the cases of the 306 soldiers who had been executed for military offences other than mutiny or murder.

Though a minority argued for the inclusion of soldiers who had been executed for murder or mutiny, the vast majority of campaigners and Andrew Mackinlay felt otherwise. The latter pointed out that mutiny and murder had been excluded from the schedule of capital offences that were abolished during the 1920s. It was generally accepted that had a contemporary civilian court instead of a court martial found them guilty, the convicted men were still liable to have been executed, albeit by hanging.

Critics, labouring under the mistaken impression that the campaign supported exoneration of the convicted murderers, repeatedly quizzed Mackinlay and *Shot at Dawn* campaigners. The MP, the families of soldiers who had been executed for military offences and their supporters all refuted the allegation, insisting their efforts were confined to securing pardons for those who had been shot for cowardice and desertion but not murder.[4]

The *Shot at Dawn* campaign attracted lots of sympathetic media coverage but Conservative historians, retired military officers and an assortment of Whitehall 'shadow warriors' persisted in drawing attention to the murder cases. The latter included Cathryn Corns and Colonel John Hughes-Wilson, whose book *Blindfold and Alone* devoted a few pages to the murder cases.[5] As part of their refutation of the legal reservations that were initially expressed by Judge Anthony Babington and criticisms ventilated in *Shot at Dawn,* Corns and Hughes-Wilson condemned of any kind of posthumous review out of hand. With reference to half a dozen murder trials cited in their book, invoking the *Manual of Military Law,* Corns and Hughes-Wilson maintained that it was, 'Up to the accused to prove why the charge of murder was not justified.'[6] They added:

> There seems little doubt that they received a fair trial and were guilty of the offence as charged. Had they been civilians they would undoubtedly have hanged, the standard penalty for military murderers at the time ... to retrospectively change legally binding decisions taken by a competent military authority over eighty years ago would set an undesirable precedent for every case of a civilian hanged for murder at the time.[7]

Although drawing on material from the declassified written proceedings, arguments advanced in *Blindfold and Alone* largely repeated points that had already been made by other supporters of the status quo. For its part, the *Shot at Dawn* campaign continued to disavow interest in the murder cases and concentrated on securing sympathetic media coverage and further support for the enactment of posthumous pardons. The news media's interest in cases of soldiers executed for cowardice or desertion was aided by campaigners' assiduous leafleting, lobbying and public meetings, and abetted by Mackinlay's legislative endeavours.

The campaign also secured support overseas. In New Zealand, Bob Cotton, a journalist working for the *Christchurch Star* drew attention to the Antipodean soldiers who had been executed. John Hipkin, the retired English teacher who founded the *Shot at Dawn* campaign, networked in Canada with the relatives of men who had been executed. John McGeehan and Peter Mulvany worked independently to draw attention to the cases of the Irish soldiers who had been executed, aided in their efforts by the historical research of Dr Gerry Oram. These individuals and a mass of other campaigners elicited a positive formal response from the governments of New Zealand, Canada and the Republic of Ireland. In Britain, after sixteen years of campaigning, a legal challenge by the daughter of Private Harry Farr (executed in 1916) and the appointment of Des Browne, a sympathetic Minister of Defence, forced a change in Whitehall's established no-pardons policy.

In 2006, the Blair government used the Annual Army Act debate to inaugurate a generic conditional pardon for all military personnel who had been executed by the British Army during the First World War. Though dubbed a 'blanket' pardon by the media, in two respects the official exoneration was very evidently a partial measure.

Firstly, the government confined its acknowledgement to the undeserving nature of the punishment of men it re-designated as 'victims of war' and refused to revoke or quash their convictions. Thereafter, to almost all the capital courts martial dossiers of men executed during the First World War under the provisions of the British Army Act there was attached a conditional pardon. Signed by the Secretary of State for Defence, it states that the soldier has been pardoned under sec.359 of the Armed Forces Act 2006, 'As recognition that he was one of many victims of the First World War and that execution was not a fate that he deserved.' Secondly, the conditional pardon excluded executed murderers.

A determined handful of families continue to press for a royal pardon and the restitution of campaign medals. But in spite of emotive polemic about the issue becoming, 'The most contentious subject casting an even darker shadow over Britain's memory of the First World War,' the intensity and scale of media interest about the posthumous exonerations has declined since 2006.[8] As a consequence, we anticipate the murder cases may now be critically appraised without our contribution becoming entangled in a skein of heated, inconclusive arguments about rewriting history.[9]

The thirteen cases featured in this work are a discrete group, comprising men who were born, educated and enlisted in Great Britain, and who were tried and executed in France or Flanders while hostilities were in progress. Though no less worthy of critical examination, the remaining ten wartime murder cases involved military personnel from South Africa, Canada, the Caribbean and China. Some of the latter were court-martialled and executed in other theatres of operations and their trials were complicated by non-judicial factors, including institutional racism. Their exclusion is informed by the need for further primary research, particularly with reference to cases in which the defendants were Chinese military labourers.

In many respects, knowledge about the thirteen men and their victims is also incomplete and likely to remain so because much official data has been destroyed. During the Second World War many official records were incinerated by Luftwaffe and Allied air raids and other material has been lost or accidentally and sometimes deliberately erased. The contents of courts martial dossiers are indispensible for reconstructing a general account of relationships and events but tend to reveal tantalisingly little about the context in which a murder was committed. The reliability of witness testimony in written proceedings often demands greater critical scrutiny than was exercised by the panel of officers sitting in judgement. The written proceedings invariably omit questions posed in cross-examination; the case for the defence was indifferently recorded, and insubstantial notes were often substituted for a verbatim statement by a Prisoners' Friend. Nothing was ever recorded about the deliberations and verdict of the President and Members of the Court, though the written notes made by confirming officers can be quite revealing about the author's moral perspectives as well as affirming their belief in the value of executions for the sake of example.

The majority of officers instructed to hear the cases and all the commanders who confirmed the death sentences were pre-war professionals and resolute authoritarians. Although they failed to endorse every death sentence awarded by courts martial convened while fighting was in progress on the Western Front, clemency was never extended to perpetrators sentenced to death for murder.[10] Since criminal courts sentenced convicted murderers to be hanged and because offences committed by military personnel on active service overseas were commonly punished more harshly than they may have been in peacetime, the confirming officers disinclination to heed recommendations to mercy and mitigating factors appears unexceptional.[11] The Army Act and official statistics confirm the latter point but there are clear and obvious differences between the wartime courts martial and contemporary trials in criminal courts.

As Judge Babington pointed out, generally many of the military officers staffing courts martial lacked legal experience and made scant allowance for a defendant's mental distress. Most of the soldiers charged with murder were provided with a Prisoner's Friend, who was usually a qualified barrister or lawyer. However, the latter had comparatively little time in which to prepare a defence and the Judge Advocate General's staff was sometimes less than rigorous in checking witnesses' depositions, even though the *Manual of Military Law* explicitly stated:

> There is not, in the ordinary sense of the word, any appeal from the decision of a court martial.[12]

If it is concluded that these murderers were accorded a less than adequate hearing, treated unjustly or punished unfairly then there may be grounds for reviewing their sentences. Bearing in mind the conditional pardons already granted to men executed for military offences and exercising a measure of consistency, it may be tempting to entertain the notion that these murderers should also benefit from a measure of historical redress – if not as victims of the First World War then perhaps as victims of British military injustice. Comforting though such an unlikely accommodation might at first appear, and notwithstanding the unprecedented success that rewarded the *Shot at Dawn* campaign, there appears little prospect of securing a review, much less belated exoneration for a Tommy who murdered his comrade. Aside from institutional opposition by the military and

Whitehall shadow warriors, in secular twenty-first century Britain, the mark of Cain endures.

Lifting the shroud of secrecy exposes not only the killers but also their victims and the plight of the bereaved. The latter's anguish and bewilderment is well exemplified by an unpunctuated letter drafted by Mary, the Irish wife of Sapper William Damper. Responding to an official notification disclosing the manner in which her English-born husband had perished, from their home in Cork she wrote:

> It is with horror I read your message to me this day Monday 9th of October that my husband died of wounds wilfully inflicted by a comrade on September 2nd 1916 [.] Could you give me any information why he did it or what country did he belong to [?] it is two terrible to think a comrade killed him [.] the men here loved him the man that killed my fond husband and I would ask no one kill if I could find him [.] any more information you might get I would be glad to hear from you [.][13]

In the file containing Sapper Damper's record of service, with Mary's grief-stricken correspondence there nestles a copy of the report of the court of enquiry into his death. There is no indication that she ever read the contents or got to find out any more details about the murder than the family of the soldier who carried out the deed.

It is open to debate whether full disclosure would have allayed her grief or relieved the suffering experienced by the killer's family. After all, untimely bereavement was a common experience for many working class households during the First World War. However, from details that emerge in the body of this book the Army's disinclination to declassify capital courts martial dossiers may be attributed to fear of public criticism about the arraignment, conviction and execution of any Tommy who killed either a fellow soldier or a French civilian during the First World War.

M.D. & J.J.P.

CHAPTER 1

Double Indemnity

Company Sergeant Major Hughie Hayes, 2nd Battalion Welsh Regiment was shot on 20 January 1915 and succumbed to his injuries the following day. The Bethune Town Cemetery register attributes his death to 'accidental wounds'. However, two of his fellow soldiers were subsequently tried and found guilty of having murdered the NCO.[1] The written proceedings of their trial have not survived but understanding how Hayes came to be killed is, in some respects, quite straightforward.

The rank and file have always had to hand the means to kill oppressive NCOs or officers but the survival of military martinets owed much to their victims' stoicism, deference to authority and the threat of draconian punishments. Even so, when harassment was potentially life threatening, some British soldiers secured summary relief by killing their tormentors.

If murderers were careless about avoiding detection or indifferent about the consequences their fate was sealed by court martial, though a contemporary narrative of the offence and trial rarely emerged. Formal announcements of the verdict and sentence via Army routine orders never involved disclosure of more than the barest details about the offence and nothing whatsoever about the condemned men's motives.

In this case the written proceedings of a court martial are unavailable so it is quite difficult to establish a wholly reliable account of what happened. However, non-judicial sources, including personal correspondence and anecdotal evidence from memoirs, provide insights and perspectives about events that are wholly ignored, marginalized or erased from official records.

An account of the killing of Company Sergeant Hughie Hayes was originally written down on 23 May 1915 in the personal diary of Robert Graves, and reproduced in his celebrated war memoir, *Goodbye to All That.* About the killers, whom he understood to be 'two young miners, in another company', Graves wrote:

> Their sergeant ... had a down on them and gave them all the most dirty and dangerous jobs. When they were in billets he crimed them for things they hadn't done; so they decided to kill him. Later they reported at Battalion Orderly Room and asked to see the Adjutant. This was irregular, because a private is not allowed to speak to an officer without an NCO of his own company to act as go-between. The Adjutant happened to see them and said: 'Well, what is it you want?' Smartly slapping the small-of-the-butt of their sloped rifles, they said: 'We've come to report,

> sir, that we are very sorry but we've shot our company sergeant-major.'
>
> The Adjutant said: 'Good heavens, how did that happen?'
>
> 'It was an accident, Sir.'
>
> 'What do you mean you damn fools? Did you mistake him for a spy?'
>
> 'No, Sir, we mistook him for our platoon sergeant.'[2]

The anecdote briefly chronicled an event that had occurred several weeks before Graves was temporarily attached to the battalion, and it retains a whiff of the kind of post-prandial yarn that would typically have enlivened a convivial supper in the officers' mess.[3] However, the pretext for the tragic killing was quite accurate and Hayes was certainly not the murderers' intended victim.

The homicide to which Graves referred was committed during the evening of 20 January by 41-yearold Private William Price, a collier from Pontypridd, Glamorganshire, whose enlistment and service with the 2nd Battalion, Welsh Regiment had commenced in January 1891.[4] Very little is known about his military career but Price's disciplinary record was decidedly patchy, though he never committed an offence serious enough to have him dismissed from the Army.

During July 1892 he was punished with a spell of twenty-eight days' detention for 'Breaking out of barracks' and on 22 August 1892, for 'Striking a superior officer' he was imprisoned for 167 days' service. On the expiry of his sentence in early March 1893, Price was shipped out to India with the battalion.

His behaviour improved for a while but on 5 May 1899 he forfeited his good conduct pay and was tried by District Court Martial for using 'Insubordinate language' and jailed for forty-two days. While stationed at Dagshai Subathu in the Simla Hills, Price was again tried by District Court Martial on 8 July 1902 and imprisoned for fifty-six days for 'Drunkenness'. After completing his sentence, Price was repatriated to the United Kingdom and discharged after having completed twelve years' service. He returned to Pontypridd and may have resumed his job as a coal miner but there is some evidence that by 1911 Price was eking out a living as a rag collector.[5]

The second soldier involved in the murder was Private Richard Morgan from Mountain Ash, Glamorganshire, who declared that he was seventeen years old when he enlisted at Pontypridd with the Militia (3rd Battalion, Welsh Regiment) in May 1898. Two years later, the entire battalion, including Morgan, volunteered to go on active service overseas and fight the Boers in South Africa, where it remained until March 1902 before returning to Wales. Morgan went back to Mountain Ash, resumed work in a local colliery, got married and became a father.[6]

When war broke out, Morgan and Price rejoined the Army, though whether as Kitchener volunteers or for other reasons remains unclear. They were sent to Flanders as reinforcements on 30 November 1914 and joined the 2nd Battalion, Welsh Regiment, in Outtersteene, where it was recuperating after having suffered very heavy casualties.[7] Three weeks later, the battalion was marched to Merville and went into action at Festubert, taking part in an abortive attempt to regain lost trenches that ended with the battalion suffering further heavy losses. On Christmas Day, instead of joining in the truce that was being generally celebrated elsewhere, the battalion mounted a raid across no-man's-land that was officially recorded as, 'A gallant effort for which the officers, C.S.M. Hayes and No.10954 Pte. Hogan received special praise.'[8]

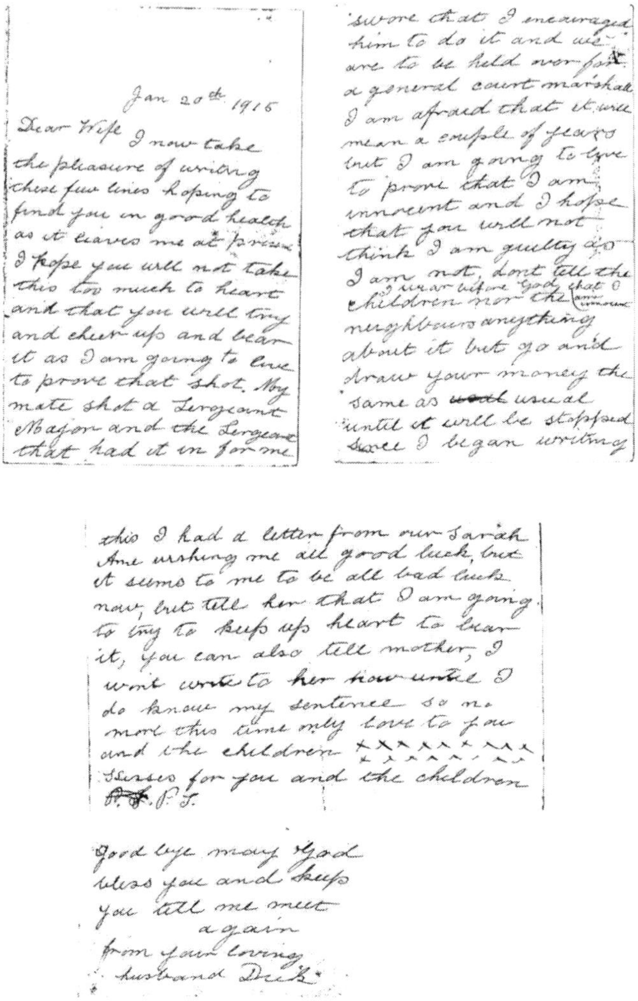

Jan 20th 1916

Dear Wife I now take the pleasure of writing these few lines hoping to find you in good health as it leaves me at present. I hope you will not take this too much to heart and that you will try and cheer up and bear it as I am going to live to prove that shot. My mate shot a Sergeant Major and the Sergeant that had it in for me swore that I encouraged him to do it and we are to be held now for a general court marshall I am afraid that it will mean a couple of years but I am going to live to prove that I am innocent and I hope that you will not think I am guilty for I am not, dont tell the I swear before God that I am innocent children nor the neighbours anything about it but go and draw your money the same as usual until it will be stopped Since I began writing this I had a letter from our Sarah Ane wishing me all good luck, but it seems to me to be all bad luck now, but tell her that I am going to try to keep up heart to bear it, you can also tell mother, I wont write to her now until I do know my sentence so no more this time only love to you and the children xxxxxxxx xxxxxxx kisses for you and the children R.J.P.T.

Good bye may God bless you and keep you till we meet again from your loving husband Dick

Conditions in the freezing trenches were appalling, as Captain Hubert Rees noted:

> The weather was atrocious, and the condition of the actual trenches worse than anything I have seen. On one occasion it took me two hours to go along 150 yards of trench and return. In many places the mud and water were nearly waist deep and the men perched on mud islands.[9]

After being relieved on 8 January the battalion enjoyed four days' rest, thawing out in Bethune before again being thrown into the front line at Givenchy, where the battalion continued to be threatened by hypothermia and frostbite as well as bombardment by enemy *minenwerfers.* Although they had only experienced five weeks at the front, under such circumstances Privates Price and Morgan and probably a good many of their comrades may be excused for seeking solace in alcohol.

The NCO whom Price intended to kill remains unknown but was most likely to have been a platoon sergeant and Private Morgan denied responsibility for mortally wounding Hayes. A few hours after the shooting, Morgan wrote a letter home in which he explained what had happened:

> Dear Wife,
>
> I now take the pleasure of writing these few lines hoping to find you in good health as it leaves me at present. I hope you will not take this too much to heart and that you will try and cheer up and bear it as I am going to hve [sic] to prove that shot. My mate shot a Sergeant Major and the sergeant that had it in for me swore that I encouraged him to do it and we are to be held over for a general court martiall [sic]. I am afraid that it will mean a couple of years but I am going to hve [sic] to prove that I am innocent and I hope that you will not think I am guilty as I am

> not I swear before God that I am innocent, don't tell the children nor the neighbours anything about it but go and draw your money the same as usual until it will be stopped. since I began writing this I had a letter from our Sarah Anne wishing me all good luck, but it seems to me to be all bad luck now, but tell her that I am going to try to keep up heart to bear it, you can also tell mother, I won't write to her now until I do know my sentence so no more this time only love to you and the children.

xxxxxxxxx

PS Goodbye may God bless you and keep you till we meet again

xxxxxxxx[10]

On 28 January the report of a court of enquiry was forwarded to 1st Corps Headquarters and a general court martial assembled to hear the case in Lillers at 10.00am on Saturday 6 February.[11] The President was Brigadier General Henry Cecil Lowther and the rest of the court was provided by 1st Division; Captain Archer Lyttleton, Welsh Regiment, conducted the prosecution but the identity of the Prisoner's Friend, if one was assigned to assist the two accused soldiers, eludes detection.[12]

The condemned men were executed simultaneously on 15 February. In memoirs that drew heavily on correspondence with his wife, Rev Harry Blackburne, the chaplain attached to 3rd Brigade recorded his own role in providing spiritual comfort to Morgan and Price:

> I have been with them frequently before the sentence was passed; now I must go and be with them to the end. Thank God, it is all over! We read together the story of the Prodigal Son and prayed, and then the sentence was carried out.[13]

Robert Graves' second-hand account of the double execution was more melodramatic:

> They were both shot by a firing squad of their own company against the wall of a convent in Bethune. Their last words were the battalion rallying-cry: 'Stick it, the Welsh!' The French military governor was present at the execution and made a little speech saying how gloriously British soldiers can die.[14]

Before 1917 the Army candidly notified the next of kin about the reason why a soldier had been executed but Richard Morgan's widow seems to have followed her husband's entreaty and did not broadcast details about her husband's death. However, Richard's parents responded to news of their son's death by directing awkward questions at soldiers who were serving with the battalion.[15]

At the end of April they received an unsolicited letter from Private Thomas Day. Though he may have been privy to a more harrowing version of events, Day's communication balanced candour with compassion:

> Having been talking to Oswald Jones, he told me you had been inquiring about your son Dick's death and that he did not know how to explain it to you, so I am taking the liberty of doing so myself, being that your son was a friend of mine there is no doubt that it all happened in drink and he happened to be in rather bad company at the time, we had the court martial read out to us on the 15th Feb, and if it is any comfort to you, I may tell you that he had no actual hand in committing the deed, Dick happened to be in company with a man named Price, he was the man that did the deed, and Dick was sentenced only for aiding and abetting, so you have the consolation of knowing that his crime was not so bad as you thought, with regards to his death I was speaking to man that helped to bury him, he told me that he died like an hero and never turned an hair, and only said that they were shooting an innocent man, please accept my deep sympathy in your great trouble it affected we Miskin Boys very much at the time it occurred, I hope you will not think me impudent in writing to explain to you unasked....[16]

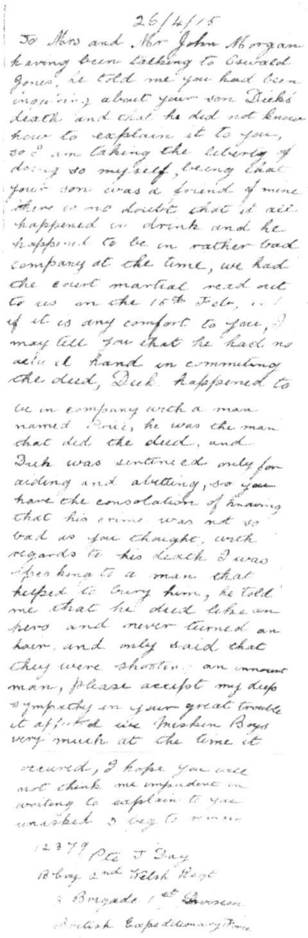

26/4/15
To Mrs and Mr John Morgan
having been talking to Oswald Jones, he told me you had been inquiring about your son Dick's death and that he did not know how to explain it to you, so I am taking the liberty of doing so myself, being that your son was a friend of mine there is no doubt that it all happened in drink and he happened to be in rather bad company at the time, we had the court martial read out to us on the 18th Feb, and if it is any comfort to you, I may tell you that he had no actual hand in commiting the deed, Dick happened to be in company with a man named [illegible], he was the man that did the deed, and Dick was sentenced only for aiding and abetting, so you have the consolation of knowing that his crime was not so bad as you thought, with regards to his death I was speaking to a man that helped to bury him, he told me that he died like an hero and never turned an hair, and only said that they were shooting an innocent man, please accept my deep sympathy in your great trouble it affected we Miskin Boys very much at the time it occured, I hope you will not think me impudent in writing to explain to you unasked I beg to remain

12379 Pte J Day
B Coy 2nd Welsh Regt
3 Brigade 1st Division
British Expeditionary Force

Further weight was added to Richard Morgan's disavowal of responsibility for killing Company Sergeant Major Hayes via a letter to the Morgan family from Private Rees Bevan, another of the 'Miskin Boys' who was unhappy about the parents' distress. Bevan wrote:

> I hope you don't think bad of him as it was not him that fired the shot only he was with the fellow that did. Dick met his death like an hero he said, I know I have got to die but you are

> shooting an innocent man and he died without a quiver poor chap.

His letter concluded on a speculative note, 'I am sorry to hear that someone has been spouting about it at home I suppose it is someone that don't know nothing about it.'[17] The Judge Advocate General and the War Office staff who were responsible for maintaining courts martial records also shared ignorance about what happened to Morgan and Price. It appears that the written proceedings and most unusually all routine reports vanished and as a consequence their cases simply do not figure in the Judge Advocate's register of cases or published official statistics.

Without further corroboration it is impossible to determine whether William Price acted out of drunken malice and had been in some way encouraged to commit murder or as Day and Bevan concurred, Richard Morgan had simply been damned because of the company he kept. As far as the *Manual of Military Law* was concerned, in order to avoid being found guilty of murder Morgan would have had to prove that he had done his utmost to prevent Price pulling the trigger.

For his part, Private Price may have felt that the sergeant's constant nagging and the burden of additional fatigues was as life-threatening as enemy fire and pleaded that alcohol had sapped his self-control. If so, many other soldiers might have sympathized with his plight but it was not a defence that would have impressed a contemporary judge and jury, let alone a gathering of officers committed to snuffing out the slightest glimmer of discontent by the rank and file.

CHAPTER 2

Alec Has Done It

On 22 April 1915 the German Army released massive clouds of chlorine gas that billowed across the front lines, breaching the defensive perimeter around the Belgian city of Ypres. As part of the British military response to the ensuing crisis, the Royal Flying Corps developed more airfields and improved facilities in which to accommodate and maintain extra aeroplanes. In the vicinity of Bailleul, flimsy canvas aircraft hangars were replaced with more robust wood and metal structures. The project involved a small groups of NCOs, craftsmen from the 20th Fortress Company, Royal Engineers being redeployed to act as managers and site foremen, supervising construction and assembly work that was carried out by locally hired civilian labour.[1]

The arrangement suited the Army because fighting troops did not have to be diverted to carry out labouring work and it was a welcome assignment for sappers already billeted in Bailleul. The latter included some who had been residing in the town since February, like Acting Corporal Alexander Chisholm and half a dozen of his comrades residing at the Estaminet du Pelican, in the Rue des Capucins. Their congenial lodgings were within easy walking distance of the hangars but appreciation of their 'cushy number' was soured by mutual antipathy that developed between Chisholm and one of his fellow NCOs, Lance Corporal Robert Lewis.

Alexander (Alec) Chisholm, a 32-year-old Tynesider from Newcastle, was a professional soldier who had been a railway steam engine fitter before enlisting with the Royal Engineers.[2] Robert Lewis, a 42-year-old from Whitchurch, Glamorganshire, was a highly skilled carpenter, latterly employed working on railway wagons.[3] Over several weeks, what started as tetchiness between the two men matured into undisguised mutual hostility, with Lewis repeatedly undermining Chisholm's authority. Though he was militarily subordinate, Lewis had a good deal more experience of construction work and used every opportunity to criticize Chisholm for being incompetent.

The aircraft hangars that the sappers were assembling consisted of large sheds made of wood, corrugated iron and canvas, built around a wooden sub-frame that was reinforced with steel angles or 'iron knees'. It was not high precision work but Chisholm made an error when procuring the iron knees. On delivery, the items turned out to be the wrong size for the job in hand, which Lewis interpreted as further evidence of Chisholm's ineptitude. Chisholm threatened to file a disciplinary charge against Lewis but the latter retaliated in kind.

Lewis had noticed for some time that some of the French labourers finished their day's work and went home suspiciously early. He was well aware that whether construction work involved hourly-rated labour or 'job and knock' piecework, sub-contracting offered a variety of opportunities for fraud. Lewis felt convinced that Chisholm was engaged in false accounting. The nature and scale of the alleged corruption was never fully exposed but it may have involved Chisholm accepting bribes, perhaps pocketing money in return for approving payment for work that was incomplete, under-paying workers or falsely inflating their hours of work. Even if Lewis was unable to produce evidence, the allegation would still have proved damaging for Chisholm.

Bailleul airfield, hangars and aircraft, 1917.

Matters finally came to a head on 4 May 1915, shortly after orders arrived from Headquarters, 3rd Corps, posting the men at the Pelican across the border to Nieppe, closer to the firing line. No official explanation was furnished but Lewis convinced himself that

Chisholm was somehow personally responsible for the move, and freely aired his suspicions to his fellow sappers.[4] At 12.50pm, the sappers' kit was loaded onto a horse-drawn General Service wagon, parked on the opposite side of the street to the *estaminet.* Chisholm went into the bar, chatted with the other sappers, and sat down at a table with Lewis, Second Corporal Thomas Freeman, and Sapper Norman Griffiths. It was an unwise move because Lewis was in a belligerent mood, so Chisholm stood up and went out into the street, to be followed shortly afterwards by the other sappers.[5]

The latter were still grumbling about the movement order when a rifle shot rang out. Lewis staggered and then toppled over onto the road, shrieking in agony. Pandemonium ensued. Some went to aid the wounded man, who was writhing in agony, moaning and cursing; others promptly seized Chisholm, who had been standing beside the wagon. Before marching him off to the guardroom, Corporal Freeman demanded to know why he had opened fire but Chisholm said nothing.[6]

Bailleul, Rue des Capucins.

Lewis remained conscious for a while but was in great pain because the bullet had blasted a hole through his guts. A British military policeman soon arrived on the scene and took Chisholm into custody; Lewis was put on a stretcher, hoisted into an ambulance and transported to the nearest Casualty Clearing Station. There was little that could be done for the wounded man, who was haemorrhaging badly. Even had it been possible to stem the bleeding, peritonitis would have developed as his intestines had been perforated and the wound would have been fouled with fragments of dirty clothing. In an era before the development of blood transfusion and antibiotics, other than administering pain-relieving doses of morphine there was precious little that doctors could do for men with such a serious abdominal wound. Lewis eventually died at 1.25pm in No.8 Casualty Clearing Station.[7]

Within a few hours Major Alexander Stevenson, the officer commanding 20th Fortress Company, began gathering witness statements.[8] Chisholm was brought from the guardroom, cautioned and allowed to ask questions after each witness had finished having their statement written down but the NCO said very little. Once the pre-trial statements had been completed they were forwarded to the Major General Sir John Keir, commanding 6th Division, who promptly arranged for a general court martial to be convened at the *mairie* (town hall) in Armentieres to try Chisholm for murder.

The trial began shortly before midday on 10 May. The President of the Court was Lieutenant-Colonel Francis Towsey, 1st Battalion West Yorkshire Regiment. The other four Members consisted of Major William Ash, 1st Battalion Middlesex Regiment and a trio of captains: Harman Potter, 1st Battalion Buffs; Francis Hamilton, 1st Battalion Cameronians, and Captain John Macartney, 2nd Battalion Leinster Regiment. The Judge Advocate assigned to advise the court on points of law and procedure was Major Edward Luard, 1st Battalion King's Own Shropshire Light Infantry, and Captain William de la Pryme, Adjutant of the 1st Battalion West Yorkshires, conducted the prosecution.[9]

Chisholm was wholly unassisted in presenting his defence. Defendants were legally entitled to be represented by a Prisoner's Friend but in practice few soldiers facing capital charges during 1915 were aided by a defending officer. In any case, having four days in which to mount a credible case for the defence would have challenged a seasoned barrister let alone an acting corporal with no legal expertise.

The trial went ahead on schedule; Chisholm entered a plea of not guilty and Captain de la Pryme called his first witness, Lieutenant Richard Charles RAMC, who formally reported that Lewis had been killed by a gunshot wound.[10]

The second witness was Second Corporal Thomas Freeman, who recalled:

> Corporal Chisholm ... tapped me on the shoulder and said that I should be wanted. He passed out of the *estaminet* into the street, I followed him about one and a half minutes later. I stood close to the door of the *estaminet* and on hearing a shot looked in that direction, when I saw the accused standing with the rifle in the firing position. He was about twenty yards off. I saw a man staggering ... Corporal Lewis, who was about 20 yards from the accused. There was no obstruction between the firer of the rifle and the man I saw staggering. The rifle was pointing in the direction of the staggering man.

Freeman continued:

> After I heard the shot he remained a few seconds in the firing position before lowering his rifle. He then threw the rifle on the ground. I went up to

> the accused and said what is the meaning of this. He said, 'I have shot my comrade, place me under arrest.'

Freeman ended by recalling that, 'There was nothing unusual in Corporal Chisholm's demeanour during lunch, or when he told me that I was wanted outside.'[11]

Freeman was then cross-examined by Chisholm:

> Q: When you came out of the *estaminet* did you see me in the street?
> A: No.
> Q: Did you look down the street?
> A: Yes.
> Q: Did you know we were moving with a G[eneral] S[ervice] wagon?
> A: No.
> Q: Did you see me near the G.S. wagon?
> A: No.
> Q: Was I standing upright when you saw me after having heard the shot fired?
> A: Yes.
> Q: How was I standing with regard to the G.S. wagon?
> A: You were standing near the tailboard on the rear side.
> Q: How high above the ground was the top of the kits on the wagon?
> A: I should say about 5 feet.

Q: Would the G.S. wagon have been visible from the Pelican door?
A: Yes.
Q: If you were standing at the Pelican door how could you see the G.S. wagon?
A: I was not standing actually in the doorway.
Q: Were you sitting opposite to me in the *estaminet?*
A: Yes.
Q: How close were you sitting to me in the *estaminet?*
A: Our knees were touching.
Q: Were you between Corporal Lewis and me?
A: Yes.
Q: Did you hear Corporal Lewis make any accusation against me?
A: No.
Q: Did you say to me 'what does he want to blab that out in here for?'
A: No.[12]

As subsequent witness testimony was to indicate, there was a good deal more that Freeman could have disclosed. However, Chisholm lacked the necessary experience to cajole Freeman into divulging more about the sensitive topic being discussed immediately prior to the shooting.

By the time Freeman ended his testimony the court rose for an hour's break. After a midday meal, the hearing resumed and the court heard evidence from

Sapper Harry Harris, who briefly stated that he had been inside the *estaminet* when the fatal shot had been discharged.[13] He added:

> At about 1.00pm on hearing a shot ring out, I went out into the street. The first man I saw was the accused who said to me 'make me a prisoner.' The accused had no rifle.

Harris was then cross-examined by Chisholm:

> Q: Where was I standing when you first saw me?
> A: Near the front of the G.S. wagon, that is near the front lock.
> Q: Was I under arrest when you first saw me?
> A: No.
> Q: How long after hearing the shot was it before you actually saw me?
> A: About two minutes.
> Q: Was anyone else near me?
> A: Not when I first saw you.
> Q: Who was the first man you saw near me?
> A: A tall sapper. I do not know his name.
> Q: How long after the shot was fired did you see this man?
> A: About three minutes.

Before standing down, Harris answered a couple of further questions posed by the Court:

> Q: Which way were the horses facing?
> A: Down the street away from the *mairie.*

> Q: What happened after the accused had spoken to you?
> A: Corporal Freeman came up called for an escort and marched the accused away.[14]

Harris's testimony and cross-examination did not add a great deal to what had already been revealed about the shooting. His reference to the unidentified 'tall sapper' eroded Freeman's claim to have been the first man to have seized Chisholm and Harris repeated the improbable allegation made in his pre-trial statement, that he had never noticed any ill feeling between Lewis and Chisholm.

The third witness for the prosecution was Driver George Williamson, an artilleryman who had been eating his midday meal in a house opposite the *estaminet* when he heard the fatal shot.[15] Williamson recalled:

> I heard a shot and immediately ran to the side door. I saw the accused bringing his rifle down from the present. I heard him mutter words to the effect either 'I have done it now' or 'now I have done it.' I then ran across the road to the assistance of the wounded man ... It was about ten seconds between the time I heard the shot and saw the accused. There was a distance of between 15 or 20 yards between the accused and the wounded man. There was no obstruction between the accused and wounded man.

In court, he did not refer to anything being said by Lewis, yet in his pre-trial statement Williamson claimed the mortally wounded man had declared, 'He's done it – the corporal – have you got him?' Given the overwhelming evidence that Chisholm had fired the fatal shot, perhaps Williamson felt it unnecessary to repeat the allegation.[16]

The following witness, Lance Corporal William Hann, in his pre-trial statement had alluded to a possible motive that lay behind the shooting.[17] Hann had been chatting in the street to Lewis a few minutes before Chisholm opened fire. In his pre-trial statement, Hann recalled:

> I said ... 'Have you decided anything about the billet? L.Cpl Lewis said, 'no not yet' and after a pause added, 'I told Chisholm this morning that I had three charges against him for falsifying accounts.' I then heard the report of a rifle and saw L. Corporal Lewis reel and fall. He remarked, 'Alec [sic] done it.' ... I had never noticed any ill feeling between the accused and L.Cpl. Lewis. I know no reason why Lance Corporal Lewis should have referred to the question of bringing charges against the accused as having anything to do with the question of billets.[18]

Hann's written statement also recorded Chisholm demanding to know exactly when Lewis first mentioned the charges, and noted Hann's response:

> Within ten days previous to the shooting, Lance Corporal Lewis said to me that the accused could not run him in because he could bring charges against the accused.

However, when Hann came to testify in court he omitted all reference to the three (sic) falsification charges:

> I came out of the Estaminet du Pelican and joined Lance Corporal Lewis. We walked off together. I noticed the accused on the opposite side of the street. He was standing behind the General Service Wagon. When we had got about thirty paces from the side door of the *estaminet,* I heard the report of a rifle. I saw Lance Corporal Lewis stagger and fall. When I turned round, I saw the accused throw the rifle to the ground. I know both the accused and Lance Corporal Lewis and have never seen any ill feeling between them. Lance Corporal Lewis was walking the further side of me from the accused. When the shot was fired, we were about twenty-five paces past the accused.[19]

Hann lied on oath. In his pre-trial written statement he had candidly admitted knowing that, at least ten days prior to the shooting, Lewis was threatening to press charges against Chisholm. In the statement he had also referred to chatting with Lewis immediately before the latter was shot but in court Hann testified he had never noticed any ill feeling between the two men. Hann concluded his evidence by denying that he had been in the bar before he encountered Lewis outside the Pelican.

Hann's evidence was followed by testimony from Sapper Norman Griffiths, who had been friendly with both Chisholm and Lewis.[20] Griffiths drew attention to developments that played an important part in prompting Chisholm to shoot Lewis. Griffiths began by explaining that on 4 May he had been outside the *estaminet,* chatting to a couple of other sappers when he saw Lewis shot. He heard the sound of a rifle clattering to the ground and saw the gun on the ground about a metre away from the rear wheel of the wagon, where Chisholm was standing. The court then set to work, cross-examining Griffiths:

> Q: Have you ever heard any arguments between the accused and Lance Corporal Lewis?
> A: Yes, frequently, about work and the time of knocking off.
> Q: Have you heard Lance Corporal Lewis use threats towards Corporal Chisholm?
> A: Yes. I have heard Lance Corporal Lewis threaten to report Corporal Chisholm over money matters.
> Q: Of what irregularity with regard to accounts did Lance Corporal Lewis accuse Corporal Chisholm?
> A: That men had signed the book for money which they had not received.

Q: Did you hear Lance Corporal Lewis threaten Corporal Chisholm on this subject on more than one occasion?
A: Yes. About twice.
Q: Did you hear this subject mentioned on May 4th?
A: No.
Q: Were you in the bar before you came from the *estaminet* and started talking to the two sappers?
A: Yes. A few sappers of the 20th Company, two men I did not know, Lance Corporal Lewis and Corporal Chisholm.
Q: Did you hear any dispute Corporal Chisholm and Lance Corporal Lewis?
A: Yes. There was a dispute about a billet, and Lance Corporal Lewis said he had three charges against Corporal Chisholm.
Q: Was this immediately before you left the *estaminet?*
A: About seven minutes.
Q: When did Corporal Chisholm leave the *estaminet?*
A: About two minutes after the dispute.
Q: Did he seem very upset at Lance Corporal Lewis's threats?
A: He did not show any signs of it.
Q: Was that the only remark Lance Corporal Lewis made?
A: Yes. All I heard.

Q: Was this threat made to Corporal Chisholm in the hearing of others in the *estaminet?*
A: Yes.[21]

Sapper Griffiths' answers directly challenged the evidence presented by Freeman, Hann and Harris, all of whom had denied hearing Lewis threaten Chisholm in the *estaminet.* Because the four men had been sitting in close proximity to one another, it is most unlikely they could have failed to hear comments made around the table, including Freeman's rhetorical comment about Lewis: 'What does he want to blab that out in here for?' Thus far in the proceedings, the entire prosecution case rested upon the evidence of three unreliable witnesses. If Griffiths was telling the truth then Freeman and Hann should have been recalled and further cross-examined about Chisholm and Lewis's relationship.

The next witness to testify was probably the 'tall sapper' to whom Harris referred in his testimony. He was Sergeant Charles Scott, a strapping 1.8 metre tall, 32-year-old military policeman who had been standing in the Rue de Capucins when Lewis was gunned down.[22] He saw Chisholm fling down his rifle and told the court what happened thereafter:

> I ... saw a wounded man lying on the opposite side of the road so I went to his assistance and found that it was not an accident, as the wounded man said 'Alec done it.' I then went towards the accused and found that he already been arrested.

> I took the names of witnesses and proceeded to the guard room to get the prisoner's particulars when he made the following voluntary statement: 'Don't trouble about evidence Sergeant, I've done it, I'll plead guilty.'

Scott admitted under cross-examination by the court that he had neither seen the shot discharged nor checked the discarded rifle to see if it had recently been fired. However, Lewis's dying declaration needed to be treated with scrupulous care by the court and Chisholm's voluntary confession was uncorroborated by any other witness. Since he was not cross-examined, it is impossible to gauge the significance of Scott's allegations but it seems likely that they were taken at face value by the Court.[23]

In the immediate aftermath of the shooting, while Scott busied himself collecting the names and details of potential witnesses, Driver William Whittaker had stood beside Chisholm until the latter was escorted away to the guardroom.[24] When it was his turn to give evidence, Whittaker explained that he had been in the street and confirmed the general sequence of events that had already been recounted by other witnesses. However, instead of being cross-examined about what Chisholm may have said, Whittaker was directed to stand down.

The rifle that fired the fatal shot was the primary focus of attention when the court heard evidence from the final witness for the prosecution, Sapper David

Kennedy.[25] Under cross-examination, he confirmed that the gun at Chisholm's feet had been recently fired but in response to a supplementary question, he flatly denied ever having heard Lance Corporal Lewis threaten or annoy Corporal Chisholm.

The case for the prosecution having been completed, Alec Chisholm opened the case for the defence. He began by presenting a narrative reflecting his own version of events on 4 May:

> At about 12.45pm, I went to the Estaminet du Pelican for the purpose of falling in a party of sappers to march to Nieppe. I sat down beside 2nd Corporal Freeman. Lance Corporal Lewis looked over towards me and said 'I see you have done it Alec, got us cleared out of the billet.' I said 'It is not my fault I left it to your officer.' He said 'All right, I will make it damned hot for you. I have three charges of falsifying accounts to bring against you.' I said 'Don't talk about that in here.' I then got up to leave the *estaminet.* 2nd Corporal Freeman took hold of my arm and said 'What does he want to blab that out in here for?' I said 'Never mind, come outside.' I went to the tail of the G.S. wagon. Lance Corporal Lewis came down the street past me and looked over and smiled. That is all I remember until the Corporal – 2nd Corporal Freeman – came and asked me what I had done. Previous to this, Lance Corporal Lewis had threatened me with exposure.

> I never knew what the charge was until the 4th of May.[26]

For de la Pryme brevity may have been the soul of wit, albeit in understanding rather than humour. However, the prosecuting officer's cross-examination of Chisholm was risibly brief. It must be almost the shortest ever cross-examination of a defendant in a murder trial:

> Q: Why did you ask Corporal Freeman to come outside?
> A: To fall in his party of sappers to march away.

Sapper Griffiths was the only witness called by Chisholm:

> For the last thirteen weeks about, Lance Corporal Lewis, Corporal Chisholm and myself have been on the same job. For the first week things went alright. Since then there have been constant quarrels between Corporal Lewis and Corporal Chisholm about the work; Corporal Lewis being a carpenter, and Corporal Chisholm not being one, though in charge of the job, each finding fault with each other's work. About three weeks ago there was a special quarrel about some iron knees. On May 4th, in the Estaminet Du Pelican, I was sitting at one end of the table. Corporal Freeman was at one end of the table, with Corporal Lewis on his right, and Corporal Chisholm on his left.[27]

The Prosecution evinced little interest in Griffiths' revelations. For Captain de la Pryme the case was wholly concerned with proving who killed Lewis and naught else; he dispensed with a closing address and the trial ended without a summing-up by the Judge Advocate, Major Luard.[28]

After closing to consider its findings, the court decided that Chisholm was guilty of murdering Lewis. On reopening, Chisholm declined an invitation to advance a plea in mitigation but the court heard a very positive appraisal of Chisholm's character and work from his commanding officer, Major Stevenson. Stevenson was unable to produce any written records but elected to make the following statement:

> The accused joined the unit under my command as a reinforcement in October 1914. Most of the time since he has been employed on detached duty under the Chief Engineer 3rd Corps [,] where he has been practically in sole charge of some construction work. The Chief Engineer has always expressed himself very satisfied with the way the accused has executed his work. And as far as I have seen I can personally endorse the above. He has had no entries against him since he has joined the company.[29]

Thereafter, the court sentenced Chisholm to be hanged, a punishment that was subsequently endorsed by all the confirming officers, including Sir John French. Alec Chisholm was duly executed in the

Asylum, Armentieres, at 6.10am on 17 May but as his death certificate confirms, Chisholm did not perish on the end of a rope. He was instead shot by a firing squad under the command of Major John Tufton, Assistant Provost Marshal, 6th Division.[30]

There is no doubt that Chisholm fired the shot that killed Lewis but whether the condemned man was given a fair trial remains open to question. Sapper Griffiths' unchallenged testimony drew attention to Lewis's practice of persistently undermining Chisholm's authority for over three months. Although 'doing that which he has a legal right to do' could not be construed as provocation, Lewis certainly did not have any right to bait, malign and undermine the authority of a superior officer. No effort was made by the court to consider whether Chisholm had temporarily lost his reason and acted 'under the influence of passion arising from extreme provocation'.

> The *Manual of Military Law* adds, the provocation:
>
> Must also be great, that is to say, practically speaking, such as might reasonably be expected to put an ordinary person, not of an exceptionally passionate disposition into such a passion that he would lose his power of self control.[31]

However, Corporal Chisholm was not 'an ordinary person'; he was a junior non-commissioned officer in the British Army. The Army did not apply the civil standard of the 'reasonable man'; Chisholm was on active service and his work and conduct had to be exemplary. It is therefore not difficult to imagine how Lewis's persistently divisive behaviour may have gnawed away at Chisholm's self-confidence and caused the latter to snap. Lewis was well aware that he had driven Chisholm to breaking point, and immediately after being wounded he had no doubt about who had fired the shot. According to Sapper William Cox, Lewis had cried, 'Do something quick – Alec has done it the coward – why did he not shoot me in the leg?' For reasons that remain unclear, Cox was not called to give evidence in person.[32]

The court was also manifestly disinterested in allegations about false accounting, so what was said in passing about the matter was insufficient to prove that Chisholm was an embezzler or part of a conspiracy that involved French civilians or fellow sappers. Certainly Corporal Freeman appeared keen to prevent the issue being discussed openly. In the Pelican *estaminet,* when he heard Lewis threaten to bring charges, Freeman had exclaimed, 'What did he want to blab that out in here for?'

What should be made of evidence from Sergeant George Ballard? Chisholm had made a confession to Ballard, one of the military police in charge of the guardroom.[33] In his turn, the NCO had told Major Stevenson, who had written down the details in a pre-trial statement that was signed by Ballard. It read:

> About one fifteen on the 4th May I went down to the cell to handcuff the accused. I said to him 'you have done a very serious thing.' He said 'Well I will tell you all about it if you won't tell anyone.' I made no reply. He said 'There are some civilians in this affair.' The accused then appeared to change his mind and he said, 'I will not tell you as I'm afraid you will open your mouth.' I applied the handcuffs and left him in charge of the guard. About 5.50pm on the 4th of May, the corporal of the guard told me the accused complained of the handcuffs being on him so I went to him and the accused asked me to remove the handcuffs. I told him that they were to stop on. He asked me for some blankets as his kit had been taken from him. I reported to the sergeant major of the platoon to get the accused some blankets if possible. Before I left him he asked me 'Is he dead?' I replied 'no but I'm afraid he will die.' I asked him where he shot him he replied 'in the back.' He said 'I levelled the rifle at his heart. I meant to shoot the bastard through the heart as he has been worrying the life out of me these last three months.'[34]

Ballard's deposition tends to erode Griffiths' contention that Chisholm appeared unconcerned at the time they emerged from the Pelican. However, the statement also challenges Chisholm's own declaration that he could not remember anything after leaving the *estaminet.* These issues remain unresolved because Ballard was not summoned to testify in court.

Having shot Lewis, Chisholm dropped his rifle to the ground and was in shock. Unfortunately, the written proceedings do not disclose the manner in which he uttered the phrase, 'I've done it now.' No less than an expression of triumphant vindication by a cold-blooded killer, it may equally have been a sigh of relief or the anguished cry of a soul in torment.[35]

Alec Chisholm did not get a fair trial and justice was not well served. Like many other soldiers who faced a court martial undefended, he received no assistance whatsoever from those who were duty bound to ensure that he suffered no prejudice. Although the Army always maintained that capital courts martial observed the standards of contemporary civil courts, the vacuity of the claim has long been demolished by the sorry treatment of soldiers who were executed for desertion and other military offences. Because Chisholm's case involved murder, a more direct comparison may be made with civilian judicial practice. If the case had been heard in a criminal court Chisholm would probably have been found guilty of killing Lewis, but with appropriate legal representation a civil court may not have sentenced Chisholm to death.

14780 CORPORAL
A. CHISHOLM
ROYAL ENGINEERS
17TH MAY 1915 AGE 31
UNTIL THE DAY BREAKS
AND THE SHADOWS FLEE AWA

CHAPTER 3

Seeing Shadows

Private No.15437 Charles William Knight, 10th Battalion Royal Welsh Fusiliers was executed for murder on Monday, 17 November 1915.[1] He had been drinking shortly before the crime was committed and he was also suffering from mental stress. However, as with the majority of soldiers who were executed during the First World War, he was unassisted in presenting his defence and executed for the sake of example.

It is unclear how a Londoner like Knight came to join the battalion at Wrexham in September 1914 but almost exactly a year later, he and his comrades were deployed with 76th Brigade near Ypres. After a month in the front line at Sanctuary Wood and Ploegstraat the brigade was transferred from 25th Division to 3rd Division and withdrawn to rest near the village of Eecke, in French Flanders.[2] During early November the weather was foul, the skies were overcast and the countryside was deluged almost daily by heavy rain. The 10th Battalion Royal Welsh Fusiliers were under cover, billeted in some damp, stinking barns and farm buildings near Eecke. In between drill, route marches and military training, efforts to generate entertainment floundered and the divisional football tournament was played in a quagmire. The chaplain, Captain Pat Leonard, wrote:

> We have absolutely nothing to do all day except watch the rain transform the farm yard into a troubled sea of mud ... the cesspool in the middle is now perfectly pestilential and the home to all the unclean beasts of the brute creation – fat odoriferous sows wallow on the marge thereof, and dead carcasses float aimlessly about the discoloured and slimy liquid.[3]

Aside from gambling and attempting to dry out in their unheated barns, the soldiers took advantage of the rural wartime service economy. Even in pre-war days, Eecke's population barely exceeded 1,000 inhabitants and many of the men in the village had been called up for military service. Nevertheless, there remained enough French civilians and refugees who were keen to provide a range of food and drinks for soldiers who had money to spare.[4] Residents improvised cafés in a room or so in their own homes and as elsewhere, local women also took advantage of opportunities to earn some francs by offering laundry and other services to troops stationed in the vicinity.

On Wednesday, 3 November, after his day's duties were done Knight decided to combine necessity with pleasure. He gathered up his soiled kit and took it to a nearby house for washing and on the way back to the barn in which his section was billeted, he visited another house in which he sat down to enjoy a coffee. Quite suddenly he had an unfunny turn; he became mentally very disturbed and began to wander about in a restless, distracted fashion. The mental commotion persisted, Knight felt completely unable to relax but he managed to eat some supper at the barn and then went to find some friends in nearby alehouse.

In early November the sun sets over the fields and villages of Flanders around 5.30pm, so night may have already fallen at the time when Knight wandered off for a beer. However, it would certainly have been dark when he returned to his billet shortly after 8.00pm. On entering the barn Knight picked up a rifle and began to behave with it as though he was engaged in fighting some invisible enemy. An unsuccessful attempt was made to disarm him but he managed to load the firearm and began shooting indiscriminately around the inside the barn. He discharged between two to three dozen shots through the walls before he was eventually disarmed by some of his comrades. Though most of the shots failed to injure anyone, before Knight could be disarmed one of his comrades was severely wounded and another lay dead.

On Saturday, 6 November, a field general court martial was hurriedly convened at Eecke to try Knight for murder. The 76th Brigade was not scheduled to move anywhere for a further three weeks, so there was time enough for its commander, Brigadier General Ernest Pratt to have ensured that pre-trial summaries of evidence were gathered from eyewitnesses but there is no sign that he did so.[5] Neither was any discernible effort put into securing expert medical testimony or arranging for a Medical Board to examine Knight's mental state.

The President of the Court, Lieutenant Colonel Percy Brown, 1st Battalion, Gordon Highlanders, was assisted by two Members: Major Charles Williams, 8th Battalion Lancaster Regiment and Major George Smith, 4th Battalion Gordon Highlanders.[6] Although Smith was an experienced Scottish solicitor in civilian life, no court martial officer or judge advocate attended the trial and although charged with a capital offence, Knight was unassisted by a Prisoner's Friend. The prosecution was conducted by Captain William Lyons, the Adjutant, 10th Bn. Royal Welsh Fusiliers.[7]

Each of the prosecution witnesses presented their account of what happened in the form of a brief narrative. The first witness was Private Thomas Richards, who recalled the beginning and the end of the shooting incident:

> Between 8.00pm and 8.30pm I was in my barn: The accused, Pte. Knight, came in staggering, evidently under the influence of drink: he picked up a rifle and started making parries towards the wall: I asked him to put the rifle down: he swung round the rifle using obscene language: I dived at him and caught him by the legs, but he somehow got away: I was on the floor when

> someone shouted out 'Look out Richards, he is loading': I then ran out, as I was by myself and went into the farm to fetch Coy. S.M. Fisher: I told him what had happened and followed him out: I waited there until later when Major Freeman ordered us to charge the door of the barn in which Pte. Knight was: I met Coy. S.M. Fisher when I got inside – I heard one shot fired after I left the barn – when I re-entered the barn Coy. S.M. Fisher was holding Pte. Knight on the floor.[8]

Sergeant Herbert Grundy had been the senior NCO on duty in C Company guardroom, which was located in a building adjacent the barn wherein Knight was discharging his fusillade. Grundy chronicled what happened to the two soldiers who had the misfortune to be wounded by some of the shots:

> I was in command of C Coy. Guard: at about 8.15pm, I was inside the guard room when I heard a man outside say that Pte. Knight was inside the barn with a loaded rifle: I left the guardroom to go into the barn, the door of which was only 4 yards away, when I heard a shot: at the same time a man inside the guardroom called out 'Oh my leg': I went back to him and found that it was No.24637 Pte. Poffley: I found he was hit in the leg, so I placed him on my knee: I then called for Coy. S.M. Fisher and when he arrived I told him there had been a man

> wounded: I also told him he had better not stand in the doorway, as some shots had come through there: I then laid Pte. Poffley on the ground and lay down beside him, as being the safest position: about ten minutes later, I heard a whistle blown outside and a voice say 'Now then, all together' and then a noise as though a charge was being made. Then someone said 'All right, I've got him': I then called for a light and stretcher bearers: On the light being brought, I found another man, No.15461 Pte. A. Edwards lying on the floor of the guardroom apparently hit: when the stretcher-bearers arrived, they examined him and found that he was dead. I heard between thirty and thirty-five shots altogether: they all came from inside the barn.[9]

The Court asked Grundy, 'Do you think the accused knew the position of the guard room?' He replied, 'Yes, he must have known.' There was no further cross-examination. The prosecuting officer then called the NCO who disarmed Knight, Company Sergeant Major Edward Fisher, to testify. Fisher remembered:

> At about 8.30pm I was in my billet when No.15617 Pte. T.E. Richards of my company ran in and informed me that the accused, Pte. Knight, was firing his rifle from the company barn: I immediately went over to the Coy. guardroom, where I saw Pte. Poffley lying wounded: at that moment Major Freeman, who commands my

> company, called me and gave me instructions to restore order and to try and locate where the rifle fire was coming from: I at once went to the sentry at the gate of the farm yard and ordered him not to allow anyone to enter the yard: I then went round the barn to find a back entrance but all the doors were locked: I then returned to the main entrance and, calling for one or two men to come with me, I entered the barn and rushed across to the back wall: from there I saw the flash of a rifle and discovered where the accused was: I jumped over a partition and moving along a wall leapt at his back and grasped him by the throat, knocking the rifle out of his hands at the same time: other men then came to my assistance: From four to six shots were fired when I was in the barn: I found that a bayonet was fixed to the rifle: the magazine contained five rounds and there was one empty case in the chamber, which the accused had fired just as I jumped on him: there were two or three bandoliers of ammunition lying in the straw beside the accused, also some loose chargers and empty cartridge cases....

After the Court enquired whether he reckoned Knight to have been sober, Fisher declared, 'In my opinion he was drunk.'

Major Edward Freeman, the officer who ordered Fisher and his men to stop Knight firing the rifle, then testified:

> At about 8.20pm I was in my billet when a man of my company rushed in and said that a man was firing his rifle in the company barn: I went towards the barn and as I came round the corner a bullet whizzed over my head: I called my Company Sergt. Major [S.M. Fisher] and told him to stop men moving about in front of the barn and then to see whether an entrance could be made into the barn from the back: this was found to be impossible: I then ordered an NCO and three men to enter through the hay in the next barn and another party under Sergeant-Major Fisher to enter by the main door: the latter party reached the accused first and secured him: I followed this party and found that the man secured was No.15437, Pte. Knight, from my company: his bayonet was fixed to his rifle, which was red-hot: there were five rounds in the magazine and one empty case in the chamber: twenty-five empty cases were picked up from the straw where the accused had been firing: there were also 120 live rounds: I placed Pte. Knight under arrest: in my opinion he had been drinking but I do not consider that he was drunk. When I went out of the barn I went to the guard room and there saw Pte. Poffley, who had been

> wounded in the leg, and Pte. Edwards, who was dead.[10]

The final witness for the prosecution was the battalion's medical officer, Captain Bernard Grellier, RAMC, who had examined Poffley, Edwards and Knight on 6 November. He recalled:

> At about 9.15pm ... I was called to the barn of C Company, 10th Battalion Royal Welsh Fusiliers, to see a man: I found that he was dead having been hit in the chest by a bullet within the previous two hours, the body being still warm: I then went to Bn. Headquarters to see a man who was wounded, Pte. Poffley by name: I found he had been wounded in the right thigh: he had four wounds, of which three were probably bullet wounds, the fourth might have been caused by a chip of something hard.
>
> I then at about 10.45pm went to the Battalion guardroom to see the accused Pte. Knight: he was lying down, handcuffed: I examined him and to me he appeared to be in a semi-conscious condition: he did not seem to fully appreciate his surroundings or those about him: what questions he did answer, he answered sensibly, except the one in which he was asked who had been talking to him: he told me his name, part of his number and his company: his breath was of the alcoholic type and his breath was tainted with liquor: I

> examined him to see if there was anything that could account for his medical condition and found nothing beyond the signs of alcohol: his eyes were constantly wandering and he was moving his hands about as if to feel something: I do not consider his mental condition was normal at that time and I consider that was due to drink.
>
> I saw him again the next morning about 9.00am and found him quite sensible: I asked him questions about the previous evening and he remembered having spoken to me then: he said he remembered going into the barn but nothing of what happened there.

The court asked only one question of Grellier: 'When you saw the accused on the morning of Nov. 4th, do you consider his mental condition was normal?' Grellier replied, 'Yes, except that he seemed to be depressed.'[11]

After each of the witnesses finished giving their evidence, Knight was formally invited to ask questions about their testimony. There is no indication in the written proceedings that he availed himself of the opportunity until the time came to present his own defence. He called one witness, Private Frank Parsons.[12] After being sworn in, Knight asked him, 'As you slept next to me, do you remember me on Nov. 2nd complaining of a headache?' Parsons replied, 'No, I cannot remember your doing so.' He then withdrew and Knight delivered an explanation for his own conduct:

> On Nov. 3rd, I went out of my barn just before tea time to take some washing to a house near[by]: on my way back I went into a house for a cup of coffee: I hadn't sat down for more than two or three minutes when a strange sensation came over me and I felt a rattling noise in my head: I had to go out into the fresh air, where I felt a little better: On my way back to my barn to tea I felt worse and could not make up my mind whether to go on or lie down: however, I went back to the barn for tea: after I had a wash and came back into the barn again, lay down and tried to go to sleep: I could not sleep, so I got up and went for a walk to the village: I met some friends there and went into a small beer house: we sat down and had a few drinks: I could not remain still however as my head was becoming worse, so I came out and sat below a hedge for nearly an hour: I then went to my billet and lay down: it was then about 8.15pm: I lay down for about ten minutes or quarter of an hour but my head became much worse, so I got up: I seemed to see shadows crossing the wall: I made a dive at something, grasped it and drove at the wall with it: I turned round and could see no one in the barn: but I saw the glimmer of a light and kicked at it and it went out: I sat down on my bed but I still had

> something in my hand: I cannot remember what it was: I remember no more until the following morning when the doctor came to see me. I had been suffering with my head for two or three years and used to take medicine for it.[13]

Although it was not entered in the written proceedings, the court withdrew at this point to consider its findings; Knight was found guilty and sentenced to death. However, the decision could not be promulgated until the confirming officers had added their comments about the case and the sentence had been approved by Field Marshal Sir John French, the Commander-in-Chief. The court reconvened and called for Captain Lyons to produce details of Knight's previous service, his conduct and disciplinary record. Lyons reported, 'His character is indifferent: he has had five cases of drunkenness during his fourteen months' service: the last case was on 5.9.15.'[14]

The written proceedings were initially forwarded to Knight's battalion commander, Colonel William Beresford-Ash, who drafted a damning assessment of Knight's character:

> Private Charles William Knight of the battalion under my command is apparently a man of very low origin, though of considerable personality. He had great influence amongst the other men, and was on more than one occasion recommended to me for promotion. He is a man who is addicted to drink, and when under its influence appears to

> lose control of his actions. He joined the BEF on 28th, September last. His conduct whilst under fire requires no comment as nothing particular occurred whilst he was under fire.[15]

Brigadier Ernest Pratt, commanding 76th Brigade, endorsed the need to have Knight killed. He observed:

> (1) This battalion is composed chiefly of miners and the state of its discipline is only fair.
>
> (2) In my opinion it is a clear case of murder and owing to the ease with which men can obtain ammunition on active service it is necessary in such cases to carry out the extreme penalty of the law.[16]

Major General Aylmer Haldane, commanding 3rd Division, had approved the execution of thirteen soldiers during the preceding twelve months and he was unlikely to have acted mercifully in Knight's case. However, the typed memorandum he produced made no direct reference to the sentence or punishment decided by the court. Instead Haldane catalogued a succession of serious reservations about the woeful lack evidence. He wrote:

> Evidence on the following points appears to be desirable:
>
> (a) Whether the Barn was crowded at the time the accused entered.

(b) Whether there was any light in the Barn at the time.

(c) Whether anyone else fired at all, or whether all the other rifles, being examined, showed no traces of having been fired.

As regards (a) there is at present no evidence.

(b) From the fact that S.M. Fisher located the man by the flash of his rifle, and that Richards called for a light in the Guard-Room, within four paces of the Barn, it appears that it was dark.

(c) The last evidence, which appears to be important, is altogether missing.

The Finding not having been confirmed, it is possible to try the man again and bring out evidence on these points, should such a course be considered necessary.

There appears to be, however, to be no doubt that the accused's conduct was such that 'any reasonable man must have known it was likely to cause grievous bodily harm,' and that therefore the charge is correct.

At the foot of the page of typed text he scrawled his signature and scribbled: 'I recommend that Pte.

Knight's offence be treated as murder not manslaughter.'[17]

What he wrote may have been a response to a conversation or some correspondence that was later weeded from the file but Haldane's addendum is the only reference in the entire dossier to manslaughter. Haldane made no direct reference to the absence of a courts martial officer but it is pretty clear from the criticism he airs that had expert legal advice been on hand then oversights and evidential flaws in the proceedings would have been avoided.[18]

In addition to Haldane's confirmation, Herbert Plumer, the General Commanding 2nd Army, also approved the capital sentence but without any accompanying reason for his endorsement. The dossier was then forwarded to the Deputy Judge Advocate General, Major Gilbert Mellor, whose duty was to scrutinize the case for legal imperfections and forward his observations to Adjutant General Wyndham Childs.[19] Mellor complained:

> The evidence in this case, as pointed out in minute (3) and in other respects is not satisfactory. I consider, however, that the court had some evidence before them that the accused was concerned in causing the death of the deceased man.
>
> The substantial question for the court to decide was whether the accused was in a state of mind

> to intend to kill or inflict grievous bodily harm or to know what he was doing would reasonably and probably cause that result, and in law it rested, in this case, upon the accused to show that he was not legally responsible for his actions.
>
> The question being one for the court, with the evidence before them, I am not prepared to say their finding is wrong in law.
>
> At the same time, as regards the infliction of the extreme penalty, there is no evidence of any premeditation or actual malice against any person, and the case should be distinguished from those where a man has with premeditation intentionally caused the death of some particular person. There is no reason to suppose that the accused, had he been sober, would have committed this or any other serious crime.
>
> In view of the unsatisfactory record of evidence, I suggest that inquiry should be made why the special officer at the 2nd Army did not act as a Member of the Court.

In addition to refusing to declare that the evidential flaws in Knight's court martial sufficed to quash the verdict, Mellor nudged away personal responsibility for the unsatisfactory aspects of Knight's court martial. The Adjutant General referred the matter to Brigadier General Wroughton, the Assistant Adjutant General,

2nd Army, and called on him to account for the absence of the court martial officer.[20] Wroughton shrugged off any personal responsibility by suggesting that criticism ought to be borne by 'all concerned'. To Childs, Wroughton despatched the following explanation:

> The services of this officer should have been applied for and all concerned have been so informed. On the date of this trial, Captain MacGeagh [Court Martial Officer] was acting as Judge Advocate on the G.C.M. [general court martial] held for the trial of Lieutenant Crowe, AVC but it could have been arranged for him to have attended Pte. Knight's trial instead, or, to have taken one of the cases the following day.

Wroughton finessed this response with a handwritten postscript to a routine advisory note to Haldane. Wroughton's addendum admonished the 3rd Division commander for failing to apply for the services of a court martial officer at Knight's trial. The routine note itself advised Haldane to promptly inform Wroughton about the promulgation, date and time of Knight's execution. Haldane's staff relayed the note to 76th Brigade Headquarters, where the advice was duly communicated to Colonel Beresford-Ash.[21]

While senior officers were composing and circulated their exculpatory memoranda about the (sic) absent court martial officer, Field Marshal French had decided Knight deserved to face a firing squad. On Thursday,

11 November, the Commander-in-Chief sanctioned Knight's execution; on following day the condemned man was visited by the 76th Brigade chaplain, Captain Pat Leonard.[22]

Leonard had been surprised and shocked when he was originally told about one of the Royal Welsh Fusiliers having 'drunk himself silly, and then loaded his rifle and run amok.' In a letter to his own family, the chaplain confided, 'the doctors seem to think that he is mentally deficient' but he trudged across the rain-sodden fields and went to visit the condemned man.[23] Leonard found Knight confined in the same place where Poffley had been wounded and Edwards had perished:

> The Guard Room is a sort of tumbledown stable, and the prisoner was lying huddled in a corner under some blankets, his handcuffed hands hidden beneath them. I sat down beside him and tried to talk to him, but it was far from easy. In the first place, the presence of the guard had a fettering effect upon my tongue, and the man wouldn't say a word. Finally I asked him, after one of two awkward pauses, if he would rather I didn't come out to see him. He shook his head so nothing was left but to clear out.[24]

However, it was not very long before Captain Leonard returned to see Knight:

> It was my duty to break the news to him and prepare him for his end. It was a terrible ordeal. He was to be shot at dawn on Monday. Most of Sunday night I spent with him; he was quite penitent and made his confession and peace with God. Monday morning I was with him for an hour before the end. He was quite composed and extraordinarily brave and faced the firing-party without the slightest sign of fear. A real white man – out of drink – and a model soldier who would as likely as not have snaffled a VC. I had to be present the whole time, and afterwards buried him. Poor fellow, the manner of his death made some atonement for the failure of his life. The whole business made me feel perfectly ill. May I never have a similar experience.[25]

Charles Knight was killed at 6.45am on Monday, 15 November. The execution appears to have been supervised personally by Colonel Beresford-Ash, and Captain Grellier certified that Knight was killed instantly by the firing squad.[26] The executed soldier's corpse was buried nearby but after the war ended his remains were disinterred by the Imperial War Graves Commission and reburied in Le Hazard Military Cemetery, Morbecque.[27]

The trial and punishment of Charles Knight were recognized to have been unsatisfactory by senior army officers and it appears that Brigadier Pratt was at fault in failing to arrange for a court martial officer to attend the trial. However, even had he done so, Pratt's failure to have Knight examined by a medical board or to ensure he was assisted in presenting his defence by a Prisoner's Friend suggests that the trial was not only hastily cobbled together but also unfair.

From the written proceedings it is clear that unqualified opinion by Company Sergeant Major Fisher went unchallenged by the Prisoner's Friend and the court accepted uncorroborated testimony about Knight's unprovoked misbehaviour inside the barn. Given that it was after nightfall and there was no illumination in the windowless barn and the doors were closed then unless Knight had x-ray vision, it is difficult to sustain the charge that he intended to injure or kill Poffley and Edwards. That Knight fired the shots from inside the barn that killed Edwards and wounded Poffley was never in doubt but as Haldane indicated, there was no evidence to discount the possibility that other soldiers also firing rifles may have injured one or both men.

Knight had not been in trouble for drunken behaviour while on active service in Flanders. He admitted having consumed some beers between eating his supper and returning to the barn on 6 November but nobody established how much alcohol he may have ingested. Yet in accounting for his murderous behaviour, the amount of booze he had consumed was an important consideration. The issue was also important because the court never clearly established whether Knight's unstable behaviour was caused by alcohol or a mental condition. Major Freeman did not think Knight was drunk and the brigade's medical officers reckoned he was 'mentally deficient'. Indeed, a medical board – had one been convened – may have concluded Knight's lethal behavior was due to mental illness rather than alcohol.

In the absence of any other medical testimony, the court relied on Captain Grellier's opinions about Knight. Grellier contended that after being disarmed, Knight was semi-conscious and mentally abnormal. Since the soldier had been drinking, in the absence of any other symptoms he concluded Knight's misbehaviour was wholly alcohol related. However, Grellier's specialism was dental surgery and although he may have known little about diagnosing and treating post-traumatic stress disorder, he never seems to have considered that Knight may have experienced an epileptic fit (petit mal) and postical fugue:

> The patient has no memory of the episode [a fugue] but can often suffer premonitory symptoms of epilepsy, either a full blown convulsion or, more likely in Knight's case, complex partial seizures. A postical fugue is also known as post-epileptic automatism and is more marked when the patient has taken alcohol. The post-ictal fugue lasts minutes or hours and this differentiates from other fugue conditions where the patient has loss of memory and has no idea who he is or where he was, lasting for months or years.[28]

It was woefully apparent that Knight's attempt to produce witness evidence proved counter-productive but it does not exonerate Grellier or the court for failing to check why Knight had to take medicine and the nature of the trouble he had been experiencing with his head. Whether Knight's condition arose from an epileptic seizure or battle stress exacerbated by alcohol it remains debatable whether expert medical testimony about the severity of his symptoms would have sufficed to sustain a defence of temporary insanity. However, Knight was certainly not given a fair trial and justice was ill served by the grounds on which the confirming officers decided to have him killed.[29]

CHAPTER 4

The Wrong Man

The experience of 30-year-old Staff Sergeant James Pick tends to contradict the superstition that a soldier is fated to be killed by a bullet with his name on it.[1] He was stationed in the Ypres Salient with 197th Company (Horse Transport), Army Service Corps and until 11.30pm on Friday, 11 February 1916 he had also been lucky.[2] Enemy artillery had spared the barrack huts and farm buildings at Zealand Farm and an air raid was not immediately likely because visibility was poor, the surrounding countryside was wrapped in a cold, ghostly shroud of moonlit mist.[3] It was also pay day, and after tea the Scotsman left camp to enjoy a drink at an *estaminet* in the nearby town of Poperinghe, where he was joined by a quartet of soldiers from the camp.

They shared a few drinks and after a couple of hours or so, they all walked together back to camp, with Pick and Driver Thomas Moore, a 24-year-old from County Durham, leading the way.[4] On entering Zealand Camp, Pick went to the farriers' quarters and Moore's party retired to their quarters in No.5 Hut, where they carried on enjoying themselves, talking loudly and noisily fooling around.[5]

Because the noise persisted for a couple of hours after Lights Out, the company's senior officer, Captain John Thompson, threatened the boisterous soldiers with arrest if they did not all settle down and be quiet.[6] He also reported the men's disruptive behaviour to Company Sergeant Major Robert Bagshaw.[7] Shortly afterwards, a rifle was discharged inside No.5 Hut and Driver Moore emerged from the doorway, rifle in hand, and began roaming around the camp, shooting, shouting and demanding a personal confrontation with Bagshaw.

On hearing the uproar, Staff Sergeant Pick snuffed out the candle illuminating the farriers' quarters and went outside. Since it was dark he called out to Moore, using the latter's nickname, 'Darky, Darky'. Moore demanded Pick identify himself but before the NCO could respond Darky shot the staff sergeant twice. Pick collapsed, fatally wounded, and expired soon afterwards from bullets that had been intended by Moore to kill Bagshaw.

Moore was disarmed and trussed up before being taken to the guardroom, where he was medically examined shortly after midnight and found to be comatose. About an hour later, he was able to speak, albeit slurring his words, and said that he had wanted to shoot Bagshaw but recalled nothing about having gunned down Pick.[8]

Major Hugh Hunter was assigned to preparing the summaries of evidence but his transcription of interviews with witnesses had to be curtailed because of an air raid on Zealand Farm camp. Though Hunter never completed his task a field general court martial was convened to try Moore on 16 February.[9]

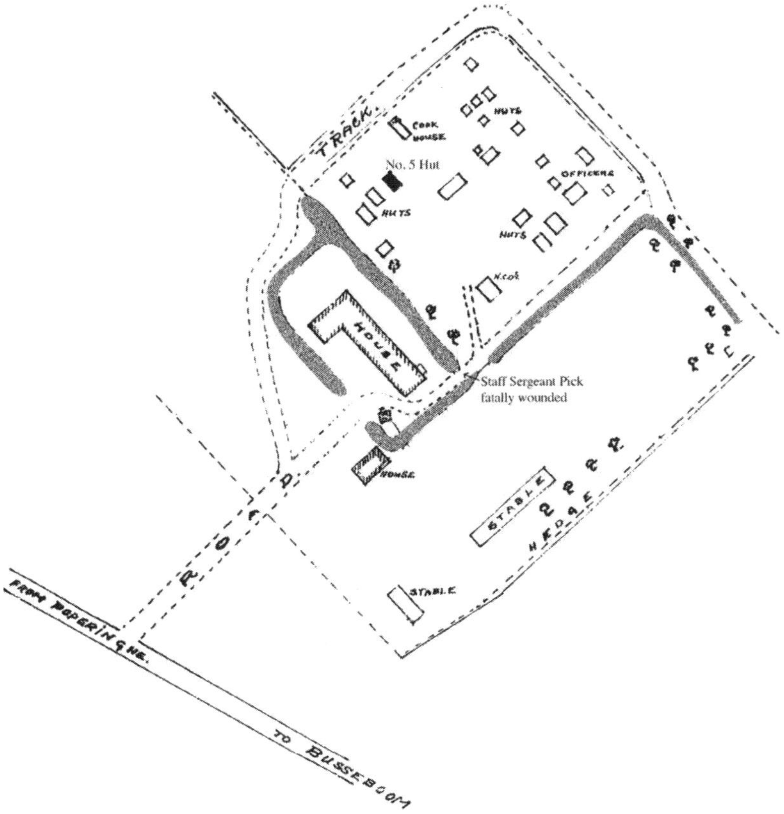

No.197 Company, Zealand Camp. Moated Farm, Busseboom

The President was Lieutenant Colonel Percy Skinner and the Members consisted of Captain Martin Alexander and Captain Reginald Hills, who was also barrister. The prosecutor was Major Hugh Hunter but the name of Moore's defending officer or Prisoner's Friend was wholly omitted or expunged from the written proceedings.[10]

The trial took place in Zealand Camp exactly a week after the shooting; it started at 10.00am and ended at 5.20pm. With patience and persistence it is possible to jigsaw together the witness testimony into a composite account of what happened at Zealand Camp on the night of 11 February 1916. The emerging narrative fits together pretty well but the completed puzzle remains both disturbed and disturbing.

After the customary preliminary rituals had been observed, Moore faced a single charge of wilful, premeditated murder and entered a plea of not guilty. The first witness for the prosecution was Captain John Thompson, who began his testimony by producing a sketch map of the camp and then presented his own recollection of what happened on the night Pick died. Thompson explained that he had been undressing before going to bed when the noise from No.5 Hut had become intolerable and he had gone over to the hut and told the culprits to be quiet. Driver Moore had responded by standing to attention and retorting, 'Yes, sir.'

Thompson reported the matter to the senior NCOs and about 11.15pm, while he was returning to his own hut, a shot rang out. He returned to No.5 Hut:

> I ... opened the door and there I saw the accused standing near the stove at the further end of the hut with a rifle in his hand. He aimed it at me, but on someone saying 'Don't shoot. It is the captain' he partly lowered it. Then he said, 'I do

> not care a bugger who it is,' and he aimed it at me again. I stepped aside out of the doorway. Several shots were then fired from inside the hut. I went round to the back of the hut and heard someone come out of the hut and fire off a rifle outside.

Thompson said that he subsequently heard a man shouting and further rifle shots. After hearing a number of other men's voices shouting, Thompson said:

> I went towards where the shouts came from and found that the accused was being secured with ropes. Lieut. Col. Ford then arrived and took charge. I then went to the Sergeant's mess and found Sergeant Pick ... lying on the table. Lieutenant Robertson an officer of the company was rendering him first aid. He was wounded through the stomach.

The night had been 'dark, misty, and still' and Thompson was adamant that Moore had not been drunk when he saw him.

On cross-examination by the Prisoner's Friend, Thompson admitted he did not know what the men had been talking about in No.5 Hut. He also named the NCOs to whom he had spoken, Staff Sergeant Bampton and Company Sergeant Bagshaw, but did not know whether either of them had subsequently visited No.5 Hut, and he conceded that no one had sought to establish whether soldiers other than Moore had fired rifles during the rumpus.[11]

The following three witnesses were men who had been quartered with Moore in No.5 Hut. The first to testify, Driver James Gray recalled that after they had been admonished by Captain Thompson, they had all prepared to go to bed but Moore had grabbed a rifle.[12] Gray explained:

> I got out of bed and knocked it out of his hand. Then he took it up and opened the bolt, and had a bandolier in his hand. A few minutes afterwards he seized another rifle and loaded it, and fired a shot through the roof and then flew through the door, and fired two or three shots outside ... as he went out I heard him say that he would do something. I am not sure what he said he would do.

When Moore eventually returned to No.5 Hut he was knocked down and disarmed by Gray and Driver Richard Clayton. In response to cross-examination by the court, Gray claimed he did not remember Thompson visiting the No.5 Hut for a second time.[13]

When his turn came to give evidence, Clayton detailed what happened inside the hut. While chatting with Gray and Moore, the latter had vainly tried to load a rifle. The weapon was confiscated by Gray, snatched back by Moore, again confiscated by Clayton and finally tucked behind Moore's bed. After undertaking to be quiet, once Thompson had departed, Moore had made more noise but then lay down on his bed. Clayton continued:

> He then got out of bed again and seized hold of a rifle and bandolier and fired a shot through the roof of the hut, and said 'I will let them know that I am alive.' The sergeant major and the quartermaster sergeant of the company then came to the door of the hut, and the accused said to them, 'If you are not out by the time I count three you will be dead men.' They ran out of the hut when the rifle went up.[14]

Because Clayton had only recently been attached to 197th Company he could not identify the NCOs. The remainder of Clayton's evidence referred to Thompson's second visit to No.5 Hut and how Moore eventually came to be disarmed:

> A short while after, Captain Thompson came in. The accused pointed his rifle at Captain Thompson and said, 'If you are not out of here in a minute, you are a dead man.' Captain Thompson then went out of the hut, and shortly after the accused went out. I then heard a lot of rifle shots going off, and some minutes after this the accused came back and asked for his cap. I got out of bed and gave him his cap outside. He was carrying his rifle and it was pointed at me. I asked him to lower his rifle before I gave him his cap, which he did. I then seized the rifle and struggled for

> it. It went off in the struggle. Someone came and helped me. While the accused was struggling with me he fired three shots at me. Driver Gray came first to help me and took the rifle off him. When I was giving the accused his cap he said, 'I have shot the wrong man. I meant to shoot Ginger.' After he was secured, I went away.[15]

Under cross-examination by the Prisoner's Friend, Clayton recalled that just before Moore caused the two sergeants to flee, the NCO with a red moustache had ordered Moore to be quiet and go to bed. In response to a question by the court, Clayton stated he did not know any NCO named Ginger.

The third witness from No.5 Hut was Driver James Rush.[16]He had been drinking in the mess before retiring to bed but when he arrived, the other occupants were 'talking and making a good deal of noise.' Rush's evidence broadly concurred with the sequence of events that had already been outlined by earlier witnesses:

> After a bit, Captain Thompson came into the hut and told us all to be quiet. The accused said he would be quiet, and went over to his bed. A few minutes later I saw him with a rifle in his hand, and he appeared to be trying to work the bolt. He and Driver Kenny began struggling with each other. After they stopped struggling, the accused fired a rifle through the roof. Then someone came to the door, I think it was Captain Thompson,

> with some others, and the accused then loaded his rifle and came to the present. I shouted, 'Darky don't fire, it's the Captain.' The accused then went out with the rifle and I heard some shots being fired near the hut. A little later I heard Staff Sergeant Pick shouting. He was saying 'Chuck it Darky.' I recognized his voice. I know him well as I worked under him in the sick lines. Then I heard a shot fired. The shot and the voice appeared to come from the same place round by the bridge. I heard the accused say 'Oh it's you Pick is it?' and then I heard another shot go off. I then heard the accused a few minutes later asking for his cap just outside the door of the hut. One of the new drivers gave him his cap. The accused told him to take the cap badge out of it. During the struggle [between Clayton and Moore] I heard a shot fired. A whistle was then blown and we fell in.

Rush was not cross-examined but in response to a question by the court, he unequivocally identified Ginger:

> The Company Sergeant Major of the Company is Sergeant Bagshaw. He is known by the name of 'Ginger'. He has a ginger moustache. I do not know any other in the company that has the name 'Ginger'.[17]

Private Joseph Tarbuck, who was responsible for managing the NCOs' canteen in the camp, heard a great deal but saw very little about events on the fatal evening. Tarbuck told the Court:

I heard him say 'I don't want to shoot the Captain or get poor old Freddy [Bampton]. It is Ginger, the bastard that I want.'

He then heard, 'Look up Ginger' followed by shot. Tarbuck continued:

> After a few minutes later I heard Staff Sergeant Pick shouting 'Darky, Darky' several times from the direction of the Farrier's Shop. This is on the roadway by the barn. We always call the accused 'Darky'. I recognized the voice of Staff Sergeant Pick which I know. I then heard the accused say, 'Is that you Pick?' and then I heard two more shots fired. I then heard Sergeant Pick groan and shout 'Bristol, Bristol'.[18]

The next witness, Driver John Stevenson was disturbed by the shouting and shooting and could clearly see Moore at the entrance of the Sergeant Major's hut:

> I heard him say 'Get out Freddy. It is Ginger, the bastard that I want' or words to that effect ... I then saw him level his rifle and fire three shots into the hut. He then went to the back of the hut, and I lost sight of him ... later on I was sent to the sergeant major's hut ... There I found a

> greatcoat lying at the foot of the bed which I examined. I found several bullet holes in it.[19]

Stevenson was not subjected to cross-examination and the court adjourned so that the Members could examine the scene of the crime. When the court reconvened, the prosecution called Private Frank Bourton, who said he had been asleep in his hut until he was roused by the gunfire:

> I heard the accused cursing and swearing. I recognized his voice which I knew. I heard him say 'Ginger come out. I want you. Be a man.' After a bit all was quiet. Then I heard Staff Sergeant Pick's voice saying 'Don't be a fool Darky. Chuck it.' Then a shot was fired. Then after about half a minute of quiet, I heard a voice which I recognized as that of the accused say 'It is you Pick, is it?' There was no answer and after a bit I heard the accused say 'Speak. Won't you speak? I will make you speak.' I then heard another shot fired. This was from the direction in front of my hut. After this, I heard more shots fired. Then I heard a shout, 'Help, help I've got him.' I then came out of my hut and made my way to the place where the sound came from. While I was on my way three more shots rang out. When I arrived at the spot, I found the accused disarmed and secured.[20]

Staff-Sergeant Frederick Hanley recounted the bloody climax of Moore's nocturnal rampage:

> I was in the saddler's hut near the barn. I heard several shots fired. Then I heard the voice of the accused which I know well. I heard him say 'Speak Staff Pick, speak.' There was no reply that I heard. I heard the accused say 'You won't speak. Well this will make you speak.' In the meantime, I had got up and come out of the hut. I heard another shot fired just as I had come out. I came onto the bridge, and there I saw someone lying. I stooped down and asked who it was. The person lying said 'It is me Fred. I am done.' I recognized the voice as that of Staff Sergeant Pick. Assisted by others, I carried him into the Sergeant's mess.[21]

The man who assisted Hanley was Corporal Patrick Driscoll, who shared sleeping quarters with Pick. In his evidence, Driscoll referred to the latter's final words:

> I was sitting in the Farrier's shop just over the bridge. I heard the report of a rifle. Staff Sergeant Pick and Driver Green and I were in the shop at the time. I heard some more shots. Sergeant Pick went to the door, and I went with him. Sergeant Pick went out. I put out the light and went up to the loft where we sleep. Then I heard Sergeant Pick's voice calling for me. He said 'Driscoll, Driscoll.' I went out and found him lying on his

> back on the bridge and I helped to carry him into the Sergeant's mess and to lay him on the table. I saw that he had been wounded.[22]

Medical testimony was aired by two officers, the first of whom was Lieutenant John Robertson, who had arrived on the scene after Pick had been shot but in time to record his death. The subaltern, who had formerly been a medical student, told the court:

> I was coming towards the camp from the headquarters mess about 11.35pm, when I heard a shot followed by another shot. The shots seemed to come from the direction of the camp of 197 Company, A.S.C. I started to run to the camp. There I saw a party of men carrying a body and they took it to the Sergeant's mess under my orders. I then tore the uniform of the man open and looked to see where he was injured. I found one wound in the front of the right hip which came out at the back of the right buttock. I found another wound in his right armpit ... I dressed the wounds. The wounded man was living when I first came. I tested his heart and found it weak. It was just beating. His breath was just audible. At 11.47pm by my watch he died .... I am unable to state from the nature of these wounds the range from which the shots were fired. The first wound described appeared to have been inflicted by a shot fired on the level. The second appeared to have been fired from above.

The court asked Robertson which of the two wounds had proved fatal, which ought to have generated an objection from the Prisoner's Friend. Robertson was not a medical doctor and was therefore not qualified to give expert testimony but since no objection materialized Robertson proceeded to answer, 'Death, in my opinion, was caused by the second wound I have described.'[23]

However, a medical officer, Lieutenant Cyril Ilott RAMC, had arrived at the sergeant's mess while Robertson was conducting his examination of Pick's injuries.[24] Ilott shared his forensic findings with the court:

> I found two wounds. One was a wound where the bullet had entered in the front of the right hip passing out of the outer side of the right buttock. In the second wound the bullet had entered at the level of the right fifth rib at the level of the armpit, and had passed out below the tenth left rib in the line of the armpit. A large loop of the large bowel which had been ruptured was sticking out of the wound of exit. I am of the opinion that death had been caused by this upper wound. The position of the second wound gave me the impression that it was the result of a shot fired from above.

Ilott's remarks about the bullet wounds on Pick's body attracted no questions but he was cross-examined by the Prisoner's Friend about Moore's condition. Ilott recalled:

> I examined the accused that night. I formed the opinion that he had been drinking. He was heavily asleep when I first saw him. This was about 12.15am or thereabouts on the morning of the 12th Feb. I saw nothing then to show whether he was sane or insane. He was not fully conscious. I shook him violently to rouse him, and when he was partially roused I opened his eyelids. I observed that his pupils were moderately dilated and did not react to light. I tried the light of an electric torch. I was able to push my fingers into his eye without his blinking.

Given the importance of Moore's mental state, it is surprising that the Prisoner's Friend was uninterested in discovering more details from Ilott. Instead, clarification was solicited by the court, to which Ilott explained:

> I formed the conclusion from these tests that he was semi-conscious. I attributed this state of semi-consciousness to the influence of drink. He gave me the impression of a man recovering from drunkenness. I do not consider that his condition could have been the result of shock. This condition might have been of the result of drugs, or of a blow on the head....
>
> I can give no opinion as to the sanity of the accused as a result of my examination of him.

Because Ilott had conducted more than one examination of Moore, the prosecuting officer was interested in finding out whether the latter's behaviour had changed over time. In response to questioning by Major Hunter, Ilott recalled:

> I saw him a second time about an hour later. He was talking rationally. I mean he was talking coherently about the events of the night, but his speech was slurred. I have seen him on three occasions since. He was not on any of those occasions in the same condition as when I first saw him....

To the Court, Ilott explained:

> I have no special experience of mental diseases. When I asked him a question the other day, he answered me in a civil, rational manner. I have not seen any signs in the accused which I could recognize as signs of insanity.[25]

Ilott had qualified as a doctor in 1906 and had worked for more than nine months as a military surgeon. However, as he clearly and unequivocally reminded the court, he had no experience in mental diseases. He was therefore under no imperative to elaborate what he understood to be 'signs of insanity'. From the outset, Ilott decided that Moore was drunk and treated him as such; poking a doctorly finger into Moore's eye to check whether he was conscious was standard procedure for verifying the consciousness of drunks. Ilott's inspection of Moore was cursory; he entirely omitted to check for concussion or marks or bruises sustained by Moore when the latter was finally knocked down and disarmed.

The penultimate prosecution witness was Staff Sergeant-Major Frederick Bampton, whose evidence partly referred to what had already been covered by others' testimony. However, he drew attention to collateral damage that Moore had caused, and complained:

> On returning to my hut I found my overcoat which I had left lying at the foot of my bed which lies on the left of the door, had several bullet holes in it. Company Sergeant Major Bagshaw lives in the same hut as I do. I do not know of any nickname which he is called among the men. His bed is on the other side of the hut.

Cross-examined by the Prisoner's Friend, Bampton added, 'I saw the accused when I came out of my hut, and called upon the men to surround him. C.S.M. Bagshaw did not speak to him while I was there.'

Bampton's addendum begs a supplementary question that was never put by the Prisoner's Friend, exactly what had Bagshaw stated earlier during the evening to Moore?

The final witness for the prosecution was Lieutenant Colonel Frank Lord, the Officer Commanding 24th

Divisional Train. Lord had arrived in the camp at 11.40pm, after Moore had been handcuffed:

> I found the accused partially secured. I gave directions as to his being properly secured, and while this was being done I heard the accused say, 'Put a bullet through me. This is purgatory.' An hour afterwards when I went to see him again I heard him say 'It was Ginger Bagshaw I wanted. I had nothing against Pick.'[26]

He was not cross-examined and the prosecution was concluded.

The Prisoner's Friend opened the case for the defence by submitting a handwritten statement that was admitted as evidence but not immediately read out in court. Then one of the soldiers from No.5 Hut, Private Thomas Kenny, was summoned to testify. Kenny recalled:

> On the evening of February 11th, 1916, the accused and I left the camp at about a quarter to six with Driver Gray and Driver Lee. We went along the road as far as the green hut. We got there about a quarter to seven. There we had a few drinks ... Staff Sergeant Pick was there when we came in and he had a drink or two along with us. Then we came down the road, Staff Sergeant Pick and Driver Moore walking together. I came along too about 20 yards behind. I overtook them by the farm next to the farrier's shop where the

> Staff Sergeant lived. Then the accused and I went up to the hut. We sat on our beds and started talking and larking just as usual. A little later Captain Thompson came in and told us that if we did not make less noise he would put the whole lot of us under arrest. After that I heard a rifle shot go off through the roof. The accused fired it. That was the first shot that was fired. Then he dropped the rifle and I went and told him to be quiet and go to bed. He laid down in bed quietly for about five minutes. He then got up again, and I gripped him and set him down in the bed again. After that I left the hut. I crossed over by the stables, and came round behind the farm where I saw Capt. Thompson ... The accused was neither drunk nor sober when I left him but between the two. He had had a good few drinks. I heard no mention of C[ompany]. S[ergeant]. M[ajor]. Bagshaw or the name 'Ginger'. When Pick and the accused left the *estaminet* they were the best of friends.

Kenny was the only witness to be interrogated about his sobriety. Major Hunter asked him if he had been drunk that night, to which Kenny replied:

> I was pretty sober when I came home. I left the hut because I thought the accused would quieten down. I heard some shots fired as I walked about the camp. I was away from the hut for about three quarters of an hour.[27]

Kenny's final recollection was in response to a question by the court. What he had to say referred to an intriguing issue that had not thus far figured in the proceedings:

> There was no chaffing or bullying of the accused that night. His mind seemed to have changed all at once.

Harassment or 'ragging' by NCOs or erstwhile comrades of weak or vulnerable soldiers was not unusual in the British or any other army but the court was wholly disinterested in finding out from Kenny exactly who may have been involved and why Moore was chaffed or bullied.

The second witness for the Defence was a 35-year-old friend who had known Moore before the war when they had both worked as labourers in Darlington. William Lee was able to provide some background information about Moore's family:

> I know the accused well. He and I come from Darlington where I know him and his family. His mother is in the asylum – the Durham County asylum – if she is still alive. His father is an eccentric sort of chap who knocks about the race courses. His brother is a wild sort of chap. I have been in the same company as the accused all along. He is a very strange chap if he gets a glass of beer. On the night in question ... I went down the road with the accused to an *estaminet*

> where we found Sergeant Pick and had some drinks together. We were all quite cheery and good friends, including Sergeant Pick.

In response to a question from Major Hunter, Lee added:

> I only know that the mother was in the asylum as a matter of common knowledge. I have met the father once or twice.[28]

He also told the court that on 11 February the drinking session in the *estaminet* had ended at about 8.00pm and that Moore was not drunk, only 'cheery'.

After Lee had answered the final question, the court adjourned to consider its verdict. It is doubtful whether the three officers spent very long deliberating about their decision; they concluded Moore was guilty of murder and then examined the statement that had earlier been submitted by the Prisoner's Friend. It read:

> Last Friday night we were paid about 5.30pm and I received fifteen francs. About six o'clock in company with Drivers Kenny, Lee, and Gray of 197 Coy. I went to an *estaminet* on the left-hand side of the road to Poperinghe. We had several drinks of English beer and stout. We were joking with each other when Staff Sergeant Farrier Pick came over and joined us. Dvr. Lee then stood the five of us a drink. We were all enjoying ourselves.

> Just after this, Staff Sergeant Farrier Pick went out. He returned in a few minutes and stood the five of us drinks. We had more drink and then it was near closing time. Staff Sgt. Farr. Pick and myself left the *estaminet* together and walked down the road towards the camp. When we got as far as the first cross-roads Pick offered me a drink out of a bottle. I drank some. The next thing I remember was wrestling with someone at the doorway of the hut where I slept. He is a man from No.1 Company and is called 'Dick'. The next thing I knew of was that I was tied to the ground and that Col. Lord shifted my legs.

The court re-opened and Major Hunter was called to provide the details about Moore's chequered disciplinary record during 1915: On 29 April for being absent from the stables overnight he was later confined to barracks for three days; on Monday 18 May for twenty-four hours absence he was confined to barracks for a week. On the night of 18 July he was punished with another week's confinement to barracks for being drunk and disorderly in camp.[29] On 20 September while en route to Loos during the forced march imposed on 24 Division by General Haking, Moore had knocked down a civilian, fought with a comrade and resisted arrest at Lebiez for which he was fined ten days' pay and awarded a fortnight's Field Punishment No.1.[30]

On 14 November, for 'Recklessly firing off a rifle' and 'Threatening to take his [own] life,' Moore had been punished with twenty-one days' Field Punishment No.1. It is tempting to infer that the two charges were directly related and that Moore's mind was temporarily unbalanced. However, in the absence of any further details all that may be surmised is that the experience caused Moore to resent the chief witness, who was Company Sergeant Bagshaw. If so, there were others in No.5 Hut who may have had very similar reasons for having a grudge against Bagshaw.[31]

The court recommended that Moore be executed but pending confirmation of sentence, the condemned man was invited to make a statement in mitigation. Moore commented, 'I was out of my mind at the time, and I don't know what happened.'[32]

For a number of reasons the outcome of the trial was never very much in doubt. The Prisoner's Friend had made a poor show of advancing the case for the defence and his cross-examination of witnesses appears to have been feeble. His failure to urge the court to summon Bagshaw to give evidence about the CSM's role in events on 11 February is frankly mystifying.

Given the case for the defence hinged on Moore's mental state, the Prisoner's Friend made no discernible effort to call for expert medical testimony, even after Ilott's admission that he had no special expertise in mental health. If genuine, what may have caused Moore's self-declared amnesia?

If Moore's loss of memory was due to intoxication then either the contents of James Pick's bottle must have been very potent or the men quartered in his hut carried on drinking after Lights Out. Certainly, witness evidence aired by men from No.5 Hut contained discrepancies about who did what, when and also to whom. Unfortunately for Moore, being drunk and shooting dead the (sic) wrong man is no defence for murder.

If Moore's amnesia was in some way linked with his mother's mental ailments then in the interests of justice, the issue should have been further pursued by the Prisoner's Friend. However, Moore had declined to give evidence under oath and risk having his personal history probed under cross-examination. Aside from a chaotic childhood, including a spell in institutional care, before the war Moore had also been an army deserter and was a convicted thief. In 1911 he had briefly served as a Special Reservist with the 3rd Battalion Yorkshire Regiment before enlisting as a driver with the Royal Field Artillery and going absent without leave after less than two months' service. He remained at liberty for two years and after a brief spell in military detention, Moore rejoined the ranks. He served satisfactorily until 21 June 1914, when he was arrested by the police for stealing a bicycle and sentenced to two months' imprisonment. As a consequence of his criminal conviction Moore had been discharged from the Army on 27 July 1914.[33]

Damaging though his pre-war antics may have been, it does not alter the fact that no evidence was produced during his trial to prove that Thomas Moore ever planned or intended to kill James Pick. Moreover, due account needs to be taken of his public humiliation by officers and men of 197th Company, including virtually everyone who gave evidence at Moore's trial. On 12 February the company was given a tongue-lashing by the company commander, Major Blakeway. The War Diary noted:

> Paraded No.197 Coy. and strafed them for behaviour when Driver Moore threatened to shoot Capt. Thompson and for not going for the man and disarming him, also for conduct generally.[34]

On 15 February, the entire company was again drawn up on parade to be personally rebuked by the officer commanding 24th Division, Major General Thompson 'Stone Age' Capper.[35] Capper did not directly order the court to find Moore guilty but as the officer responsible for convening the court martial, it was unnecessary for him to have done so. Brave indeed or foolhardy would have been anyone who would have sought to delay or interfere with the speedy execution of Moore.

Woolwich, S.E.

15th. March, 1916.

Madam,

I have to inform you that No.T/4/040862 Driver Thomas Moore, Army Service Corps, was sentenced after trial by Field General Court Martial to be shot, and the sentence was duly executed at 5.40 a.m. on the 26th. day of February 1916.

I am,

Madam,

Your obedient Servant,

Lieutenant.

Asst: for Colonel i/c A.S.C. Records.

Mrs. N.Dixon,

2, King Street,

DARLINGTON.

The Secretary,
War Office, S.W.1.

T4/040862 Drver T.Moore.

With reference to War Office letter 45/Gen.No./1728, B.M.4281 (A.G.I.R.) dated 17th.July, I beg to report that the above mentioned man enlisted in the R.A.S.C.on the 7th.January 1915, was convicted and dealt with as shown on the attached copy of 24th.Division Routine Orders.

Will you please favour me with a decision as to whether his misconduct should debar the next-of-kin receiving the Memorial Plaque and Scroll.

Colonel.

Woolwich Dockyard,
6th.August.1919.
Casualty Branch.

i/c R.A.S.C.Records.

[redacted] ...fications on this ...ressed to – ...War Office, London, S.W.1. ...number quoted

WAR OFFICE,
LONDON, S.W.1.

August 1919.

B.M.4281 (A.G.1.R.)
Enclo to 45/Gen No/1728.

WOOLWICH DOCKYARD
R.A.S.C. RECORDS
5 AUG 1919

Officer in Charge,
R.A.S.C. Records,
Woolwich Dockyard.

With reference to your letters CR/22843/Cas/16 and CR/77520/Cas/16 dated 6th instant, concerning the issue of the Plaque & Scroll to the next of kin in respect of the undermentioned:-

No T1/4135.	Driver W.J.Laws.	Issue approved.
T4/040862.	Driver T.Moore.	Issue <u>not</u> approved.

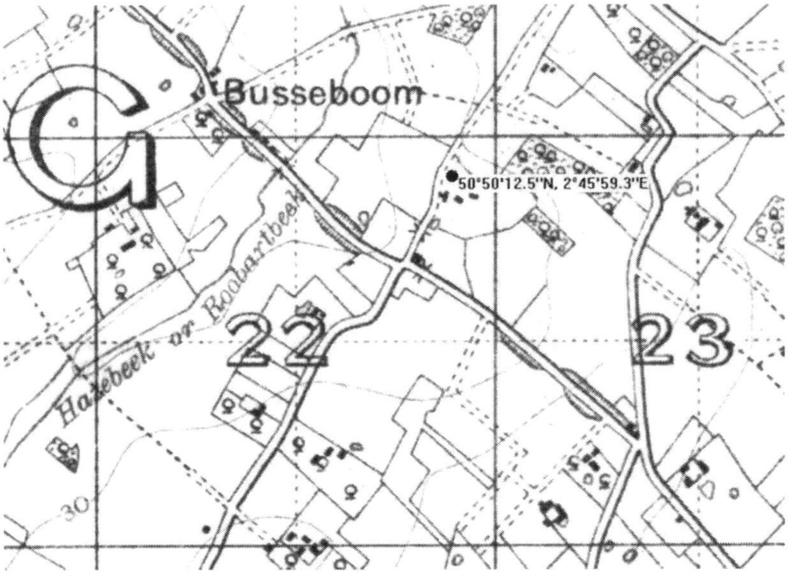

Driver Thomas Moore, buried at Devonshire Farm, Busseboom but recorded as Missing on the Menin Gate Memorial, Ieper.

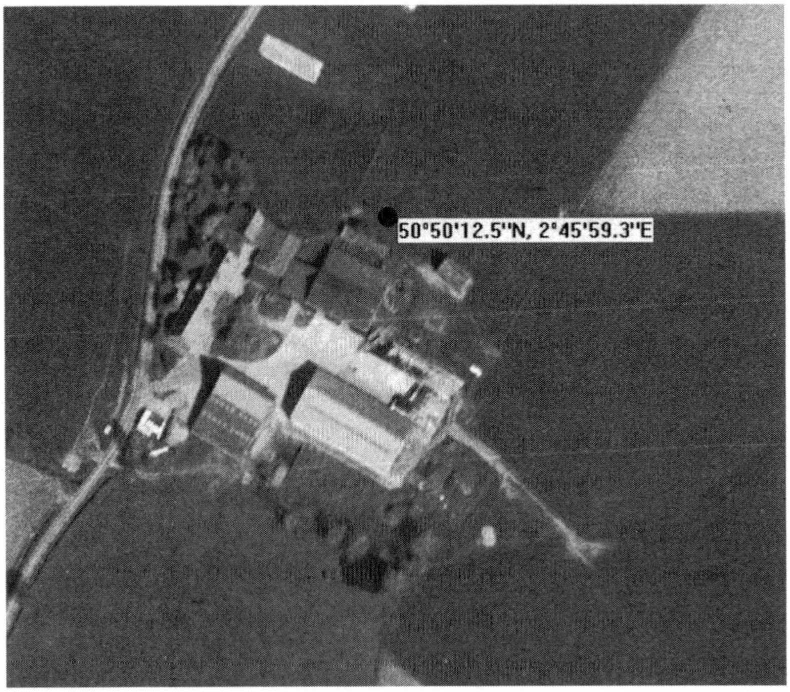

Moore's execution was supervised by Lieutenant Colonel Lord and carried out by a firing party composed of men from his company at Devonshire Camp, near Busseboom, at 5.35am on 26 February. Captain Ilott signed the death certificate and Lord sent a memorandum to HQ, 24th Division, reporting where the executed man's corpse was buried.[36] As next of kin, Moore's sister, Nelly Dixon, was officially notified about his death, but it was to Kathleen Finch, his 11-year-old niece, that he bequeathed all his worldly possessions.[37]

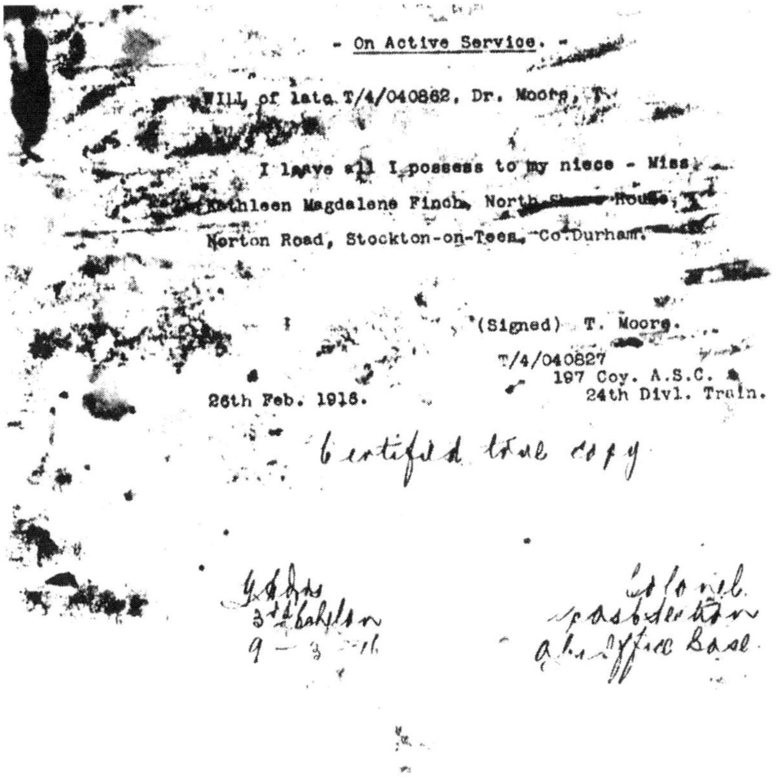

- On Active Service. -

WILL of late T/4/040862, Dr. Moore, T.

I leave all I possess to my niece - Miss Kathleen Magdalene Finch, North [illegible] House, Norton Road, Stockton-on-Tees, Co. Durham.

(Signed) T. Moore.
T/4/040827
197 Coy. A.S.C.
24th Divl. Train.

26th Feb. 1916.

Certified true copy

3rd [illegible]
9-3-16

Colonel
[illegible]
[illegible] Base

CHAPTER 5

Accidentally Inflicted

When war broke out, Arthur Dale, a 46-year-old Royal Scots reservist was working as a labourer in Belper, Derbyshire.[1] He rejoined his regiment in November and was posted to 13th Battalion Royal Scots, with whom he landed in France on 4 August 1915. He saw action during the battle of Loos, and was lucky to survive after the battalion was strafed by British artillery firing short and latterly by enemy guns during the struggle for Hill 70.[2]

The battalion spent the chilly winter months enduring week-long tours of duty at the front, alternating with a week's rest in the 15th Division reserve lines. Sleet and snow showers persisted after the New Year, and it was still bitterly cold at the beginning of February when the Dale and other men from his dozen-strong section were billeted in the hayloft of a disused brewery adjacent to the rue d'Arras, Noeuxles-Mines. Situated about 8 kilometres behind the British front lines, Nouex-Les-Mines was a grubby, war-battered town on the Gohelle Plain, a coal-mining region with an abundance of slag heaps. Many of Nouex-les-Mines 8,000 citizens had fled and although notionally afforded some relief when in reserve, routine duties allowed soldiers precious little free time in which to sample what remained of the town's leisure facilities.

On the morning of Monday, 7 February, after having completed their spell of guard duty at the company's blanket store, two of Dale's comrades, Private Henry Wickham and Lance Corporal James Sneddon, who was also the NCO in charge of the section, decided to visit a nearby *estaminet.*[3] After a while they were joined by Private Robert Hutchinson and a decidedly inebriated Arthur Dale, who settled down at a table and quaffed a couple of bottles of stout apiece.[4] Sneddon then asked Dale if the latter had carried out some unspecified work and after eliciting an assent nothing further was exchanged between them until shortly after 11.00am, when the NCO declared that it was time for them all to move out. He approached Dale and Hutchinson and ordered them to gather their kit and equipment from the billet and prepare to march to Philosophe, a village about a kilometre and a half distant from Noeux-les-Mines. Dale initially said nothing but did as he was told, albeit cursing obscenely, and assisted in making his exit by a push from Sneddon.

Dale managed to stagger back to the courtyard at the rear of the brewery but access to the entrance of their sleeping quarters in the hayloft was via a 10-foot long ladder from the courtyard at the rear of the brewery. Sneddon grasped the collar of Dale's greatcoat and led him to the foot of ladder but the soldier managed to climb to the top without further assistance and disappeared inside. Sneddon and the two soldiers waited for Dale, who re-appeared after less than a minute at the doorway and addressed the NCO, saying, 'Here you are, Corporal.' A shot rang out and the bullet hit Sneddon in the belly; he immediately collapsed and lay moaning on the ground in front of Wickham and Hutchinson. The latter glimpsed Dale standing at the top of the ladder, loosely hanging onto a rifle, the muzzle of which was pointed down towards the courtyard, before busying himself trying to staunch Sneddon's wounds, while Wickham dashed away to summon medical assistance.[5]

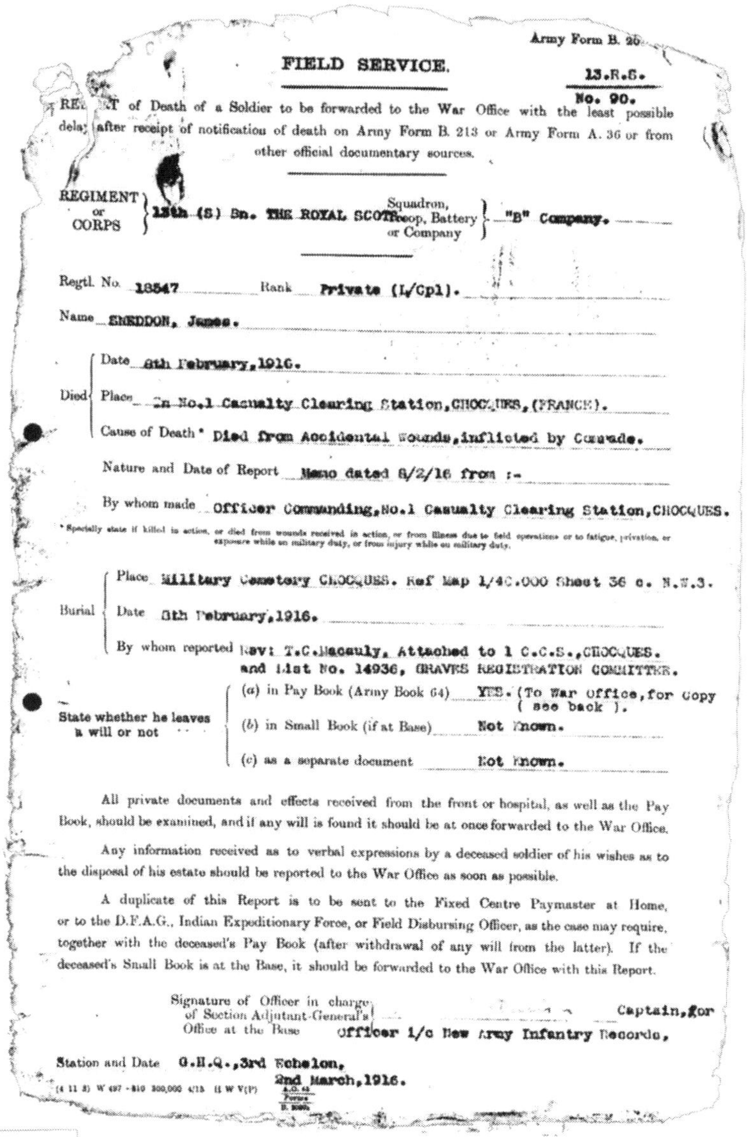

Army Form B. 20

FIELD SERVICE.

13.R.S.

No. 90.

REPORT of Death of a Soldier to be forwarded to the War Office with the least possible delay after receipt of notification of death on Army Form B. 213 or Army Form A. 36 or from other official documentary sources.

REGIMENT or CORPS: 13th (S) Bn. THE ROYAL SCOTS. Squadron, Troop, Battery or Company: "B" Company.

Regtl. No. 18547 Rank Private (L/Cpl).

Name SNEDDON, James.

Died — Date 8th February, 1916.
Place In No.1 Casualty Clearing Station, CHOCQUES, (FRANCE).
Cause of Death* Died from Accidental Wounds, inflicted by Comrade.

Nature and Date of Report Memo dated 8/2/16 from :-

By whom made Officer Commanding, No.1 Casualty Clearing Station, CHOCQUES.

*Specially state if killed in action, or died from wounds received in action, or from illness due to field operations or to fatigue, privation, or exposure while on military duty, or from injury while on military duty.

Burial — Place Military Cemetery CHOCQUES. Ref Map 1/40.000 Sheet 36 c. N.W.3.
Date 9th February, 1916.
By whom reported Rev: T.C.Macauly, Attached to 1 C.C.S., CHOCQUES. and List No. 14936, GRAVES REGISTRATION COMMITTEE.

State whether he leaves a will or not —
(a) in Pay Book (Army Book 64) YES. (To War Office, for Copy (see back).
(b) in Small Book (if at Base) Not Known.
(c) as a separate document Not Known.

All private documents and effects received from the front or hospital, as well as the Pay Book, should be examined, and if any will is found it should be at once forwarded to the War Office.

Any information received as to verbal expressions by a deceased soldier of his wishes as to the disposal of his estate should be reported to the War Office as soon as possible.

A duplicate of this Report is to be sent to the Fixed Centre Paymaster at Home, or to the D.F.A.G., Indian Expeditionary Force, or Field Disbursing Officer, as the case may require, together with the deceased's Pay Book (after withdrawal of any will from the latter). If the deceased's Small Book is at the Base, it should be forwarded to the War Office with this Report.

Signature of Officer in charge of Section Adjutant-General's Office at the Base — Captain, for Officer i/c New Army Infantry Records,

Station and Date G.H.Q., 3rd Echelon, 2nd March, 1916.

Even before Wickham returned with a doctor, another medical officer had begun to attend to treat Sneddon's wounds and an ambulance arrived, whisking the NCO away before a couple of British mounted military policemen arrived at the scene.[6] By the time the policemen had arrived, all that remained in the courtyard was a puddle of Sneddon's blood on the ground at the foot of the ladder and a crowd of soldiers milling around the vicinity, some of whom told the policemen where they might find the gunman.

The two policemen climbed up the ladder and entered the hayloft, where they found Dale lying, curled up on the floor. They attempted to interrogate him but Dale did not appear to understand anything and had to be picked up and lowered down the ladder by the collar of his greatcoat before being escorted away and detained in custody.[7]

Meanwhile, Sneddon had been transported for more than an hour along 10 kilometres of bone-jolting, cobbled road to No.1 Casualty Clearing Station at Chocques, where he was examined at 1.00pm. Although he was still conscious, the traumatized NCO was in agony and the bullet wound was so grave that there was nothing medical staff could perform by way of remedial surgery. The bullet had smashed through Sneddon's upper abdominal cavity, penetrated his intestines and exited through his buttocks. Even had it proved possible to stitch up his guts, Sneddon would have been doomed by massive internal infection and contamination caused by bullet-impacted fragments of clothing and dirt. Though he survived for a further twelve hours and his suffering was alleviated with doses of morphine, there was nothing more that could have been done for the stricken man.[8]

Dale was charged with murder and tried by FGCM at Mazingarbe on 20 February. The President of the Court was Lieutenant General Charles Henning, 7th Royal Scots Fusiliers; the two Members were Captain James Farquhar, 6th Cameron Highlanders and Captain James Mitchell, 11th Argyll and Sutherland Highlanders. A court martial officer, Lieutenant Neville Anderson, London Rifle Brigade, was appointed to advise the court and the prosecution was probably conducted by the Adjutant of 13th Battalion Royal Scots, Captain Christopher Francis. Another captain from Dale's battalion, Captain Charles Yule, was assigned to assist the defendant, who had entered a plea of not guilty.[9]

Private Wickham was the first witness to give evidence for the prosecution. He recalled what had happened during the fatal morning, confirming that Dale was very drunk but understood Sneddon's orders and had managed to climb up the ladder to the hayloft without any assistance. Wickham explained that he had heard Dale call out to the NCO and seen 'He had his rifle up to his shoulder, and immediately fired a shot' at Sneddon.[10] Since neither the court nor Yule cross-examined Wickham about his testimony, the next witness, Private Hutchinson, was sworn in.

Hutchinson broadly corroborated much of what Wickham had to relate about Dale being drunk even before they had entered the *estaminet* but recalled that although unaided, the latter had 'staggered' up the ladder. Hutchinson also heard Dale declare 'Here you are corporal,' but he did not see him take aim or fire, and he recalled how Sneddon had fallen at his feet and cried out, 'Oh my poor wife and bairns.' Hutchinson had looked up and seen Dale, 'Holding a rifle with the butt under his right armpit and the muzzle pointing down' before he vanished into the hayloft. After three or four minutes Hutchinson and another comrade, Private Rush, clambered up the ladder and found Dale lying behind the door, crying and in a delirious state.[11]

Under cross-examination by Yule, Hutchinson confirmed that he had not at any time heard Dale direct foul language at Hutchinson. In fact, he asserted that the two men were good friends.

The third witness was one of the two military policemen who had arrested Dale. Corporal William Howarth explained to the court that the ladder was about 10 feet high and did not have a handrail. On entering the hayloft he discovered Dale lying prone behind the door and his rifle was propped up against the wall some 2 feet away. Howarth added:

> I spoke to the accused and told him he would be a prisoner for having shot the Corporal. He made no reply at this time. He was drunk. I don't think he understood what I said to him.... I handed the rifle to Corporal Rogers, and afterwards I examined it. There were four live cartridges in the magazine and one empty case in the breech.... The accused did not seem to realize that he had shot Lance Corporal Sneddon.[12]

Yule decline to cross-examine Howarth and the court proceeded to hear the second military policemen, Corporal William Rogers. Rogers testified that Dale:

> was very drunk and crying, and mumbling in a stupid way. Corporal Howarth told him he had come to arrest him. I can't say whether the accused understood what Corporal Howarth said to him ... I saw a rifle leaning against a wall near the accused. The accused said it was his rifle. He told us this when we had got down the ladder and before we left the yard. We asked him for his equipment and rifle. He then told us that the rifle was his. We found four live cartridges in the magazine and one discharged one in the breech. The cut-off was closed.[13]

Rogers was not cross-examined and the prosecution called its final witness, Captain Haycraft, an experienced military surgeon serving with No.1 Casualty Clearing Station. He recounted details about the nature of Sneddon's fatal wound, and in response to an enquiry from Captain Yule, recalled, 'Lance Corporal Sneddon stated that he had been accidentally wounded in his billet.'[14]

With that, the prosecution rested. It was now the turn of the defence.

Yule did not call Dale to testify on his own behalf but summoned a couple of character witnesses. Corporal Robert Bain testified briefly about the cordial relationship that existed between Dale and the dead NCO:

> I was in the same platoon as Lance Corporal Sneddon and the accused and knew them both. They were very friendly with each other and I never knew them to have a quarrel.[15]

It was very rare for a Regimental Sergeant Major to testify in court, let alone to speak positively about a soldier accused of murder. As an experienced, highly trusted professional soldier and the most senior warrant officer in a battalion, William Price's opinion of a soldier's character would usually have carried considerable weight with the officers of 13th Battalion Royal Scots. Of Dale, Price declared, 'I know the accused and have known him from 1890-1898 when soldiering in the 2nd Battalion, Royal Scots. He was a good soldier and a good character.'[16]

Yule's concluding remarks were paraphrased in the written proceedings, in which he reminded the court, 'The evidence shows no premeditation or malice aforethought. The deceased L/Corp. himself said it was an accident.'[17]

The court was unimpressed; Dale was found guilty of murder and sentenced to death. The convicted soldier made no statement in mitigation but as was customary, 46-year-old Dale's disciplinary record was attached to the proceedings. His record of service was unblemished by any misconduct and his character was classified therein as 'Good'.[18]

The written proceedings were then passed along the chain of command and a succession of increasingly senior officers was required to express their personal opinion about the case. The papers were forwarded without comment by 45th Infantry Brigade headquarters to Major General Frederick McCracken, the officer commanding 15th (Scottish) Division, who observed, 'There appears to be no doubt that No.4437 Pte. A. Dale was drunk at the time of the occurrence.'[19]

The commander of 4th Corps, Lieutenant General Sir Henry Wilson, commented:

> Three things:
>
> (a) The man was drunk
> (b) There was apparently, no motive for the crime.
> (c) The man has a very good character.
>
> I do ***not*** think this a case [for] the extreme penalty.[20]

However, the recently appointed Commander of 1st Army, General Sir Charles Monro, disagreed.[21] Instead of advancing any justification for his opinion, Monro took the opportunity to draw attention to his own review of routine orders:

> I recommend the execution of the sentence in this case – Enquiry is being made as to the Rules in place governing the question of arms in Billets so as to ensure that magazines do not remain charged in the circumstances.[22]

Field Marshal Sir Douglas Haig simply scribbled 'Confirmed' on the court martial schedule, entered the date and, via a couple of pencilled addenda, inferred criticism of the failure by the brigade and divisional commanders to enter their opinions about the case.[23]

Voluntary intoxication was not regarded as a valid defence but it could be taken into account by the court when considering the vitally important element of intent to commit murder.[24] From the written proceedings it appears pretty clear that Dale was too drunk to form the legally necessary intent to murder Sneddon and no evidence of premeditation was produced during the hearing. Testimony favourable to the defence was even presented by prosecution witnesses, including the victim, albeit indirectly via the testimony of Captain Haycraft.

From the written proceedings, Yule's advocacy appears rather less than robust and may be partially excused by his lack of legal training or experience of courts martial. Nor, as was also the case in a number of other capital courts martial, does the notionally verbatim written record of the trial appear to record in full what the defence stated. Even so, it is unclear why Dale himself did not give evidence. Although he may have been unlikely to recall much about the shooting, Dale was plainly remorseful and an expression of contrition may have induced the court to return a verdict of manslaughter. Much else about the hearing is mired in surmise because the written exchanges include neither a record of the court's deliberations nor advice offered by Captain Anderson, the courts martial officer. However, if the officers of the court were instructed on the issue of manslaughter, it certainly did not arise because of anything that was advanced by Yule in his defence of Dale.

Major Kenneth Beatty, the Assistant Provost Marshal, 15th Division, choreographed Dale's execution in the abattoir at Mazingarbe. The firing squad was composed of men from the condemned man's battalion, who duly carried out their task and the condemned man's death was recorded by Lieutenant Arthur Jekyll as having occurred at 6.35am on 3 March 1916.[25]

Dale was interred in Mazingarbe Communal Cemetery, his family were notified about his fate and rather unusually they were permitted by the military authorities to retain the dead man's 1915 campaign medal. James Sneddon was buried in Chocques Military Cemetery but rather ironically, his personal service papers reveal that six weeks before embarking for service overseas he had been sentenced to twenty-one days detention for striking an NCO while drunk, and the entry recording his cause of death states: 'Died of wounds No.1 C.C. Station accidentally inflicted by a comrade - 8.2.16.'[26]

CHAPTER 6

The Missing Kilt

Pioneer battalions were unglamorous pick and shovel auxiliaries responsible for maintaining and constructing trenches. Companies from pioneer battalions also worked independently and were frequently detached to serve with other formations.[1] Thus, at the end of August 1916, Private Francis Murray and an unspecified number of fellow pioneers from 9th Battalion Gordon Highlanders and other Scottish battalions came to be lodged in a barrack hut at the 173rd Tunnelling Company, Royal Engineers depot on the outskirts of Noeux-Les-Mines.[2]

In cold weather or when trench digging, Scottish kilted battalions sometimes wore trousers but otherwise all ranks were required to wear kilts, and if a Gordon Highlander lost his kilt the cost of a replacement ran to two or three weeks' pay. Victims of kilt theft were understandably upset and disposed to recover their property as soon as possible.

Such emotions certainly informed Murray's behaviour early on 2 September 1916, when he could not find his kilt. Convinced that he knew the culprit, Murray promptly accused and then assaulted Private James Glen, Royal Scots.[3] He then left the depot and went to Noeux-les-Mines, where he was later spotted drinking stout in an *estaminet* and by the time he returned to camp it was dinnertime (circa 1.00pm) and Murray was thoroughly drunk.

During the early afternoon Murray began to behave in an erratic and unsettling manner. Private William Lynch recalled:

> About 2.00pm he came into the hut and drew a bayonet, after standing a few minutes threw it on the ground. He then picked it up and went and got another bayonet. Pte. Maguire went up and took the bayonets from him ... [Murray] then came and got his rifle and went to the door. Another man then took the rifle from him and threw it back on his bed.

Murray then went over to his bed but this time it was Lynch who acted:

> I noticed him handling his rifle, I went over and took away the bolt and told Corporal Rogers what I had done. He [Corporal Rogers?] went into the hut and I then left.[4]

It is not clear what happened immediately after Lynch departed but Murray seems to have also gone out and returned to the hut at about 3.30pm, still in a very drunken state. On re-entering the hut Murray spotted Private Glen but instead of acting aggressively, Murray shook hands and made friends again. Glen then left and was seated outside the hut when a dishevelled Murray emerged with a loaded rifle and fired five or six rounds at random.

Murray staggered around the camp, crossed over the barbed wire perimeter fence and went into an adjacent garden. He noticed that a handful of unarmed soldiers was stalking him and fired a couple of rounds in their direction. The shots struck a hut but also wounded two sappers.

Attracted by the commotion, a further hundred soldiers emerged on the scene and began to hurl stones at Murray, who staggered around for a while, waving his rifle and motioning soldiers to come on. After having fired a further couple of rounds, he tripped over the guy rope of a tent and was pounced upon by a dozen soldiers and disarmed.

While Murray was being handcuffed and taken into custody, attention turned to the two wounded men, Lance Corporal Lionel Woodthorpe and Sapper William Damper. Woodthorpe had been struck by a single round that injured his back and right elbow but Damper sustained two body wounds from a ricochet and died of an internal haemorrhage shortly after being admitted to No.6 Casualty Clearing Station at Barlin.[5]

Murray was tried by a field general court martial convened by Major General Harold Ruggles-Brise, the Officer Commanding 40th Division. The trial took place on 24 September in a hut at the 173rd Tunnelling

Company camp, less than 100 metres away from where Murray had been rampaging. The President was Major Robert Bell Turton, a barrister who was also second in command of the 12th Battalion Yorkshire Regiment, the Pioneer battalion of 40th Division. The two Members were Captain Leslie Burbidge, Army Service Corps and Lieutenant Edward Graham, Royal Field Artillery. The court martial officer, Captain Edward Chapman, Yorkshire Regiment, and the Prisoner's Friend, Lieutenant Joseph Healy, Army Service Corps, had been barristers.[6]

With reference to Damper, Murray was charged with murder and an alternative charge of manslaughter. He was also charged with shooting Woodthorpe with murderous intent and two lesser, alternative charges of inflicting grievous bodily harm and unlawful wounding. After Murray had pleaded not guilty to the charges, the prosecuting officer, Captain Bryan Freeland, 173rd Company Royal Engineers, summoned as his first witness one of the men under his command, Corporal Richard Dobson.[7]

Dobson produced a roughly sketched scale plan of the 173rd Company camp that was accepted as evidence by the court. The corporal was not cross-examined by Lieutenant Healy nor did the court demand the original plan of the camp be produced instead of the scale drawing that had been specially created for the prosecution.

If the original document was available then Dobson's sketch constituted secondary evidence and may even have been unnecessary, since the scene of crime was readily visible from the hut in which the trial was being conducted. However, the second witness, Corporal Frederick Wells, made use of Dobson's map to trace the movements of individuals and to deliver his account of the sequence of events:

> At about 4.10pm on 2nd Sept. 1916, I was in the yard of the 173rd Company, RE, at Noeux-les-Mines. I was in [the] rear of the parade ground. I saw the accused come from the hut marked **A:** he was carrying a rifle; after leaving the hut, I saw him capering about outside the door of the hut; about two minutes later I saw him fire his rifle; he brought the rifle up to his shoulder and fired in the direction of the cookhouse, **B,** at the end of the parade ground.
>
> I went into the Sergeant's mess, and from the doorway I saw him fire four more rounds. When he had finished the five rounds, I, Corporal Woodthorpe and Sapper Todd, made for the accused, who was getting through the barbed wire at the point **C** on the plan. The accused saw us coming. I saw him sink down on one knee and point his rifle at us. Woodthorpe and I ran round the corner of the cookhouse, by the Sergeant's mess, **D** on the plan. Todd was on the wire.

> I went into the cookhouse of the Sergeant's mess and observed the accused through the window. Corporal Woodthorpe and Sapper Damper were outside the cookhouse. I saw the accused repeatedly put his rifle to his shoulder and point it towards the cookhouse. I then saw the accused bring his rifle to his shoulder more deliberately than before: I dropped down in the corner of the hut and heard two shots fired in rapid succession. The first shot entered the hut immediately above my head, through the corner of the hut and I heard Corporal Woodthorpe shout, 'I've got it Freddy.' The second shot passed just underneath my chin, it passed through the hut and I saw Sapper Damper fall. I could see him through the open door. When I saw the accused just before firing the two shots referred to, he was in my opinion pointing his rifle at Todd.
>
> I think that I and Woodthorpe were at that time not in view of the accused. Damper was also out of sight of the accused at the moment the two shots were fired. Todd was at **E.** Woodthorpe was at **F.** Damper was at **G.** I was at **H.** The accused was at **I,** in the middle of the garden, about 50 yards away from us.[8]

Healy did not cross-examine Wells but the court wanted to hear more. In response to questions put to him by the President, Wells provided further details:

When I saw the accused come out of the hut **A,** he seemed as though he were mad drunk and silly. He was shouting out, I could not hear what. He had on a pair of trousers, and a shirt; one arm only was in his shirt; I think he had slippers on. He was dancing about; I thought he was drunk because he was acting in such a strange manner. I never saw him fall down. The first two shots went towards the cookhouse at the end of the yard; the next two shots were fired towards **X** [the room in which the court was sitting]. The fifth shot was fired down the parade ground in front of the huts. Each time he fired, he put his rifle to his shoulder and fired at once, apparently without taking any aim. Men were walking about in the yard at the time. During the whole of the time I never was able to distinguish what he was saying. I saw no one near him nor did I hear anyone say anything to him. I never saw the accused reload his rifle.[9]

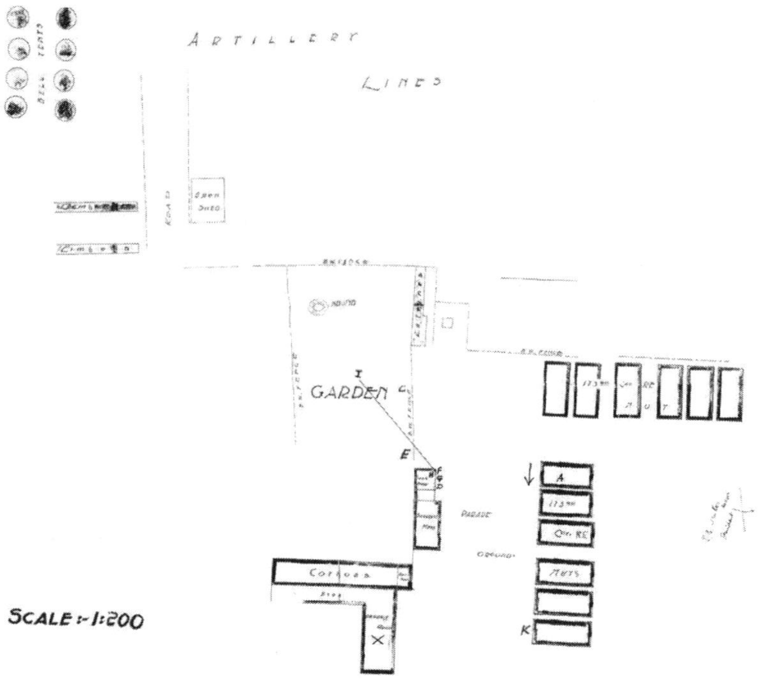

173rd Depot, Royal Engineers, Nouex-les-Mines (for greater clarity, letters A to X reorientated)

The ensuing testimony from Corporal Hugh Rice, 173rd Company, also included an account of how Woodthorpe and Damper came to be wounded:

> At about 4.00pm … I was in the hut marked **K.** I heard rifle shots. I went out and found the accused with a rifle in his hand and taking aim now and again. I saw only one shot fired: he was then in the yard. I and some other men rushed towards him. He went towards the garden and went through the barbed wire into the garden. We were then at the corner of the Sergeant's mess. I attempted twice to get through the wire

to him but whenever I did so he aimed his rifle in my direction: this happened twice.

I then lay down behind the corner of the Sergeant's mess. While there I heard two shots fired in succession. On looking round I found Woodthorpe and Damper lying down beside me wounded. I don't think the accused could see the result of his two shots: I don't think he could see either Woodthorpe or Damper fall.

I then got up off my belly and saw the accused walking away towards the other side of the garden in the direction of the artillery limbers. He then fired his rifle again pointing it in the air. I saw him leave the limbers and go towards the bell tents. I saw him trip over a tent rope and fall face downwards and I saw an artilleryman catch him.

As soon as I looked round after the firing of the two shots, I saw that Damper had a wound near the small of his back it was bleeding slightly. Before the accused left the yard and entered the garden I saw men throwing stones at him.[10]

Under cross-examination by Healy, Rice admitted that he never got any closer than 20 yards away from Murray but concluded:

> The accused was not in full possession of his senses. He never stood very long in one position.

In response to a request from the court for further clarification about the stone throwing and Murray's lurching progress across the camp yard and into the garden, Rice stated:

> I first saw men throwing stones at the accused after he had fired the shot in the yard before he got into the garden. I should think that something like a hundred men were throwing stones at him from all directions. This went on for about a minute. There was no stone throwing when I first came out of my hut. There was not much shouting going on.
>
> I could not hear the accused say anything. When I first saw the accused he was staggering about in the yard; it was the sort of staggering that one sees in the case of a drunken man. He got through the wire very easily. They did not throw stones at him when he was in the garden. I saw him load from the magazine for the first shot; he loaded from his magazine on each occasion: if he had loaded any of the shots, which I saw fired, otherwise than from his magazine, I must have seen him do it.[11]

Rice's testimony about the timing and nature of the stone throwing hinted that Murray might have been further confused, intimidated or infuriated by the missiles. However, the stone throwers had certainly not provoked Murray into discharging the fatal shots.

The significance of Rice's remarks about the way in which Murray loaded the rifle is rather difficult to interpret. When very drunk, manually loading and firing single rounds may have been more difficult for Murray than using the bolt to discharge ten rounds from the fully charged magazine of a Lee-Enfield rifle. However, the distinction is rather eroded if Murray may also have been lucid and dexterous enough to have filled the gun's magazine with two five-round chargers before emerging from the hut.

Captain Arthur Pritchard, Royal Engineers, recounted his own role in events:

> On 2 September 1916, at about 4.15pm, I was in the orderly room 173 Coy. R.E. at Noeux-les-Mines. I heard four shots fired. I then left the room and saw the accused in the garden; he was in the act of leaving the garden in the direction of the limbers. I called out to him: 'Put your rifle down.' He turned round, brought his rifle to his shoulder and fired at me. I ducked into the cabbages and heard the report of a rifle. I heard no bullet. As I was getting up, a few seconds later, I heard another shot. The accused was then a good deal nearer the [artillerymen's] tents. I went to the side of the limbers: and as

> I came out from the limbers I saw some ten or twelve men holding him on the ground.[12]

Pritchard accompanied Murray as the latter was escorted to the Royal Scots' guardroom:

> On the way he complained that he was only one among many and that they were handling him roughly. He complained that the man who had him by the neck was hurting him. I saw him tied up. He was distinctly excited and I should say he had been drinking. I think he was quite capable of realizing what he was being tied up for. I answer to his questions to me, I told him that as he had shot four men he would have to be tied up, and he said to me: 'Yes. If you let me loose I'll shoot you too, you fucking officer.' He also offered to fight his way through the lot of us, if he were let loose. When he was tied up he tried to pull himself up to his feet by catching hold of some woodwork with his mouth.[13]

Pritchard's opinion that Murray had been fully aware why he was tied up was highly prejudicial. However, Healy did not call for the remark to be struck out; instead he conducted a perfunctory cross-examination that yielded from Pritchard an admission that Murray had been 'blind fighting drunk'.[14] Murray's mental state was a critically important issue that ought to have attracted more vigorous interrogation by Healy.

Metaphorically, Pritchard's testimony had unpicked the lock of a door that once opened, could not easily be shut. Major Turton proceeded to push the door open by declaring:

> The court proposes to ask the witness whether in his opinion the accused was so drunk that he was incapable of realizing what was going on; i.e. that men were throwing things at him and that he [the accused] was firing shots at them.

Healy objected to the question 'on the grounds that this question is for a medical expert and should not be put to the witness, as it is his opinion. M.M.L., para.15.'[15]

The relevant paragraph in the *Manual of Military Law* (1914) stated:

> It has been remarked ... that there are certain rules which exclude from consideration on judicial inquiries classes of evidence which would be taken into consideration on ordinary inquiries. The most important of these negative or exclusive rules may, with reference to criminal proceedings, be stated as follows:
>
> I. Nothing shall be admitted as evidence which does not tend immediately to prove or disprove the charge.

> II. The evidence produced must be the best obtainable under the circumstances.
>
> To these may be added, subject to important qualifications:
>
> III. Hearsay is not evidence.
>
> IV. Opinion is not evidence.[16]

But it was too late; Healy's objection was overruled by Turton, for the *Manual of Military Law* (1914) also stated:

> At any time before the time for the second address of the accused, the Judge Advocate, and any Member of the Court may, with the permission of the court, address through the President any question to the witness.[17]

Turton was thereby permitted to ask any questions he wished, even if it entailed him acting *de facto* as a prosecutor. Any Member of the Court questioning a witness could be overruled by Turton but if a question was posed by Turton he was hardly likely to overrule himself.

Captain Pritchard therefore went ahead and answered Turton's question, declaring:

> I think the accused did realize what was going on: for he recognized me as an officer, he

> complained about being hurt as he was taken to the guard room, and he made a threat of what he would do in the event of his being set loose.[18]

The factual observation about Murray's inebriation was admissible but Pritchard was not medical authority and what he stated about Murray's mental condition should not have been accepted by the court as expert testimony.[19] Also, because military law presumed that a person was sane at the time the offence was committed unless the opposite could be proved, the burden of proof rested with the defence. However, at this point in the proceedings the case for the defence had not yet been advanced; the prosecution was still in progress. It was therefore improper for the court to inquire into Murray's mental state and in overruling Healy's objection the President had undermined Healy before any defence testimony had been presented.

After a witness had answered a question put to them by the court, the *Manual of Military Law* permitted any party to question a witness, so Healy also had an opportunity to challenge Turton. However, to do so required the permission of the court and the question could not be addressed directly. Instead, Healy would have been required to express his criticism obliquely, via a question to the witness, Pritchard. However, regulations required the question to be put to the witness via the President of the Court, Major Turton. Unfortunately for Healy, Turton could not legally be compelled to pose the question if he considered it inappropriate. In a civil court, Healy may have had grounds for lodging an appeal with a higher court but the Army Act made no similar provision and at best, Healy could only hope that due allowance for Healy's dilemma would be made by the Deputy Judge Advocate General during the post-trial review of the written proceedings.[20]

The prosecution next called one of the men who felled Murray, Driver George Alexander, Royal Horse Artillery:

> At about 4.20pm ... I was in the artillery lines at Noeux-les-Mines, grooming my horses. I saw the accused in our gun park. He came from the direction of the R.E. Coy. He went towards our tents. As he was behind one of our tents, I made a rush for him and got hold of him. We both fell to the ground when his rifle went off.[21]

Though Healy did not ask any questions, Alexander was cross-examined by the court and responded with further details:

> When I saw him first, there was a crowd of people following him. That is why I rushed at him. I am almost positive the man was drunk and did not know what he was doing. He was staggering about, waving his rifle about and motioning people to come on. I said nothing to him, he said nothing to me. I could not say if he smelt of drink. I was at grips with him for about 1/2 [a] minute. I did

> not accompany him to the guardroom. He had no jacket on; I cannot say what he had on his feet.[22]

Yet again, the court accepted opinion as evidence. Alexander contradicted what Pritchard had related about Murray's mental state and possibly also the extent to which the latter was inebriated.

The sixth prosecution witness was Sergeant James Currie, whose evidence appeared to endorse the impression that certainly by the time he was detained, Murray had taken leave of his senses. Currie told the court:

> At about 4.35pm ... I was on duty at H.Q. gate of the Company, in Noeuxles-Mains. The accused was handed over to me. I confined him in the guard detention room. He was very violent. I had to handcuff him and tie him up. In my opinion he was drunk. In my opinion, he was not capable of realizing what was going on. He did not know where he was. He did not recognize me as a Sergeant. He had known me before. He was threatening to shoot everyone. I think he did not know where he was because he did not mention any names.[23]

Currie's observation about Murray's mental state carried more weight than mere opinion, if only because the latter had failed to recognize the sergeant with whom he was acquainted. Healy did not cross-examine

Currie but the court picked up the point and questioned the Sergeant more closely:

> The only reason why I think the accused did not realise where he was, was because he did not mention any names. Captain Pritchard was there at the time. He [Murray] said to Captain Pritchard 'You are a fucking officer, and I will shoot you and all.' He said he would shoot the fucking lot if he were let go.[24]

Captain Pritchard was again summoned to briefly confirm he had been at the guardroom, adding that he subsequently inspected Damper's corpse and attended his funeral at Barlin.[25] It was then the turn of Captain Owen Richards, RAMC, who confirmed the nature and cause of Damper's demise:

> On 2nd September 1916 ... a man labelled Sapper Damper was brought in to No.6, Casualty Clearing Station, at Barlin. He had a wound over the lower left ribs and another smaller one on the buttocks. He was moribund. The hole was small and irregular, consistent with it having been caused by a ricochet bullet. There was no sign of exit. I think the man had been hit by two separate fragments. He had scarcely any pulse when admitted. I infused him, he did not rally. He died shortly afterwards. I saw him after he was dead. In my opinion the cause of death was internal haemorrage [sic], the haemorrage [sic] having been caused by the fragments which caused the

> wounds. The state of things which I found was quite consistent with the deceased having been hit by a bullet which had ricocheted off a shed. I cannot say from which field ambulance the deceased had come.[26]

The final witness was Private James Glen, Royal Scots, the first man to suffer from Murray's wrath on 2 September.[27] He said very little:

> At 8.30am, on 2nd September, 1916, the accused accused me of having stolen his kilt: he struck me and was annoyed. At about 3.30pm I saw him again: coming into the hut. He was drunk at the time. He came up and shook hands and made friends with me again.

Glen was not quizzed about his own erratic behaviour or how he had reacted to being assaulted by Murray. Private Duncan Scully, who saw Murray in the hut shortly before he went on the rampage, quite unaccountably failed to give evidence in court. Yet in a pre-trial written statement Scully had recalled:

> On the Morning of Sept. 1st 1916 I came in from the trenches and that evening saw the man, whom Accused charged with stealing his kilt, come into the hut drunk. The next morning the accused and this man had a fight about 8.00am. Between 3.00 and 4.00pm I saw the accused in his hut drunk. He was going about with his rifle so we hid some

> of the [rifle] bolts. The next thing I heard were shots being fired.[28]

Neither Private Lynch nor Corporal Rogers were invited to give evidence in court and no attempt was made to establish how much alcohol Murray had consumed. What Murray had been doing between 2.00 pm and circa 3.30pm remains open to conjecture. He could have been drinking more alcohol or he might have been asleep or he may even have been provoked in some way by soldiers who were upset about his disruptive behaviour.

However, the court considered that it had heard enough, and before adjourning at 1.05pm for lunch a halt was called to further testimony from prosecution witnesses. Turton announced that it was:

> Unnecessary to call any other witnesses whose evidence was not taken at the summary; nor does the accused's friend desire their presence.

When the court reconvened an hour later, Lieutenant Healy opened the case for the defence; he produced only one witness, the defendant. Murray told the court:

> I joined the army in August 1914. I joined the 9th Gordons. I came to France in July 1915. Since then, I have been doing regular night work in the trenches. I have had only one spell of rest in seven days. I remember [the] morning of 2nd

> September 1916. When I got out of bed, I struck Glen and accused him of taking my kilt. At about 12.05 I went to an *estaminet;* I drank stout and white wine: I cannot say how much. I drank a lot before I left. The *estaminet* was in Noeux-les-Mines. I don't remember anything until I found myself in the Royal Scots Fusiliers' Guard-Room.

Murray was not cross-examined by the prosecution but the court questioned him about what he could remember about developments that occurred after he had been arrested. He answered:

> As far as I can recollect I was brought from the Royal Scots Fusilier's Guard Room to my own Guard Room in a motor lorry. I think this was on the next day. I don't remember talking to Captain Pritchard. I remember Sergeant Currie coming to the Royal Scots Guard Room on the 3rd September in order to take me to my own Guard Room. I don't remember firing any shot. I don't remember shaking hands with Glen, and making up our quarrel. One of the Gordons was drinking with me in the *estaminet;* his name is Smith. I don't know his number. He is in the 8/10 Battalion and is attached to the 173rd Tunnelling Company. He is with the Company yet. I have no spite against any man in the Company and I did not know the two men who were shot.[29]

When Lieutenant Healy rose to deliver his closing address, he drew the court's attention to the *Manual of Military Law,* paragraph 10, and advanced a defence of insanity:

> The accused was not merely drunk but mad. The continual strain and the drink had made him mad. He had made friends with his only enemy, Glen. What explanation is there as to his subsequent actions except that the accused was mad?[30]

With that, the defence rested its case.

Lieutenant Healy's performance had been less than dazzling but he was outclassed, outmaneuvered and outranked by two experienced barristers. There is little doubt that Healy appreciated the merits of his client's case but he simply lacked the resources and testimony that was essential to develop the meagre opportunities afforded the Prisoner's Friend at a field general court martial. Even so, Healy made some worthwhile points that would have been noted by Turton and Chapman.

Turton and Chapman knew Healy was right to insist that only a medical expert could pronounce authoritatively about Murray's state of mind on the day Damper was killed. Healy could have recalled and cross-examined Captain Richards, even though the latter was a surgeon and not an authority on either alcoholism or battle stress. However, Healy had no guarantee that Richards would have been a sympathetic witness, given that contemporary medical judgement was often flawed by eugenic and moral perspectives about drunkenness and madness.

Healy could have sought reinforcements by summoning witnesses. For example, it should have been a fairly straightforward matter to find out how much alcohol had been consumed by Murray in the *estaminet* at Nouex les Mines by tracing Private Smith, his drinking companion. Though Smith is a common enough name, he would have easily been identified in the ranks of the 8/10th Battalion Gordon Highlanders attached to 173rd Tunnelling Company at Noeuxles-Mines. Nor would it have been difficult for Healy to have contacted the owner of the *estaminet,* let alone Privates Scully, Lynch, Maguire and Corporal Rogers.

From the available evidence, Murray directed his animosity only towards James Glen. Privates Lynch and Scully's statements make no reference to Murray specifically threatening to shoot or kill anyone inside or outside the hut. On the other hand, Scully, Maguire, Lynch and others sharing the hut were patently aware of the potentially lethal consequences of Murray grabbing a gun and blindly discharging it inside the hut. Their thoughts and responses were never solicited by Healy or tested via cross-examination of their testimony.

It is not likely that the soldiers sharing the hut with Murray conspired to remain silent but their reticence to volunteer information was understandable. Some would have regarded Murray as a disruptive nuisance, a proverbial pain in the arse, and felt sorry for the men whom he shot. Others may have simply not wanted to get involved, fearing self-incrimination, for not doing their utmost to restrain Murray before he began shooting on 2 September.

While Healy could easily have solicited further assistance, Murray's behaviour on 2 September and the nature of the crime meant there was little guarantee that Healy would have persuaded them to disclose information that could be useful in defending Murray.

The court found Murray guilty on the primary charge of having murdered Sapper William Damper, and because there was consequently no need to proceed with them, Murray was found not guilty of all the other charges. As a consequence, a brief written deposition from Corporal Woodthorpe that had been dictated to Pritchard was never tested in court:

> At about 4.15pm ... I heard a shot in the yard and rushed out to see what the matter was. I saw Pte. Murray with his shirt torn, lying down in the field at the back of the latrine. He took aim at me and fired, the bullet hitting me in the right elbow and back. I am quite certain he aimed at me.[31]

Neither Murray nor Healy made any further statements but before passing sentence the court was acquainted by Freeland with Murray's disciplinary record.

Murray's character was generally classed as 'Good', but there were a number of entries that drew attention to a propensity for getting drunk and upsetting his comrades. An entry in the company conduct record noted that he had been drunk on Friday, 9 October 1914, but it was not until the battalion was in training at Perham Down Camp on Salisbury Plain that Murray's misbehaviour was penalized by the Gordons' commanding officer. On Friday, 14 May 1915, Murray got drunk and made a disturbance in his hut about 11.15pm, for which he was punished on 17 May with ten days' confinement to barracks.

On Friday, 21 May he again engaged in, 'Highly improper conduct and creating a disturbance in his hut at about 11.00pm,' before slipping out of camp and remaining absent overnight, for which he forfeited a day's pay. On Friday, 4 June Murray was yet again 'Drunk and creating a disturbance in his hut about 10.30pm' and 'striking a comrade,' for which he was later fined 10/- and confined to barracks for twenty-one days. On some Friday nights it appears Murray was inclined to drink and disturb comrades with whom he was billeted but while on active service in France he appears to have been a good, sober soldier.[32]

The two barristers, Chapman and Turton, may have considered Murray had the elements of a passable defence, albeit weakly presented. Thus the court sentenced Murray to death but added:

> The court strongly recommends the accused to mercy on the grounds that he committed the act while under the influence of drink and that his conduct in France during the past fifteen months has been good.[33]

The written proceedings were forwarded to Major-General Harold Ruggles-Brise, commanding 40th Division.[34] In addition to carrying out his duties as one of the confirming officers, Ruggles-Brise had been responsible for convening the court martial and selecting officers to try the case. Evidently unimpressed by the court's recommendation to mercy, he commented:

> I recommend that the sentence of death be carried out. This man committed murder, taking the life of a soldier, and shot at – with intent to murder – an officer, and I do not consider that the fact that he was drunk at the time of committing the offence in any way lessens the gravity of that offence. His official age is 22 years 2 months. The man now states his real age to be 21 years 2 months.[35]

Even if Ruggles-Brise had decided to recommend the death sentence be commuted, there was no guarantee that Murray would have escaped execution. However, in casually brushing aside the court's recommendation to mercy, Ruggles-Brise also distorted the evidence. Murray was never charged with attempting to murder an officer nor was there any proof that Murray fired at the officer. Pritchard himself testified that Murray only pointed his rifle at him, adding that he had not heard a bullet being fired in his direction and Murray was 'blind fighting drunk'. Nor could Murray even be charged with cursing Pritchard, for according to the *Manual of Military Law:*

> Mere abusive and violent language used by a drunken man as the result of being taken into custody, should not be used as a ground for framing a charge of using threatening or insubordinate language to a superior officer.[36]

The only offence committed against Captain Pritchard by Murray involved threatening behaviour at a time when Murray was tied up and could therefore not have physically harmed Pritchard. Yet it was the only evidence produced to support the prosecution's contention that Murray ever intended to kill anyone in the camp.

Ruggles-Brise forwarded the written proceedings to, Major General Henry Havelock Hudson, who was the officer commanding 1st Corps between 4 and 29 September 1916. When the latter had commanded 8th Division earlier in 1916, he became quite accustomed to lots of soldiers under his command being killed, and Murray's case demonstrated that his indifferent judgement as a military commander also extended to his knowledge of military and civil law.[37] In his endorsement of the decision to execute Murray, Hudson wrote:

> I recommend that the sentence be carried out. This is a civil offence and in civil law drunkenness is not, I believe, held to be an extenuating circumstance in a case of conviction for murder.[38]

The Major General was correct about murder being a civil offence but he was wrong about drunkenness. At the time Murray was found guilty of killing Damper, voluntary intoxication was clearly acknowledged in the *Manual of Military Law* as a defence analogous to the defence of insanity.[39]

There was never much of a prospect that the court's recommendation to mercy would be entertained by General Sir Richard Haking, who was the officer commanding 1st Army between 7 August and 29 September 1916. He was already regarded as a red tabbed butcher because of his role in the deaths of thousands of men under his command in ill-starred offensives at Aubers Ridge and Loos during 1915, and latterly the slaughter of Australian troops at Fromelles.[40] Haking examined the written proceedings on 27 September, and commented:

> I recommend that the sentence of death should be carried out. I consider that there are no extenuating circumstances and that it is highly desirable to make an example in this case.[41]

On 29 September, Field Marshal Haig confirmed the death sentence passed on Francis Murray. The condemned man was executed at 6.58am on 1 October at Bully Grenay by a firing squad under the command of Major Alexander Maxwell, Assistant Provost Marshal, 40th Division.[42]

In reviewing Murray's crime, it is clear that he had previously got drunk and been disruptive but he had never before used a weapon and prior to 4.00pm on 2 September, the only person with cause to fear Murray was Glen, and then only until Murray shook hands with him. There is insufficient evidence to prove conclusively that Murray was being harassed or ostracized by his fellow soldiers, so what else may have caused Murray to go on the rampage with a rifle?

His personal history yields a few clues. Francis Murray was born in Eastfield, Lanarkshire; he was unmarried and lived with his parents and siblings at Calderbank, where he worked as a labourer before joining the Army.[43] His disciplinary record drew attention to the possibility that he may have been alcohol dependent, if not a full-blown alcoholic, before he went to France. Murray had also served at the front in the midst of some of the heaviest fighting of the war. He was at Loos in 1915 and at Hulluch and the Kink in late April and early May 1916, and during August 1916 he had been working in the vicinity of Becourt, Contalmaison and Fricourt on the Somme battlefield.

Fourteen months of arduous labour in a fighting zone certainly could change men's behaviour and cause many to act impulsively. However, there is a further, rather mundane contributory factor to which Murray alluded in his testimony: the effects of sleep deprivation. In court he complained, 'I came to France in July 1915. Since then, I have been doing regular night work in the trenches. I have had only one spell of rest in seven days.'

Sleep loss does not usually turn sufferers into murderers but sleeplessness erodes rational thinking and alcohol is known to induce mood swings, including paranoia, hallucinations and loss of memory. War or no war, chronic sleep deprivation and booze would have been enough to transform Murray into an incoherent, capering lunatic with a persecution complex.

CHAPTER 7

A Rum Affair

The Battle of the Somme ended officially on 18 November 1916 and massive losses sustained by infantry formations including the 16th Battalion, Highland Light Infantry were made up by drafts of reinforcements. The latter's ranks included battle veterans like 23-year-old Private Alexander Reid who had already seen action and been wounded while serving with other formations.

Reid enlisted on 17 August 1914 and claimed that he had initially been sent to France in March 1915 with a draft of reinforcements to 10th Battalion, Highland Light Infantry. He maintained that he served with the formation until May 1916, when it was amalgamated with 11th Battalion but he had been transferred to 12th Battalion, Highland Light Infantry, 46th Brigade and 'served at [sic] Armentiers, Hulluch and the Somme' until August 1916, when he had been wounded in the lungs. His injuries were so grave that he had to be shipped back to the United Kingdom for surgical treatment and convalescence. By November he was passed as fit for duty and at his own request, 23-year-old Reid was again sent to France, where he joined the 16th Battalion, Highland Light Infantry in mid-December.[1]

The 16th Battalion, Highland Light Infantry, nicknamed 'The Holy Second', had originally been composed of volunteers from the notionally teetotal Glasgow Boys' Brigade. However, the battalion had been eviscerated during the Battle of the Somme and Reid was one of the non-teetotal reinforcements sent to replace the hundreds of dead and wounded.[2]

When Reid joined the battalion it was temporarily billeted behind the lines in the vicinity of Franqueville and Rubempré, a couple of villages situated roughly 14 kilometres north of Amiens. In spite of the bitterly cold, wet weather, the military authorities made an effort to revive morale via a programme of robust training, plenty of sporting activities and instead of freezing in tents, troops were accommodated in vacant or derelict buildings. A couple of sections, including Reid's, were bedded down in wooden bunks that had been installed at No.2 Billet, Corbie Road, Rubempré.[3]

Soldiers were awakened at 4.30am, four hours before sunrise, and ate their final meal of the day at about 4.30pm, roughly half an hour before sundown. In the absence of anything else to do during the long, dark winter nights, many soldiers would have gone to bed well before Lights Out at 9.30pm. Efforts were made by officers to arrange some entertainment: impromptu concerts were organized and everybody feasted well at Hogmanay. Otherwise, at the end of a day's duties and when not in the front line, soldiers lucky enough to have money for the purpose could also purchase drink or food and enjoy local amenities. Others, lacking cash to buy booze were able to console themselves via the routine issue of dollops of rum that constituted a much appreciated nightcap.[4]

At the end of an afternoon's strenuous trench digging on Friday, 5 January 1917, Reid and a couple of men with whom he was billeted, James Kean and William Cumberland, decided to go out for a drink after they had eaten their supper.[5] The trio went to a nearby *estaminet,* consumed several bottles of stout and purchased three bottles of white wine as a 'carry out', to share with a couple of friends. They left the *estaminet* at about 6.00pm and went to the guardroom, where two other pals, Privates John Kelly and Hector McLean, had been detained. The duty corporal, being himself fond of a drink, was content to allow the visitors and detainees to consume the wine. After about thirty minutes, Reid, Kean and Cumberland returned to the *estaminet* and resumed drinking stout until 8.00pm, when they returned to the guardroom, and generously shared the contents of a couple of bottles of stout with the two detainees.[6]

At about 8.30pm, Reid, Kean and Cumberland left the guardroom, intending to be back at No.2 Billet in time for the evening's routine issue of a tot of rum and Lights Out. En route, they popped into another billet, occupied by No.12 Platoon, where Reid, Cumberland and possibly also Kean managed to get issued with a tot of rum. On finally arriving at No.2 Billet, Kean and Reid secured a further two double issues of rum apiece; Cumberland saved up his tot and gave it to Reid. With the rum issue completed the supervising officer and his assistant, Lance Corporal Spence, departed but were intercepted in the street by Reid and Kean. After successfully complaining that neither had received any rum, the latter were each rewarded with a further tot apiece.[7]

By 9.00pm, when all the men had bedded down for the night a violent altercation suddenly erupted between Kean and Reid, who occupied adjacent bunks. They got out of their beds and a tussle ensued between them for possession of a rifle that Kean had grabbed from a nearby wall. The NCO in charge of the No.2 Billet, Lance Corporal George Thompson, intervened; he confiscated the firearm, hung it back on the wall and with assistance from Lance Corporal Peter Spence, ordered both men to get back to their respective beds. They backed away from one another and remained standing beside their beds for about twenty minutes, when Reid surreptitiously re-appropriated the rifle. Again, Thompson attempted to seize the firearm but before he could do so a shot was discharged and Kean dropped to the floor, mortally wounded.[8]

During the morning of 15 January a field general court martial was convened in the small French village of Bus-lès-Artois to try Reid for killing Kean. The President was Major Edward Rigg, 2nd Battalion, King's Own Yorkshire Light Infantry, and the Members of the

Court consisted of Captain John Muir, 17th Battalion, Highland Light Infantry, and Captain John Griffiths-Jones, General List.[9] The prosecution was conducted by Lieutenant Andrew Macfarlane, the Adjutant of 16th Battalion, Highland Light Infantry, and Reid was assisted by Lieutenant Charles Bell Buddle, a qualified barrister who was serving with the Army Service Corps.[10]

After Reid had pleaded not guilty to murder and an alternative charge of manslaughter the prosecution called on Captain Vincent Badcock, the medical officer attached to 16th Battalion Highland Light Infantry.[11] Badcock recalled arriving at the scene around 11.30pm, where he found the deceased:

> Lying on the floor of the men's billet, I examined him and found that he had been shot in the back just below the left shoulder blade in the region of the heart ... from the appearance of the wound I formed the opinion that death had been caused by a rifle bullet discharged at very close quarters.

Badcock had then visited Reid in the guardroom. He continued:

> I formed the opinion that the accused was sober. He was standing swaying gently from side to side and he refused to speak. I was with the accused for about ten minutes.

Buddle quizzed Badcock in detail about his examination of Reid, inferring that in the candlelit guardroom the medical officer may have overlooked marks on the intoxicated soldier's face. However, the inspection had been carried out with the aid of an electric torch, Badcock declared Reid's face was unblemished and reckoned Reid to have been shamming:

> I came to the conclusion that the accused was purposely swaying in order to give me the impression that he was drunk. I could smell no liquor on the accused. I tried to get into conversation with the accused but he refused to speak.

Badcock had conducted a further examination during the morning of 7 January and noted Reid's face was very swollen, and reflected:

> It is quite possible that in the first occasion that I saw the accused he might have had a blow on his face, and that there had not been sufficient time for the swelling to have developed. It is quite possible that the swelling might have been due to a blow from a heavy instrument, such as the butt of a rifle, but there was no discolouration.

In response to further questioning by Buddle, Badcock also conceded:

> It is possible that a sudden shock would sober a man up to a certain extent but there would be

> indices of his having been drinking such as dilated pupils and not reacting normally to light. In this case accused's pupils were quite normal. It is possible that a man might take a considerable amount of rum and yet his breath not smell of it, so far as I know.[12]

The court then heard testimony from the NCO in charge of No.2 Billet, Lance Corporal George Thompson. He broadly confirmed the sequence of events, maintaining that Reid and Kean had been chums and on good terms with one another at supper time and when they returned to No.2 Billet at 8.15pm. Thompson remembered, 'They were both sober and friendly when they returned. Both the men appeared as if they had had a drink or two but did not appear to be the worse for it.'[13]

Thompson noticed Reid being issued with a double ration of rum by Lieutenant Temple, and remembered Kean and Reid arguing about an incident that had occurred when the latter had served together with the 3rd Battalion in Haddington. After successfully wresting the rifle from Reid and Kean, Thompson said it had taken half an hour for himself and Lance Corporal Spence to establish peace and quiet. Twenty minutes later, immediately after Kean had been shot, Thompson had remonstrated with Reid. Thompson recalled:

> The accused replied, 'It is all right Corporal: don't you trouble.' The accused added, 'He called me

> a German....' When I took the rifle from the accused after the deceased had fallen I saw a cartridge clip in the accused's left hand. I took the clip from the accused and found four cartridges in it. The clip was one that held five cartridges. I then examined the rifle and found one empty cartridge case in the breach [sic] which became extracted as I opened the bolt. The magazine was empty.

Under cross-examination by Buddle, Thompson conceded that he had not personally witnessed Kean getting a rum ration and that light from two candles was sufficient to illuminate the sleeping quarters, and for issuing rum. All the men had drunk their rum in front of the officer except Reid, who carried his mess tin over to Kean's bed. Thereafter, Thompson did not remember seeing them again until 9.20pm, when he heard the two men arguing. As for physical violence, in response to a couple of further questions posed by Buddle, Thompson denied witnessing Kean attempting to either strangle or strike Reid with a rifle butt. At no time during the early evening, the NCO added, had he noticed any cuts or bruises on Reid's face. However, he conceded that it had been a dark night and a solitary candle had latterly illuminated the billet. Even though it had been a dark night and illumination was restricted, Thompson insisted that it would have been sufficient to illuminate the billet.[14]

Finally, in response to queries from Major Rigg about the rifle, Thompson noted that the barrel had been 'dirty' and since the platoon had not been shooting on 5 January, there would have been no reason for the weapon to have been loaded.

In his testimony, Lance Corporal Spence generally corroborated the evidence that had been presented by Thompson, and recalled what had ensued after they had tried to get the two soldiers to undertake to settle down:

> I heard Thompson exclaim 'Now that will do Reid,' and with that I heard a shot fired ... I saw Thompson dart forward. The accused had a rifle in his hands and before Thompson could reach it the shot was fired and at the same time the deceased gave a cry and fell back.

When cross-examined by Buddle, Spence stated that Reid and Kean had both been sober but reckoned the latter to have been 'an aggravating man in drink or not'.[15]

The rifle that Thompson had successfully wrested from Reid and Kean belonged to Private Robertson, the third prosecution witness. Robertson had been in bed at 9.00pm on 5 January and heard Kean quarrelling with Reid as they entered the billet:

> I heard Corporal Thompson order both the accused and Kean to be quiet, as the men could not get to sleep. They however did not obey and ...

> continued to quarrel for at least half an hour afterwards over what each had done since they had been out in France. I heard Keen call the accused, 'A German'. Kean then invited the accused outside the billet, 'To finish it out.'

Robertson recalled Reid being disarmed by Thompson and the rifle being put back in place on the wall. He then witnessed Reid, with a five-round clip of ammunition in his hand, re-appropriating the gun, which Robertson insisted had been unloaded. Though Robertson had been lying in his bed and could not see Reid load or fire the weapon, he heard them repeatedly exchanging taunts and declared that there was enough candlelight to see both men standing about 5 yards apart from one another. He witnessed Reid assuming a loading position, and calling Kean a German, two or three times before the latter was shot. Robertson maintained that stricken man took a couple of minutes to die and that after Thompson had declared Kean was dead, Reid had said, 'He deserved it.'

Under cross-examination by Buddle, Robertson corroborated Thompson's evidence. He conceded that his field of vision had been limited and that the room had been poorly lit but after the shot had been discharged, he was adamant that he also spotted only four rounds in the ammunition clip borne by Reid. In wrestling for possession of his rifle, Robertson told Buddle that no blows had been exchanged between

Reid and Kean. Since the quarrelsome pair had joined the battalion while he had been elsewhere, Robertson said he had never seen either until the fatal evening and when they made their entry at 9.00pm, and in his opinion both men were drunk.[16]

After Robertson's evidence, the court adjourned until 10.00am the following day, when the three remaining prosecution witnesses presented their testimony. Company Sergeant Major James Allison, who had briefly visited the scene soon after the killing, said that he found Reid calmly standing in the billet, apparently sober and smoking a cigarette, and ordered him to be detained in the guardroom.[17]

The court next heard from the NCO who had taken Reid into custody, Peter Lavelle, the Lance Corporal of the Guard at Rubempré. Lavelle reported that at the time of his arrest, Reid had been sober enough to make his way under escort but without assistance to the guardroom. Reid had not initially been handcuffed but by the time he had bedded down in the guardroom his hands and feet had been tethered by straps. Notwithstanding rain pouring through an adjacent hole in the wall, Reid had fallen asleep until awakened for his medical examination by Captain Badcock.

Some evidence had to be coaxed out of Lavelle via cross-examination by Buddle, who went on to press the NCO to confirm details about the drinks session that had taken place in the guardroom. Lavelle refused to admit he had permitted Reid and Kean to ply Kelly and McClean with wine and stout, until he grudgingly conceded they:

> Did come to the Guard Room and drink wine and stout which they may have brought with them, between the hours of 6.00pm and 9.00pm, with the Prisoners in the Guard Room.

Lavelle sought to minimize his own complicity by insisting that he had personally only shared a drink with Private Cumberland but certainly not with the prisoners or Reid.

The final witness for the prosecution was Sergeant Marr, who had relieved Lavelle in the guardroom when the latter went off duty. Marr testified that Reid slept soundly through the night until Reveille at 4.30am on 6 January. In response to questions from Buddle, the NCO felt unable to express an opinion about the soldier's sobriety and acknowledged that with reference to Reid's face, because it had been dark, and because the guardroom had been poorly illuminated by a solitary candle, on Reid's face, 'There might have been a swelling without a contusion but had there been a cut or discolouration I should have noticed it.'[18]

The case for the prosecution ended; Buddle opened the case for the defence by summoning Reid as the first witness.

Private Reid began by outlining his own war service and informed the court that his three brothers were also serving with the Army.[19] He also explained how he had raised the money to pay for drink:

> We first went to a French house and sold some goods such as a razor and socks, which belonged to me. The deceased Kean sold some stuff as well.

Reid's recollection of what happened subsequently was reasonably accurate. In addition to an unspecified but substantial quantity of stout, by his own account he and Kean must have also consumed at least half a bottle of white wine, and between 8.30pm and 9.00pm the equivalent of about half a dozen drams of SRD overproof rum.[20] Moreover, neither man had eaten very much since their midday meal of bully beef, other than bread and butter with tea at 4.30pm. Without knowing more about their physical size and alcohol tolerance it is impossible to accurately assess the extent to which either man's faculties may have been addled by drink. Nevertheless, Buddle's persistence in drawing attention to Reid's intoxication appears to have been well grounded.[21]

Quite understandably, Reid's recollection of the sequence of events in the billet differed from other witnesses' but the verbatim account of his testimony does not indicate any intervention or prompting by Buddle. Reid declared:

> Kean and I ... returned to the billet and we both went to bed, our bunks being next to one another.

> The next thing I remember was that someone had hold of me by the throat telling me 'that I am a German.' I was sound asleep but woke up and found the person to be Kean. I got up and felt dazed. I remember little after this but I have a faint recollection of struggling with Kean for the possession of a rifle and feeling a blow on my left cheek with the butt of the rifle. The next thing I remember after this was waking up in the Guard Room and finding that I had a pair of handcuffs on and my legs tied. I also have a recollection of someone holding a torch in front of my face. I remember nothing more until the morning when I was wakened up by the Sergeant and I wanted to know what I was in the Guard Room for. The men in the Guard Room then told me that I had been fighting on the previous evening and that the deceased Kean had been shot. In the morning I found myself lying on wet ground right in front of the hole in the wall.

Reid told the court that he had only met Kean about a month prior to the shooting but they swiftly became inseparably close friends. Kean, he estimated to have been about thirty-eight years old and although they had never quarreled, when influenced by drink his bosom pal could be rather an unstable character. Reid explained:

> I had been drunk about two or three nights before the 5th Jan. We got paid that day and I had

> several drinks. We had been drinking with a French soldier. I went away with the French soldier and left Kean. On my return the deceased Kean and I had further drinks. Another Frenchman came in. The deceased Kean being drunk hit the Frenchman without the slightest warning because the Frenchman had, earlier in the day by way of a joke, twiddled the deceased's moustache. The deceased Kean and I then went back to our billet and Kean rose up that night and shaved his moustache off without knowing what he was doing, or having the slightest any recollection of it the next morning. This same night he rose out of bed rolled up his sleeves and slipped out of the billet with the avowed intention of pursuing the same Frenchman. I followed him into the road and persuaded him to come back. That same night, deceased Kean smashed up a lot of timber planks with a hatchet until one o'clock in the morning, during the whole time talking to himself. The following morning, the deceased had no recollection of any of these incidents.

In response to a brief cross-examination by the prosecution, Reid confirmed that Kean and he had downed all the rum and that while he had been tied up in the guardroom he had been unaware that he was examined by the battalion medical officer. Reid left the court and Buddle then summoned the first of six further witnesses for the defence.

Private John Kelly stated that Kean, Reid, and Cumberland had briefly visited the guardroom after supper, and confirmed sharing wine and stout during their two subsequent visits. Kelly also witnessed Reid's subsequent incarceration, and believed Reid was drunk because he had staggered, fallen down and gone to sleep beside a hole in the wall, with rain beating in on him. According to Kelly, Reid did not stir until he was woken up by the sergeant major and tied up.

The following morning, the prisoners heard soldiers outside the guardroom discussing the previous night's events and Reid showed Kelly his jaw, which was swollen and remarked that, 'There was not a soldier in the billet, if there had been we would have been separated.'

Prompted by a question from Lieutenant Macfarlane, Kelly confirmed Reid's comments were uttered after they had overheard the other men discussing the night's events.[22]

Of the following two witnesses for the defence, Private Hector McClean's evidence generally supported Kelly's testimony but otherwise added little of further substance; Private William McCheyne presented an eyewitness account that broadly endorsed the established sequence of the events in the billet. McCheyne stated that he had jumped up from his bed and gone to aid Kean as the latter lay dying on the floor. In response to McCheyne recalling Kean 'nagging' and referring to Reid as a 'German', Buddle demanded to know more about Kean's behaviour. McCheyne replied:

> Kean was a very peculiar man. When in drink he was very quarrelsome. On New Year's evening, the deceased Kean came into the billet drunk. There were some logs of trees. He started to chop them with an axe and continued to cut them for an hour and a half. Whilst doing so he was talking and swearing the whole time.

As for Reid's conduct at the time of the shooting, all McCheyne could recall was Thompson telling Reid to put down the rifle and go to bed.[23]

The following witness, Private John Simpson, had known Reid and Kean for about five weeks and recalled that they had been 'great chums' although he considered Kean was inclined to be very quarrelsome when he was drunk. Simpson had been in bed when Reid and Kean entered the billet; he remembered they were both drunk but otherwise quite friendly until the latter began to quarrel with Reid. Simpson said:

> I heard the deceased Kean call the accused 'a fucking German'. A good while after I heard this remark I heard a rifle shot. I jumped out of bed and found the deceased Kean on the floor. I went to his assistance.

Under cross-examination by either the court or Lieutenant Macfarlane, Simpson was called on to estimate how much time elapsed between the rifle shot and Kean's grossly insulting reference to Reid. He replied:

> It was a good while after the deceased Kean called the accused a 'fucking German' that I heard the rifle shot. I cannot say how long but it must have been an hour at the very least.

Because the surmise offered the prosecution an opportunity to argue that Reid had exercised premeditation in killing Kean, Buddle immediately sought clarification from Simpson. Under cross-examination by Buddle, Simpson admitted Kean had repeatedly called Reid a German but insisted a full hour passed between the time he heard the final 'fucking German' curse and the fatal shot. That said, Simpson conceded that he was half asleep at the time and had initially not taken much notice of events.[24]

The penultimate witness, Private Alexander Gallagher, had already been in bed at No.2 Billet, from where he witnessed Kean and Reid's drunken entry on the fatal evening. He recalled they were initially quite amicably disposed but after they had gone to bed, Gallagher had heard them arguing and gained the impression that Reid was trying to avoid a quarrel. Gallagher also witnessed Reid being throttled and struck by Kean, and estimated that between an hour and a half and two hours elapsed before the rifle shot was discharged.[25]

The final witness, Private William Grant, also reckoned Kean and Reid to have been friendly enough when they entered the billet on 5 January. However, Grant added:

> After they had gone to bed about 9:30pm I heard them arguing in bed. I saw the deceased Kean get out of bed and he made a rush towards the corner of the billet. He appeared as if he was going for a rifle. I saw the Corporal and other men run after him. I saw them take a rifle from the deceased Kean. The accused was in his bed the whole of the time. Kean then went back to bed. About half an hour later I saw the deceased Kean catch the accused by the throat: I was then in my bed which was just above their beds. I saw through the wire mattress of my bed. The deceased Kean then again got out of bed. He called on the accused to come outside and fight him. The accused did get out of bed. I heard the accused say, 'It's a wash-out.' The accused appeared as if he did not wish to fight and made this remark. They then continued to argue on the floor and I heard the deceased call the accused 'a German'. That was all I heard until about half an hour later when I heard a rifle shot in the billet and I saw the deceased Kean drop at the foot of my bed. In my opinion both the men were drunk.

According to Grant, it had been Kean who acted provocatively and not Reid. Under cross-examination by Lieutenant Macfarlane, Grant added that a few minutes after the shooting, he had also seen Reid without a rifle in his hand.[26] Evidently satisfied, the prosecuting officer posed no further questions.

There being no more witness testimony, Buddle was directed to sum up the case for the defence. Unfortunately, no verbatim record was made but an informed appreciation of the points he raised can be deduced from a scribbled page of notes that Buddle submitted to the court.

He began by airing two key questions about the charges: 'Is he guilty of murder or manslaughter, or either?' and 'If murder, it must be proven conclusively that he fired the shot and intended to kill or injure somebody.' Buddle then proceeded to review the evidence.

He maintained that there was no direct evidence that Reid had loaded and fired the rifle; Grant and Gallagher had testified that there had been confusion in the billet, and Thompson, Spence and Robertson all agreed that the billet was poorly illuminated.

Buddle reminded the court that they must consider whether Reid was capable of forming the intent to kill, and drew their attention to testimony from Cumberland, McClean, McCheyne, Kelly and Simpson that indicated Reid had been drinking heavily. Buddle also went into detail about the volume and rate at which Kean and Reid had been drinking, and testimony about Reid's comatose state in the guardroom.

In the event that the court chose to conclude that Reid has fired the fatal shot, Buddle maintained there was unchallenged evidence that Kean had been persistently and wholly unreasonably been aggressive and Reid had not acted provocatively. Both Grant and Gallagher heard Reid being called a 'fucking German' by Kean, who had first grabbed the rifle and struck Reid in the face. Buddle queried whether Kean had personally loaded the rifle, intending to shoot Reid.

Though there was universal acknowledgement that Reid and Kean were pals, none of the witnesses had a positive word to say about Kean's character, and the deceased was referred to as being 'quarrelsome' when drunk. Notwithstanding his age, Kean was given to immature, idiosyncratic behaviour, exemplified by his unprovoked assault on the French soldier; his inability to recall shaving off his moustache after the attack, and his shouting and swearing to himself when chopping wood. Yet Reid had cared for Kean after the assault on the French soldier; he had had acted responsibly as a friend; he had taken care to guide Kean back to their billet and put him to bed, and made an effort to keep his pal out of trouble.

Buddle argued that Reid's assertion that Kean 'deserved it' was evidence that Reid had been provoked beyond reason. He contended that the outburst was impassioned and that if the court accepted such an interpretation then Reid could only be convicted of manslaughter. Buddle supported his advocacy by citing legal authority:

> In considering ... whether the killing upon provocation amount to murder or manslaughter, the instrument wherewith the homicide was effected must also be taken into consideration; for if it were effected with a deadly weapon, the provocation must be great indeed to extenuate the offence to manslaughter ... the mode of resentment must bear a reasonable proportion to the provocation to reduce the offence to manslaughter.[27]

However, he also pointed out:

> It was not every slight provocation, even by a blow, which will, when the party receiving it strikes with a deadly weapon, reduce the offence from murder to manslaughter ... he left it to the jury to say, whether, in the interval during which the prisoner was absent, there was time for his passion to cool and reason to gain domination over his mind: if not, they should find him guilty of manslaughter only.[28]

The duration of the 'cooling off' period was for the court to determine because there had been a range of estimates about the time that elapsed between Reid being struck with a rifle butt by Kean and the latter being killed: between twenty and thirty minutes

(Thompson and Grant); an hour (Simpson) and between an hour and a half and two hours (Gallagher). Buddle maintained that Thompson's estimate was likely to have been correct. He inferred that since Reid had not had time enough in which to cool down before firing the rifle at Kean, the court should eschew returning a conviction of murder.

Moreover, Reid had been drunk at the time, and were the court to decide he was guilty of manslaughter, in the light of Reid's intoxicated state, Buddle urged the exercise of leniency in sentencing, citing the *Manual of Military Law* (1914):

> Where intention is of the essence of the offence, drunkenness may justify a court martial in awarding a less punishment than the offence would otherwise have deserved, or reduce the offence to one of a less serious character.[29]

Finally, referring to Reid's war service and completely unblemished disciplinary record, Buddle observed that if the court accepted there was no criminal intent and Reid were found guilty of manslaughter, he would be jailed. Rather than imprisoning Reid, Buddle enquired, 'Would it not be better to allow him to go on fighting for his country?'[30]

In addition to addressing the court, summing up for the prosecution, Lieutenant Macfarlane submitted a handwritten list of points:

> The Charge is murder.

Evidence conclusively proves that accused was sober and knew what he was doing.

Drunkenness – if proved – is not a palliation but an aggravation to the crime.

Indifferent behaviour of accused after the crime.

Accused knows how he was handcuffed in the Guard Room but did not recognize the Medical Officer.

Loaded the rifle with one round only.

Evidence of Kelly and McClean unreliable in that they were confined in the Guard Room awaiting trial by Court Martial when accused was brought in and any tale could be made up among them while there.

There is no way of knowing how Macfarlane elaborated these points during his address to the court but the evidence certainly did not conclusively prove that Reid was sober – quite the contrary. Reid may have been sober at 8.00pm but that had been before he began drinking rum, and in any case nobody had questioned Reid about how much stout and wine he consumed during the early evening on 5 January.

Macfarlane's reference to Reid's 'indifferent behaviour' on the night of the killing is rather intriguing. The evidence shows that he told Thompson that Kean 'deserved it' and was then escorted to the Guard Room, where he passed out on the wet floor. He remembered somebody shining a torch in his face and he recalled that his hands and feet were tied up but he was not aware of Kean's death until he was told about it the next day.

Kelly and McClean knew nothing about the killing; they simply told the court about Reid's visits to the Guard Room with the wine and stout. If Macfarlane had suspected that Kelly, McClean, and Reid had collectively fabricated a yarn, he made no effort to expose their duplicity via cross-examination. He taxed Kelly with only one question and declined the opportunity to cross-examine McClean. The written proceedings do not feature any evidence that the three men had acted together to concoct a story.

In law, drunkenness is not an 'aggravation'. Voluntary intoxication might even negate intent when it is an essential element of the crime and insobriety never has been of itself a defence for murder but as Buddle had already pointed out via his reference to the *Manual of Military Law,* intoxication ought to have been taken into consideration by the court.

After the court retired to consider their finding and determined that Reid was guilty of murder, Lieutenant MacFarlane revealed Reid's disciplinary record contained only one 'minor entry' but noted his character was 'indifferent'. Macfarlane added:

> The accused joined this Battalion quite recently with a draft from the base. He has been in no actions with this Battalion, but I have heard that he has been serving in France before.[31]

Reid was permitted to submit a plea in mitigation. He began with an apology, 'I am very sorry that this has happened. If I had not been under the influence of drink it would not have happened,' and went on to remind the court of his own war service: battalions, battles and the serious wound he had suffered and his decision to volunteer for a further spell of active service. He ended his plea with a reference to his three brothers, who had also enlisted in fighting formations.[32]

The confirming officers were divided in their opinions about the case. The convening officer, Brigadier General James Jardine, agreed with the verdict and sentence but Major General Sir Reginald Barnes, the officer commanding 32nd Division felt otherwise, and commented:

> I am of the opinion that the evidence bears out the charge of manslaughter and not of murder – For the following reasons–
>
> (1) Malice aforethought is not established and he ***doubtless*** had provocation.

(2) Although drunkenness is ***not*** proved, there is no doubt that both men had been drinking heavily.

(3) Everything points to the fact that the act was committed in a ***moment of anger.***

I recommend that the sentence be commuted to penal servitude.[33]

In airing his views, Lieutenant General Sir Edward Fanshawe, commanding 5th Corps, was brusque and brief. He scribbled, 'The Court has found the accused, Private A. Reid guilty of murder, and not manslaughter. I am of opinion [sic] that the sentence should be carried out.'[34]

The case elicited a contrary response from the 5th Army Commander, General Sir Hubert Gough, who commented: 'The case is undoubtedly one of murder but it is equally clear that he was goaded by the deceased, and that murder is not the prevalent offence. Under the circumstances, I recommend that the sentence is commuted.'[35]

On 28 January, without indicating any reason why he desired to confirm the death sentence passed on Reid, Sir Douglas Haig scrawled his confirmation on the Court Martial Schedule. Reid was executed by firing squad in the village of Bertrancourt, just over a kilometre away from where he had been court-martialled. Captain Charles Dickson, RAMC, certified that Reid died instantly at 7.11am on Wednesday, 31 January.[36]

Details about Reid's crime and punishment were circulated to other military formations via Routine Orders and a letter from the War Office duly notified his next of kin. His family's reaction was recorded after the war via the inscription on Alexander Reid's gravestone in Bertrancourt Cemetery:

> Thy purpose Lord we cannot see,
> But all is well that's done by thee.[37]

CHAPTER 8

Is Anyone Dead?

At Gosport in 1913 Sergeant Thomas McCain, 4th Company, Royal Engineers, was awarded a Good Conduct Medal in recognition of his exemplary military service. He had been a 17-year-old unskilled lad from Gloucestershire when he enlisted in 1894 but after initially being trained as a submarine miner, he became an experienced engine driver, operating steam engines and latterly, motor vehicles. He had served in Bermuda and Malta, and at harbour and coastal defence establishments in the West Country and in Scotland.

Because McCain was classed as 'A thoroughly trustworthy and hard working NCO with a good knowledge of motor car work and driving' at Gosport, he was responsible for the searchlight wagons and lorries and training young soldiers at Stokes Bay.[1] When war was declared he remained in post and may not have been sent overseas had it not been for the escalation of enemy air raids on civilians and military installations during 1915.

In the United Kingdom and Northern France more searchlights were urgently needed to assist antiaircraft gunners in dealing with night-time incursions by enemy bomber aircraft. Appropriately experienced personnel were drafted in to train and command units intended for service with the BEF. So, in September 1915, McCain was promoted to Company Sergeant Major and transferred to 50th Field Searchlight Company.

Sapper Arthur Oyns joined McCain's unit on 11 January 1916. He had originally volunteered for service as a signaller, but after nine months' training at the Royal Engineers Base in Chatham, Oyns was directed to exercise his skills as an electrician. He had previous experience of working as an electrical wireman in Bristol and Avonmouth, which was just as well because during April, 50th Searchlight Company was shipped out to France and attached to 4th Army Troops on the Somme, where it was to remain until mid-1917.[2]

Field Marshal Haig's plans for a massive summer 1917 offensive against the German forces around Ypres and a hush-hush naval operation on the Flanders coast meant many Fourth Army formations had to be dispatched to replace French and Belgian Army units in the vicinity of Coxyde and Nieuport. However, on Friday 13 July, when the ill-fated British offensive was underway in Flanders and Fourth Army Headquarters had already moved to Dunkirk, the 50th Field Searchlight Company was still lodged in Nissen huts at the Royal Engineers camp, Brie. Their accommodation was situated in woodland, immediately adjacent to the Athies-Ponts de Brie road, on the west bank of the river Somme and there was not much available by way of leisure facilities for the troops.

However, the camp did boast a 'wet' canteen, which was where Arthur Oyns had downed some beers before proceeding to make a lot of noise outside the Nissen hut in which his section was quartered.

It was 9.00pm, about an hour before sunset, and he wanted to attract the attention of a chum. However, anyone within earshot who knew him would have been deterred from responding because when drunk, Oyns was not a congenial companion. The bellowing also disturbed Sergeant McCain, who was seated on the end of his bed outside another hut, situated about 10 metres behind the Nissen hut. The NCO got up, went over to Oyns, admonished him for being noisy, and then walked back along the flank of the Nissen hut to his bed.

Oyns disappeared inside the hut and about half an hour later, he went over to one of a pair of windows at the rear end of the Nissen hut, from where he could see McCain. He put a rifle to his shoulder and from the windowsill Oyns fired twice, wounding two NCOs: McCain, who keeled over with a wound in his neck, and Company Sergeant Major Beresford Finniston.[3] Although suffering from a gunshot wound in his back, Finniston sprinted away out of the line of fire and Oyns was immediately pounced on and pinned to the floor by Sapper Horace Anson.[4]

Sapper Anson had been inside the hut when the shots were discharged and actually witnessed the second shot being fired but had not acted quickly enough to prevent Oyns pulling the trigger. After a couple of minutes, Sergeant Finniston entered the hut and although weakened by loss of blood, he briefly assisted Anson to hold down Oyns until other soldiers came to their assistance. Finniston and McCain were then driven away to get their wounds treated; Oyns was trussed up and at about 10.00pm he was marched away to the guardroom.[5] Finniston's wound eventually responded to hospital treatment but McCain's was fatal. At Lucknow Casualty Clearing Station, Peronne, the medical staff could do nothing to prevent McCain bleeding to death; he expired shortly after 2:15pm on 14 July and was buried nearby.[6]

For reasons that remain unexplained the Army postponed Oyn's arraignment until after 50th Field Searchlight Company had moved to Bray Dunes, on the Belgian coast. It was not until 8 October that a field general court martial finally convened at the headquarters of 123rd Brigade, 41st Division in the tiny Belgian hamlet of St Idesbalde, near Coxyde.[7] The President, Lieutenant Colonel Sydney Beattie and Members, Major Noel Sim and Captain Charles Cotesworth were all serving with units attached to the brigade.[8] Captain Oscar Dowson, a barrister serving with the RASC was the Court Martial Officer; a Cardiff solicitor, Major Ernest Green, Welsh Regiment, conducted the prosecution and Oyns was assisted in presenting his defence by another barrister, Lieutenant Gonne Pilcher of the Intelligence Corps.[9]

Without tarrying for a preliminary address, Major Green called the first of four prosecution witnesses, all sappers who had been quartered with Oyns in the Nissen hut at Brie camp. Horace Anson, who supported what he had to relate with a roughly-sketched plan of the crime scene at Brie camp, presented an account of events that damned Oyns:

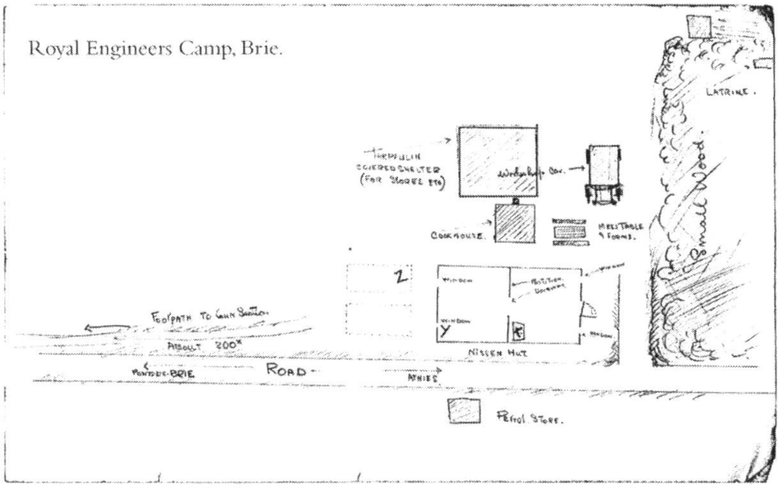

> On July 13th about 9.30pm I was in the Nissen hut at Brie shown on the plan. The hut is divided by a partition. I was in one part of the hut marked 'X'. The accused was in the hut on the other side of the partition. The door between was open. I heard a shot go off – the sound came from this part of the hut. I went at once to the door of the partition. I saw accused holding his rifle to his shoulder. It was pointing out through the window – marked 'Y' on the sketch. He then fired a shot through the window. I saw the flash of the rifle. I saw CQMS Finniston rush past the

> window – 'Y' – outside the hut. The accused was standing by the window resting his rifle on the windowsill and pointing it outside. The accused was alone in the hut. I ran across to accused and caught hold of him. I bore him down to the floor and then took the rifle off him. I called for assistance. After a minute or two CQMS Finniston came and took charge of the accused. CQMS Finniston is now away from this unit wounded. I went out then. I saw CSM McCain lying on the ground outside the hut in the position marked 'Z' on the sketch. This was about 10 yards from where I saw accused fire the shot. I saw McCain wounded in the neck.[10]

Under cross-examination by Pilcher, Anson's positive references to the deceased NCO made it apparent that McCain was well regarded by the men under his command and that the killing had been deliberate and akin to patricide:

> I saw CQMS Finniston run past immediately after the first shot. I had seen accused earlier in the evening. He seemed in an excited state and quarrelsome. This is not his normal state. This was about an hour before. I noticed no bottles of beer in his pockets. I have seen the accused drunk on a previous occasion. He was then rather violent. His actions were not then the same as his actions on the evening of July 13th. SM McCain was popular in the Section. SM McCain

> was friendly to the accused and seemed like a father to him.[11]

Answers to questions posed by Major Green during his re-examination of Anson ensured that in focusing on McCain's demise, Finniston's suffering was not overlooked. Anson continued:

> The window through which accused was pointing the rifle was open. I do not know whether CQMS Finniston was wounded when he came into the hut. I had seen him twenty minutes before; he was not wounded then. I had seen SM McCain and CQMS Finniston sitting together outside the hut about twenty minutes before the shot. I saw CQMS Finniston ten minutes after the shot: he was wounded then. I mark with a stroke on the plan the direction in which the rifle was pointing when I saw accused fire it from the window.

At this point Anson wrote the letter 'Y' on the plan before the court. 'The rifle was resting on the top of the lower half of the window.'[12]

Lance Corporal Lewis Boyce was the second sapper to testify for the prosecution. He described what happened inside the hut after the shooting had taken place:

> I returned to the hut at 9.00pm and left to go for a walk at 9.20pm. I had not gone many yards down the lane when I heard two shots. I returned

> to the hut and found Sapper Anson and CQMS Finniston holding the accused down. I noticed CQMS Finniston was very weak. I saw a rifle on the floor. I kicked it to one side: shortly after I examined it and found three live rounds in the magazine and nothing in the breech. I can't say if the bolt was shut. I found two empty cartridge cases on the floor. I noticed the rifle had obviously been fired not long before. The accused was in the hut when I left to go for a walk at 9.20.[13]

As with Anson, so with Boyce, Pilcher could have directed attention on getting witness testimony aired about Oyns' mood and the sapper's relationship with McCain:

> The accused was in an excited condition when I was in the hut between 9 and 9.20pm. It is not his usual condition – only when he has had some beer. I have seen accused drunk and he was then in a very excited condition. The accused's normal condition is quiet. CSM McCain was always very nice to him. I have heard accused had a grudge against McCain. I can't say whether SM McCain has done any good turns for accused. I say accused had a grudge against SM McCain because accused had spoken to me about it. He grumbled to me about him. It was quite ordinary grousing. I have not heard other men make the same remarks to me about SM McCain as accused

> made. I never noticed any partiality in SM McCain's manner towards the men. I was holding accused down for ten minutes or quarter of an hour.[14]

Under cross-examination Major Green pressed for Boyce to clarify the nature of the grudge to which the latter had referred. If Oyns had a grudge against McCain, it could provide a motive for killing McCain. However, Boyce was unable to add much of substance to his allegation:

> The remarks accused made to me about CSM McCain were made about a month before. He said, 'I will go up against the wall for one bloody man.' I don't know that the accused was referring to SM McCain when he said this.[15]

Green then called Sapper Daniel Lawlor, who had been the person whose attention Oyns had sought to attract by shouting. Lawlor also presented a view from outside the hut:

> On July 13th, 1917 at Brie, shortly before 9.00pm, I was chopping wood outside the Nissen hut. Accused came out of the hut and shouted my name. SM McCain was sitting at the back of the hut near the point marked 'Z' on the sketch. The accused went back into the hut. He again came out shortly afterwards and shouted my name again. SM McCain went to him and said something to him. He [McCain] then went back to position

> 'Z'. Accused went into the hut again: and then there was quietness for a while. I then heard two shots go off one immediately after the other. I saw SM McCain fall to the ground. I could see him from where I was. CQMS Finniston then rushed round and pulled me into the wood. Half a minute later, I then ran up to where SM McCain was. I found him lying doubled up. I found he was bleeding from his neck. About five minutes later I saw CQMS Finniston was wounded between the shoulder blades. Before the shots went off I saw CQMS Finniston beside the SM.[16]

Pilcher's cross-examination probed Lawlor's estimate of Oyns' character and relationship. Lawlor admitted, 'I know accused fairly well.... He is very easily roused,' and explained that, 'the only reason I know why accused was shouting for me was that I had been down to get some beer.' He reckoned Oyns to have been 'in a boiling temper,' adding, 'I have seen accused drunk and he was then violent.'

Lawlor had seen Oyns drinking in the camp canteen earlier in the evening, and gained the impression that:

> He seemed more calm and deliberate on this occasion than when I had seen him drunk.... I say he was more deliberate on 13th of July because when he came out and shouted my name he said it deliberately.

With reference to Oyns' character and relationship with McCain, Lawlor revealed:

> Accused was a man who always had a grudge, imaginary or otherwise. He was not friends with the SM but I took what the accused said as just the ordinary grousing of the ordinary man. I say he was not friends with SM McCain because he told us the SM was responsible for him getting fourteen days. He said that the SM was against him. He said this sort of thing several times to me. I can't say how recently.[17]

Generally, little information survives in official archives about soldiers who served with 50th Field Searchlight Company but Oyns' disciplinary record was preserved in his court martial dossier. It shows he had been punished on two occasions for disciplinary offences. On 20 April 1916, he was sentenced to seven days' Field Punishment No.2 for hesitating to obey an order, and for being drunk and creating a disturbance on 9 March 1917, Oyns was awarded a fortnight's Field Punishment No.1. In both cases McCain had been responsible for reporting Oyns misbehaviour to the company's commanding officer.[18] If Lawlor's reference to 'fourteen days' was reliable then it was probably the latter experience that caused Oyns to resent McCain's authority.[19]

The only witness who heard what McCain had said to Oyns was Sapper Sydney Hathaway. His testimony was brief:

> I was sitting in the hut at Brie at 9.00pm when accused came in. He was shouting out for Lawlor. I heard SM McCain tell the accused to keep quiet. SM McCain was outside the hut. I went to the latrines then – 40 yards away. While away I heard two shots fired. I went back into the hut and saw CQMS Finniston holding accused down in the hut. CQMS Finniston's coat was ripped a bit in the shoulder.

Pilcher's cross-examination failed to establish whether Oyns appeared to be drunk but like Anson, Hathaway referred to Oyns' inclination to be violent when drunk:

> SM McCain called out to the accused because the latter was making such a noise. Accused did not appear to be the worse for drink. I did not notice particularly but he did not seem to fall about. When not in drink the accused is quiet. I thought the reason why the accused was noisy was that something had upset him. On the occasion previously when I had seen him drunk the accused was noisy and violent.[20]

None of the remaining witnesses were sappers, and the evidence they produced was mostly concerned with what had happened after the two NCOs had been shot. Thus, Bombardier William Pritchard, an artilleryman, was approximately 200 metres away from the Nissen hut when he heard the two shots fired. He arrived on the scene shortly after Finniston had been relieved from assisting Anson and Boyce to hold down Oyns. Pritchard told the court:

> I found a CQMS and CSM lying on the ground wounded. I then went into the hut close by and found accused being held down by two men. I tied his hands and legs and handed him over to the guard. Accused appeared to be quite conscious of what he was doing and what was going on around him. He might have been drinking but he was not in my opinion drunk. I spoke to the accused only once – a quarter of an hour later. The accused was swearing whilst I was tying his wrists. Otherwise, he did not appear to be excited. He said nothing to me about why he was being taken away.[21]

Pilcher did not cross-examine Pritchard, but the court wanted to know how much time elapsed between him hearing the shots and seeing McCain and Finniston lying on the ground. Pritchard reckoned:

It was about three minutes from the time I heard the shots to the time when I saw the SM and CQMS wounded on the ground. Much of Pritchard's testimony was surmise; he simply could not have known whether Oyns was conscious or not about his actions. However, Pilcher did not voice any objection and so the Bombardier's answer was allowed to stand.[22]

A fellow artilleryman, Bombardier Thomas Windebank had been one of the camp guards. He recalled:

> I took charge of the accused. I marched him down from the R.E. camp at Brie with assistance. The accused was the worse for drink. He did not appear to have a clear idea of what he had done. During the night, in the guardroom I heard the accused make statements. He said 'I think something has happened. Is anyone dead?' He also said 'No, not you Finn, you're one of the best – But that bugger. If I had a Lewis gun I would wipe the whole lot out.'

Pilcher sought clarification about Oyns' inebriation from Windebank, and was told:

> I consider the accused was drunk. He was staggering when I took him to the guardroom. He smelt strongly of drink. He was sick during the night.

Reviewing what was alleged about Oyns' utterances, it is surprising that Pilcher did not question Windebank's powers of recall, yet summaries of evidence had not been gathered until about 20 August and three months had elapsed since Oyns' arrest. Moreover, no notes or any other corroboration was produced in court to substantiate what Windebank alleged. Nor did Windebank reveal to whom Oyns had addressed his remarks. If it was not the bombardier then was Oyns talking to himself or somebody else in the guardroom?

Three witnesses briefly testified about the transport of the two wounded NCOs to Lucknow Casualty Clearing Station and the death of Sergeant McCain. Bombardier Pritchard was then recalled to testify but was unable to remember whether Oyns had smelled of drink.[23] The fourth witness, Captain James Smalley, was the surgeon who examined McCain and concluded that there was nothing that could be done to save his life. On the nature of McCain's injury, Smalley stated:

> He was suffering from a gunshot in the neck and upper half of the chest. The entrance wound was halfway between the left jaw and the collarbone. The exit wound was in the middle line at back – 3rd dorsal vertebra. The wound was a typical high velocity bullet wound.[24]

In presenting the case for the defence, Pilcher was faced with a very difficult task. He could have picked away at inconsistencies in prosecution witnesses' evidence but there was no doubt that Oyns had fired the rifle that killed McCain and wounded Finniston.[25]

Oyns, giving evidence in his own defence, repudiated any suggestion that he had a grudge against McCain but admitted that he suffered from alcohol-related amnesia, possibly linked in some way with concussion he had suffered:

> On July 13th after tea I went up to the canteen and had several drinks. I remember this but don't

> remember leaving the canteen. Drink always affects me in this way. About seven months ago I got fourteen days for being drunk – this had nothing to do with SM McCain. SM McCain always got me out of scrapes. I never bore him any grudge for the specific reason that he never did me any harm. I have always been with SM McCain since I have been in the Company. My work before the war has been interfered with by drink. I was an electrical worker. I had to leave places on account of drink. My defence to my charge of drunkenness seven months ago was that my mind was a blank. I could remember nothing that occurred. My father is dead: I support my mother. I had a blow to the head twelve years ago in the Liverpool riots. Since then whenever I drink I remember nothing of what happens. I only know by being there afterwards. I have never done anything more than ordinary grousing about SM McCain, just as the other fellows did. SM McCain was not the sort of man fellows have a grudge against. I never had any grudge against SM McCain. If others formed a different view, I know nothing about it.[26]

Cross-examined by Major Green, Oyns summarized what he could (not) remember:

> I drank English beer on the 13th July. I don't remember Sapper Anson coming. I don't remember being bound up. I have not to my

> knowledge made statements against SM McCain when I was sober. I don't remember saying what Bombardier Windebank says I did about the SM. I know of no reason why Windebank should say this; I don't know anything about the incident. I don't remember what occurred.

After the court enquired whether his rifle had been loaded before he picked it up to shoot McCain and Finniston, Oyns replied:

> I can't remember my rifle being in the hut on this day, July 13th. I can't say if it was loaded. I had not had it loaded for months previous. There was ammunition in the equipment in the hut.[27]

Oyns' evidence achieved little by way of rebutting the murder charge but further testimony for the defence came from an unexpected quarter, Captain Douglas ffrench-Mullen, the Officer Commanding 50th Field Searchlight Company.[28] Unfortunately for Oyns, ffrench-Mullen's contribution was rather a mixed blessing:

> The accused has been in my unit nearly two years and during nearly all the time he has been under me as Company Section Commander. He is hardworking and good at his trade. He did not appear to get on well either with the other men or the NCOs. Company Sergeant-Major McCain took some interest in the accused and considered

> that his difficulty in getting on with the other men was due to his being new to the army. He always tried to settle any difficulty into which the accused had got by settling it without bringing it up before an officer. The SM was extremely popular and as far as I know there was no exception to this. When accused was brought up on a charge of being drunk previously he stated he c[oul]d not remember anything about it. I gathered from the SM on this occasion that he had arranged that a milder offence sh[oul]d be made the subject of the charge than might otherwise have been made. From reports made to me I had gathered that the accused was violent and uncontrolled when drunk – both in his actions and language.[29]

Pilcher's final address was very brief:

> I contend on the evidence that the Court is not justified in finding the accused guilty of murder. I do not contest any of the facts as to the shooting, the position of the rifle etc. It is clear that SM McCain was shot by the rifle accused was holding. I suggest that the accused was drunk; and that in that condition, he was not capable of forming the intention of shooting to kill. There is no evidence that the accused had any motive whatever. The evidence shows only that the accused groused in the ordinary way.

Oyns was found guilty and the court heard from Major Green details about the two offences for which the sapper had been punished while on service with 50th Field Searchlight Company. Pilcher responded with a plea in mitigation that Oyns was not altogether bad, and was a troubled soul who had already been punished:

> The accused has been a good son to his mother though he has been in trouble from time to time owing to drink. There has been great delay in this case and accused was left for five weeks before a summary was taken; and he has suffered suspense and he has been subjected to trying conditions while in confinement for twelve weeks.

On 17 October, the death sentence was confirmed by Field Marshal Haig and Captain Simms, Assistant Provost Marshal, 41st Division proceeded to arrange for Oyns to be executed simultaneously with another soldier at St Idesbalde on 20 October.[30] Oyns' companion in death was Private Frank Cheeseman, a straggler who had been condemned to death for desertion.[31]

What motivated Arthur Oyns to kill Thomas McCain remains a mystery. The references by his fellow sappers about the executed man's hostility towards the dead NCO are rather contradicted by ffrench-Mullen's testimony about McCain's pastoral concern for Oyns. However, the commanding officer's reference to McCain's indulgence over Oyns' indiscipline inferred that the condemned man had a worse reputation for misbehaving than what had been entered on his disciplinary record. The latter may also account for Oyns' poor rapport with his fellow sappers.

Oyns' personal record of military service before he was posted to 50th Field Searchlight Company tends to lend further weight to the impression that he was a disruptive if not a disturbed sapper. On 13 September Oyns was punished with eight days' confinement to barracks for creating a disturbance after Lights Out and using improper language to an NCO. On 12 October he was awarded a further four days for overstayed his pass, and on 13 December he was drunk and got fined five days' pay for refusing to leave the guardroom and smashing a window pane with a cup. He had also forged a pass to visit Portsea, where his elderly mother was living, for which he was punished with ninety-six hours' Field Punishment No.2 on 31 December. On 10 January 1916, at Woolwich Barracks, on the day he was posted to 50th Field Searchlight Company, Oyns was fined a further week's pay for creating a disturbance in his barrack room and wilfully damaging government property.[32]

The conundrum of whether Oyns was afflicted by a malady that drove him to drink or whether it was alcohol that triggered his inappropriate behaviour is impossible to resolve. However, Oyns' physique was certainly less than impressive. When inspected at Portsmouth in April 1916, a medical officer noted that Oyns weighed 54 kilos; his chest was 81 centimetres

(88 centimetres expanded) and his height was 1.6 metres, and his teeth were in such poor condition that he had to be fitted with dentures.[33] Oyns would not have needed much beer to get drunk and on 13 July his authority as Section Commander would have been undermined after being publicly told to pipe down by McCain.

The Royal Engineers promptly notified 71-year-old Isabel Oyns about her son's execution. However, it was not until March 1918 that Thomas McCain's Good Conduct Medal was forwarded to his widow, Mabel.[34]

CHAPTER 9

Murder in the Rue Racine

The British military presence transformed Northern France and the Channel ports, including Le Havre. Berths reserved for merchant ships or ocean liners were monopolized by battleships and military transports, disgorging men and war materiel. The arrival of masses of foreign military personnel had a mixed impact on the social fabric of Le Havre and a hinterland that was already strained by war mobilization. Military conscription, increased taxation, soaring inflation, enemy submarine and aerial operations combined to dislocate the city and regional economy. However, the hundreds of thousands of military transients and establishment of vast encampments in the vicinity of Le Havre and nearby Harfleur also generated commercial opportunities and provided employment for the local civilian population, including prostitutes.

Prostitution always extended beyond the confines of Le Havre's officially licensed *maisons tolérées* or the debauched *maisons d'abbatage* in the vicinity of Rue d'Albanie and Rue de Galions.[1] Aside from promiscuous encounters in railway stations, theatres and dancehalls, as in many pre-war provincial towns, prostitutes' services could readily be secured in large and small hotels, restaurants, cafés and a range of notionally respectable retail establishments. Notwithstanding the British official efforts in early 1918 to have 'blue lamp' or 'red lamp' establishments placed out of bounds in Le Havre and elsewhere, it was patently impossible to prevent a soldier casually interacting with streetwalkers and prostitutes operating from private residences.[2]

Henriette Tremerel, a *fille de soldat,* was a well-dressed 52-year-old widow who supported herself by working as an unlicensed prostitute. Although she spoke very little English, almost all of her clients were British or Australian soldiers, some of whom she casually accosted in the street. However, a few regulars also made their way independently to No.4 Rue Racine, a lodging house on the corner of the junction with Rue Emile Zola, where she lived alone in a single room on the first floor.

Her apartment was comfortably furnished, with a pair of French windows that overlooked the Rue Racine and another pair that gave her a view across the Rue Emile Zola. A common hallway and stairs provided access to all the furnished rooms occupied by a further ten lodgers. They included Mme Palmyre Defraey and Arthur Bergilez, a Belgian Army corporal, who occupied the only other apartment on the first floor landing, and Mme Marie Lemoine, who lived on the second floor. Mlle Virginie Gremond, the principal tenant and proprietress, lived on the ground floor, immediately beneath Henriette's room. The two women were friendly; they regularly ate an evening meal together in the latter's kitchen and Virginie maintained that she was generally unconcerned about the latter's activities or clients and was familiar with some of the regular visitors. However, it was understood that a rap or two on the floor of Henriette's room was a summons that required a rapid, personal response from Virginie.[3]

Virginie later recalled that shortly before 9.15pm on Wednesday, 19 December 1917, as they were dining on cabbage and potatoes, Henriette heard a noise in the hallway. Assuming it was one of her clients, she went into the unlit hallway, from where she could hear the sound of voices from an upper floor.[4] The visitor turned out to be a British Army NCO who had mistakenly knocked on the door of Mme Marie Lemoine's apartment. Mme Lemoine, with a lighted candle in her hand, opened the door but only briefly glimpsed the man before he turned and went back downstairs in response to Henriette, who shouted (in French), 'You are mistaken as I told you to ask for me on the first floor and not on the second.'[5]

Speaking in French, Henriette remarked, 'This little fellow came to see me at six o'clock,' as she ushered him into the kitchen, where he waited for the two women to finish their meal with cups of tea. Virginie later remembered the man's name was Arthur, and his breath disclosed he had already been drinking before accepting the women's offer of a small glass of rum. He could communicate in broken French, and gesturing to a scar on his neck, he said, *'Trois fois blesse a la guerre'* (three times wounded in the war). According to Virginie, he appeared rather excited; Henriette had also mentioned that it was very warm and unbuttoned the man's greatcoat.[6] In French, when Henriette had enquired, 'Will you sleep with me?' He responded, *'Oui'.*

Henriette then asked if he had a pass. He answered, *'Oui, me permission,'* and allowed her to fish around in the left pocket of his tunic pocket. Her efforts yielded a couple of small notebooks, two Christmas cards and couple of photographs, but no pass. After he revealed where he was stationed, Henriette urged him to return to Harfleur camp but he insisted, 'Me sleep with you.' She demanded to know if he had any money; she was shown four francs and told, 'I will have more money tomorrow.' With that, Henriette and the man stirred; Virginie lit an oil lamp to illuminate their ascent upstairs and then returned to the kitchen.[7]

Henriette unlocked the door of her apartment, and after she and the NCO had entered, as was her custom with clients she then locked the door, leaving the key in the lock. Virginie remembered about half an hour later being startled by a sudden, very heavy thud, followed by a less pronounced noise and three sharp raps on the floor of Henriette's room. Pausing only to lock the kitchen door, Virginie rushed up to the first floor landing and demanded, 'Mme Tremerel, Mme Tremerel, will you open the door?'

On hearing some moans from inside the room, Virginie attempted unsuccessfully to open the door with a master key and shouted, 'Please open the door, Sir.' From the other side of the door a man's voice replied in English, 'Yes! Yes! *Toute de suite, Madame tres bonne.*' After fifteen minutes' knocking on the door, Virginie decided to summon the police. She hurried away, leaving a terrified Mme Defraey to keep an eye on the landing while Bergilez, from a window in his room, monitored the windows of Henriette's room in case the man made a move to escape via one of the windows that faced onto the Rue Racine.[8]

The junction of Rue de Mailleraye and Rue Emile Zola.

Tables, fireplace and mirror. East side of the room.

During the afternoon, Fitzpatrick and Roberts visited the guardroom and formally arrested Wickings on suspicion of murder. Roberts rummaged through the soldier's clothing and found a khaki handkerchief, a picture postcard and some photographs; the NCO's greatcoat was confiscated and sent away to be examined for bloodstains. Captain Ralph Rimmer RAMC examined Wickings and noted three parallel scratches about 2 or 3 centimetres long extending down from the sergeant's mouth and some superficial abrasions on the knuckles of his left hand.[21]

On Christmas Eve, Mme Lemoine and Virginie were invited to attend an identity parade and although Mme Lemoine picked out another man, Virginie identified Wickings as the sergeant who had been in her kitchen on the night of the murder.[22] Three days later a further identity parade was held, in which he was again picked out on a second attempt by Mlle Germaine Gueroult, a waitress whom Wickings claimed to have served drinks to him at a café in the Rue Jules Masurier.

Mlle Gueroult recalled Wickings arriving at the café at 6.00pm, where he had purchased a glass of Dubonnet and a bottle of stout, and that after about ten minutes he was joined by three other soldiers. The four men had then retired to the back room, where they remained until shortly before 8.00pm, when all British military personnel were required to vacate the café.[23] The three drinking companions were Rifleman Binks, who had known Wickings since 1915, and Riflemen Hawes and Johnson.[24] Hawes and Johnson then departed, leaving Wickings and Binks chatting in the street for about a quarter of an hour before the latter walked away.[25]

By 4 January 1918, data from the French police having been collated in Wickings' presence, Second Lieutenant William Jefferis ASC began compiling summaries of evidence. These written statements for the prosecution were gathered over four days from twenty-two French civilians and British military personnel.[26] Conrad Sasso, who had been assigned by the French Army to assist APM Havre, was on hand to translate what French-speaking witnesses had to say. Somewhat unusually, Wickings quite voluntarily made a statement to Jefferis, in which he openly admitted to having had a brief sexual encounter with Henriette Tremerel on 19 December. However, he insisted that at the time she was being murdered he was on a tram, en route to Harfleur.[27]

A field general court martial was convened to try Wickings on Monday, 4 February 1918. The President was Brevet Colonel Godfrey Massy, Norfolk Regiment, and the Members were Major Lord Louth, commanding 831st Area Employment Company, and Captain John Grindley, Royal Welsh Fusiliers. Captain William Crowdy, Devonshire Regiment, was assigned to serve as the court martial officer.[28] Second Lieutenant William Jefferis conducted the prosecution; Captain Hugh Gatehouse, a barrister and experienced court martial officer, defended Wickings and Conrad Sasso acted as interpreter.[29]

During his pre-trial preparations, Gatehouse expressed concern about Second Lieutenant Jefferis having secured a written statement from Wickings. In spite of assurances to the contrary, Gatehouse was worried that Wickings may not have fully appreciated that he was under no obligation to submit or initial any kind of a witness statement.[30]

In her testimony Mlle Gueroult recalled Wickings arriving at about 6.00pm and said that he had remained in the café until 8.00pm, adding, 'I remember the time because immediately after his departure I had to warn the other British soldiers that it was time to close the café.' She also recognized Wickings because of a distinctive scar on his neck: 'His companions in the café had explained to me it had been caused by a wound. I also recognized him by the shape of his nose.'

She disclosed to Gatehouse, 'I was first questioned about the accused on December the 26th 1917, at the café. I was able to remember all the details.' However, she conceded:

> A great many soldiers use the café. It was full on the night in question. It was not busy from 6.00pm to 7.00pm but was busy between 7.00pm and 8.00pm as the soldiers were drinking more between 7.00pm and 8.00pm than between 6.00pm and 7.00pm.

She added, 'The three soldiers with whom the accused conversed walked in together. They and the accused then went into a back room together. I had no difficulty recognizing the accused.' She excused her subsequent inability to immediately pick out Wickings at the identity parade by explaining, 'I did not recognize the accused at first in the room because it was too dark. I recognized him at once when he came out into the open. It was in a big dining hall but the light was not clear.'

Gueroult stated, 'I was in the back room between 6.00pm and 7.00pm. The accused remained in the café all the time between 6.00pm and 7.00pm.' After the President of the Court, Massy, enquired how she was able to remember what the quartet had been drinking, Gueroult replied, 'I specially remember what was drunk that night as we do not sell much stout and it was because of the quantity drunk that evening that we had to renew our stock the next day.'[31]

However, Gueroult's testimony was at odds with her pre-trial witness statement, in which she had stated Wickings had arrived shortly before Binks, Hawes, and Johnson entered the café. In other respects her memory was decidedly impressive. Although she did not speak with the police until Boxing Day, she was able to recall what an individual customer had been drinking seven days previously, during a seasonally busy week. However, her explanation of Wickings' acquisition of the scar on the right side of his neck was inaccurate. The disfigurement was, in fact, the legacy of a mundane but large abscess, as had been noted on Wickings' attestation papers by a medical officer in 1908.[32]

Rifleman Binks testified that he had been pleasantly surprised to encounter Wickings, an old acquaintance. Binks also recalled Wickings saying, 'He [Wickings] had been here since 5.00pm, but I don't know whether he meant the café or Le Havre.' However, in response to cross-examination by Jefferis, Binks was certain that, 'The accused had no scratches on his face; it was quite light in the café'. The quartet had all enjoyed their drinks until, Binks recalled, 'We all came out, including the accused, at 8.00pm. Hawes and Johnson left us outside and I remained in conversation with the accused for about five or ten minutes. Accused asked me whether I could go to Le Havre on Boxing Day and told me if so, he would see I had a good time. I went to a place three or four doors away and the accused went towards the Quai de Southampton.'

Cross-examined by Gatehouse about the time they had moved into the café's back room, Binks said, 'It would have been about 7:15pm when the accused and I entered the back room. Accused told us about himself quite freely'. He added, 'I should have noticed if the accused had had any scratches or small marks on his face, such as might have been caused by shaving but I would not have recollected this fact a week later.' And had Wickings said anything about catching a tram? Binks replied, 'We were almost the last to leave the café. We were turned out at closing time. I do not remember anything said about a tram, but I am a bit deaf. I think the camp where the accused is, is about 5 miles from the Hotel de Ville, Le Havre.'[33]

The other two riflemen broadly endorsed one another's testimony. On entering the café, Hawes said he been accompanied by a woman and had not noticed any scratches or marks on Wickings' face, nor had the NCO appeared anxious, upset or behaved in an abnormal fashion.[34] Rifleman Johnson reckoned that Wickings drank three or four bottles of stout, and as they left the café the sergeant had purchased a further bottle, saying that it 'would do for a livener in the morning.' Under cross-examination by Gatehouse, Johnson was asked if he had seen marks on Wickings' face. He answered, 'If I had noticed small scars on a man's face I think I should remember it a week later, if I knew the incident which caused it.'[35]

Taken individually or collectively, the three soldiers' booze-up in the café and sex thereafter may account for the speculative quality of their evidence. In responding to questioning on Christmas Day, it would have been surprising if they had remembered a small scar on a stranger's face. In sum, their testimony amounted to confirmation that they had enjoyed a few drinks in Wickings' company and thereafter he had chatted with Binks outside the café.

The key witness for the prosecution was Virginie Gremond, who gave evidence in French; Conrad Sasso translated what she said into English. Translation, the formal etiquette of military justice and the nature of the crime erode what at first sight appears to have been an informal, friendly personal relationship. Virginie and Henriette are universally referred to by their surnames in the written proceedings and though not themselves on trial, implicitly and at times explicitly in the narrative their relationship and lifestyle attracted critical scrutiny.

Virginie Gremond briefly outlined her relationship with Henriette Tremerel, and related how the evening meal came to be disturbed between 9.00pm and 9.15pm. She then formally identified Wickings as the visitor who had gone to the wrong floor at her lodging house on the night of 19 December.[36]

In her initial statement, Gremond said that Tremerel had recognized the visitor because she had seen him earlier that evening. She claimed, 'The accused and Mme Tremerel entered my room. Mme Tremerel said to me in French, "This little fellow came to see me at six o'clock this evening."'[37] The passage was struck out because it was hearsay but Gatehouse insisted that it be read out to the court. Gatehouse also failed to raise hearsay as an objection when Gremond testified about the alleged conversation between Tremerel and Wickings:

> Mme Tremerel said to the accused in French, 'Will you sleep with me?' and the accused replied 'yes'. She then asked him if he had a pass. He said '*Oui,* me permission.' She took a small pocket book from his left-hand pocket and looked at it and said to him, 'I don't see any pass here.' She did not produce a pass. She then said, 'Oh his name is Arthur.' Mme Tremerel then withdrew from the pocket of the accused a second pocket book. I do not remember the colour of these pocket books but one was longer than the other. She also found two picture cards, one of which is produced.[38]

Gremond told the court that shortly afterwards Tremerel had expressed unease and tried to persuade Wickings to return to camp but he had been insistent so they had gone upstairs to her room. Gremond recounted how she had been startled and alarmed between 9.40pm and 9.45pm by the sound of three raps and a sudden thud from Tremerel's room.

Gremond described what she saw in Tremerel's room after Waugh and his men had managed to break in:

> The room was in darkness. I obtained a lamp from Mlle Defraey. I noticed the window opposite the door looking onto the Rue Emile Zola was open and on the bar outside were tied a sheet and a counterpane which were hanging out of the window. There was also a khaki coloured handkerchief on the windowsill.

She went on to recall the appearance of the corpse on the deathbed before remarking about Tremerel's jewellery and the state of the room:

> The deceased was wearing around her neck a gold chain with a heart-shaped pendant which had been pressed into the scars on her neck. The deceased was also wearing her wedding ring and earrings. The marble top of the table was on the floor and the table itself was upset. A small portable bookshelf was also on the floor. The bookshelf was standing up straight but the books were all awry. This bookshelf usually stood on a table in front of the right-hand window looking into the Rue Emile Zola. The clothes of the deceased were strewn about the floor. The deceased was a very tidy woman and usually folded up her clothes very carefully. On picking up the table I found a small

> black purse with two or three compartments containing a few coppers perhaps about five. The purse was lying open ... the one the deceased usually brought down to my room in her handbag. In my presence the examination was conducted by the French police and I handed them the key of the wardrobe as I knew where it was kept. I cannot say anything was definitely missing as I was not present at the examination of the deceased's jewellery.[39]

In response to a question by Jefferis, Gremond insisted that she had never seen Wickings prior to 19 December. Captain Gatehouse began his cross-examination by enquiring about the number of tenants lodging at No.4 Rue Racine and went on to suggest that Gremond was operating an unlicensed brothel. She rejected the suggestion but her denial was rather ambiguously expressed. Her response, 'I had no interest with Mme Tremerel's prostitution,' could be interpreted as an expression of disinterest about what her lodger did in her own apartment or a dismissal of the imputation she was benefiting financially from immoral earnings. Gatehouse did not need to press the issue; it was apparent that Tremerel was a prostitute whose activities were known to fellow lodgers and whose clients were given drinks by Gremond.

Given Wickings' inability to comprehend French, Gatehouse then asked how Gremond and Tremerel managed to communicate with their visitor. Gremond admitted, 'Mme. Tremerel spoke a little English only; she could just make herself understood. I understand just a few words of English only.' However, according to Gremond, her lodger's language skills sufficed to secure 'sometimes three to four visitors a day, not many regular visitors. They were all English and Australians. She had two or three visitors that afternoon. I am acquainted with a few of her visitors, chiefly two Australians.' She was not asked to explain how often Tremerel's clients tarried in her kitchen but Gremond conceded that they could easily escape her notice while en route to the first floor of the lodgings.

When quizzed by Gatehouse about how her lodger had been dressed on the fatal night, Gremond recalled that Tremerel had been wearing 'a long dark brown coat with a fur stole and a muff when she left the house at 1.30pm to 1.45pm. The coat had two rows of buttons on it.' Since Wickings had claimed in his statement that shortly after 6.00pm he had been accosted by a streetwalker dressed in a black fur coat and had gone to her home, Gatehouse put it to the landlady that she was mistaken about the exact time that Wickings had been in her kitchen on 19 December. However, Gremond was adamant:

> The conversation with the accused which I have stated took place between 9.00pm and 9.15pm did not take place at about 6.15pm. I was in my kitchen between 6.00pm and 7.00pm. I did not see the accused with Mme Tremerel in my kitchen

> at about 6.15pm. We did not have a drink together at 6.15pm; it was at 9.15pm.

Chivvied by a succession of further questions from Gatehouse, Gremond recalled the conversation that had been exchanged between Wickings and Tremerel in the kitchen:

> I understood Mme Tremerel asked the accused what age he was and he said twenty-five. Nothing was said about the length of the accused's [military] service.... It was the deceased who took the two pocket books out of the accused's pocket. Accused showed us two photographs or two Christmas cards. I remember the accused showing me the scar on his neck and he said he had been three times wounded.[40]

Whether due to her restricted comprehension of English or a lapse of memory, the landlady was wrong about Wickings' age and wounds. Arthur Wickings was born in early 1890 and although he had three scars on his body, only two were the consequence of war wounds.[41] However, neither discrepancy attracted further intervention by Gatehouse. Instead, he asked if Wickings had shown her a pass, to which Gremond replied, 'There was a question about the accused's pass.' She did not elaborate any further but her pre-trial written statement featured a reference to the murdered woman being concerned about 'Arthur' not having a pass.

Gatehouse shifted tack and directed a series of questions about what had happened on the first floor landing and the killer's behaviour and activities as the crisis developed. Though she never actually saw the man inside the room, Gremond confidently asserted, 'When the accused spoke to me through the door his tone seemed to be a jeering one.' He had also remained in the room with the dead woman for some time because just as she was about to re-enter the lodging house with Sergeant Waugh, she had drawn his attention to the room's electric light being extinguished. Normally, Gremond explained to Gatehouse, she herself turned off the house electricity supply at the meter at 10.00pm and had 'turned it off that night when I returned with the police.' With reference to footsteps she heard inside Tremerel's room, Gremond explained that she had not mentioned the noise to the gendarmes at the time because Mme Defraey had already done so.[42]

Gatehouse then referred to the khaki handkerchief that had been appropriated by Fitzpatrick. Had she been the first person to notice the item? She replied:

> I saw the khaki handkerchief on the sill immediately I entered the room and pointed it out to the three policemen and later the French police. I left it lying where it was. Someone closed the window, I cannot remember who.

In her pre-trial statement she claimed the room was dark and she noticed the handkerchief after she had obtained an oil lamp. However, Waugh had never made any reference to a handkerchief.

At this point Lance Corporal Charles Ford, MFP, was fetched into the court and Gremond was asked by Gatehouse where and when she had previously seen Ford. She responded:

> I do not recollect having seen this military policeman before. I was so excited at the time. I cannot recollect. I do not recollect having a conversation with this policeman between 10.30pm and 11.00pm. Several persons questioned me with regard to a description of the man who had gone to the deceased's room. I never said to any of the police that the man who entered the deceased's room had a moustache.

She was evidently flustered. However, Ford had been the first British military policeman to arrive on the scene that could converse in French and was therefore able to gather a description of the fugitive killer.[43] The lance corporal had noted Gremond stating that the wanted man had a moustache. However, her patent inability to remember either Ford or the conversation they had exchanged undermined Gremond's hitherto impressive capacity to recall details about much else of what occurred on the fatal night.

Gatehouse finished his cross-examination but the prosecution posed a final question. Jefferis asked Gremond in what language she had communicated with Sergeant Waugh, who spoke no French. She replied, 'When I pointed out to the police about the light being extinguished, I spoke in French.'

Seeking further clarification of her evidence, at this point the court intervened. The questions posed by the court were not recorded in the written proceedings but her answers draw attention to anomalies in her earlier testimony. On Wickings' grasp of French, she explained, 'The accused appeared to understand a few words in French. When he pointed to his scar he said: "Trois fois blesse a la guerre."' She reiterated, 'The accent of the man speaking inside the room was undoubtedly that of an Englishman.'[44]

Because nobody on the first floor landing had been able to see through the door, her identification of the killer relied to a great extent on Gremond's comprehension and familiarity with spoken English. However, it is apparent that the landlady's command of English was restricted to a few words and phrases. Even without the benefit of hindsight, it is doubtful whether in her 'excited' state she would have been able to distinguish between English regional accents or the accent of a soldier from Portsmouth, England, and another from Portsmouth, Australia.[45]

Concern about resolving further inconsistencies may be inferred from the court's subsequent cross-examination of Gremond about her facial description of the alleged killer. She insisted, 'When questioned about the identity of the man who had entered the deceased's room, I used the expression *"sans moustache".'* Since Lance Corporal Ford was the only witness to have referred to a moustache, her unequivocal response suggests she had developed an enhanced recollection of what had been said, though not about the NCO himself.[46]

The court then enquired about Gremond's initial impressions of the room immediately after the door had been forced open. She recalled, 'I found the room in disorder, it gave me the impression that someone had been searching for something.' The 'something' may have been a box that she maintained had gone missing from the room: 'The box referred to containing letters was a small inlaid wooden box about seven inches long. I have seen in this box, a pocket book containing the addresses of Englishmen. I have not seen this box since December 19th.'

Gremond also revealed that she had 'heard footsteps in the deceased's room between 6.00pm and 7.00pm, but I cannot say if it was one or more persons.' Wickings may have derived a crumb of comfort from the admission, for it indicated a visitor or visitors to the lodging house could have made their way upstairs unnoticed by Gremond. The court concluded by asking her how she could be certain that it was 9.15pm and not 6.15pm when she first encountered Wickings. Gremond answered, 'I looked at the alarm clock in my kitchen when Mme Tremerel went upstairs to see who was there.'

The quality of the landlady's testimony had been rather variable but due allowance needs to be made for her distress over the murder and having her testimony dissected by a highly formal gathering of British Army officers. Though Sasso translated the questions and her responses, and Jefferis may have been marginally more sympathetic in his manner than Gatehouse, as a French woman she would have inevitably been regarded as being their social inferior. That said, in her final answer to a question posed by the court, Virginie was rather miserly with the *actualité* when she said, 'I do not know of the deceased having had any trouble with any of the soldiers who used to visit her.' Her own evidence suggested otherwise.[47]

Conrad Sasso's services as translator were again employed for the next prosecution witness, Marie Lemoine.[48] She recalled:

> Between 8.30pm and 8.40pm on the 19th December, someone knocked four times on the door of my room. I opened the door and saw a British soldier by the light of a candle which I was carrying. The man was of average height and wore an overcoat with stripes on the arm. I cannot say how many. He was clean shaven.

In spite of his close proximity, she added, 'I could not recognize his features.'

Lemoine had failed to pick out Wickings at an identity parade and selected another man, Sergeant No.476111

F. Mills, Rifle Brigade, who was wholly unconnected with the case. Jefferis summoned Mills into the courtroom and Lemoine said:

> I recognize this sergeant as one of those on the identification parade, and I pointed him out at the time judging from his height and build, not from his features, that he might have been the man who knocked at my door.[49]

Mills then withdrew and Jefferis proceeded to enquire whether she had seen any other soldiers in the house on the fatal night. In a rather blasé fashion she commented, 'I did not notice whether any other soldiers came or not that evening, so many soldiers used to come, I did not take any notice.'

The court then asked how she could be certain of the time that the man arrived at her door. She replied, 'I knew the time because I looked at my clock and had just finished my dinner.' There being no further questions, Mme Lemoine's contribution ended.[50]

However, Gremond had recollected 'Arthur' arrived at around 9.15pm, circa thirty-five minutes after the latest time recalled by Lemoine. Reconciling the discrepancy invites speculation: was the landlady's clock too fast or was Lemoine's too slow? Did one man visit on two occasions or may two men have independently visited Tremerel's room that night?

There was a prospect that the next witness, Mme Palmyre Defraey, may have resolved the matter. She related her version of events; she had gone to bed at about 8.45pm and about half an hour later she had also been disturbed by sudden noise from the other side of the first floor landing.[51]

Both Lemoine and Defraey agreed that the disruption occurred at circa 9.15pm. However, if the landlady's recollection was correct, Defraey could not have heard any noises from across the landing because Gremond, Tremerel and 'Arthur' were together in the kitchen at that time. On the other hand, Defraey's sense of time was at odds with Woodgate's. When it came to recalling how long it took for the door of Tremerel's room to be battered open, Defraey reckoned that it had taken twenty minutes, whereas Woodgate said he took between five and ten minutes.[52]

The following witness, Corporal Arthur Bergilez, testified that he had arrived at the lodgings between 6.30pm and 7.00pm and had gone to bed at 9.00pm. About fifteen minutes later he heard 'three taps on the floor as if made by a stick ... a few minutes afterwards a noise, as if something heavy had fallen.' Bergilez confessed he did not speak English but that while he had been on the first floor landing he had also heard a man speaking French with an English accent. After the three British military police gained entry, Bergilez had spotted the sheet dangling from one of the French windows of Tremerel's room. However, his efforts to alert military police came to naught, probably due to his own nervous stress but also because of Sergeant Waugh's inability to understand French.[53]

Waugh's involvement in the case began at 10.30pm at the eastern end of the Rue des Ramparts near the Place Richelieu, which was where Tremerel had sought his assistance. Waugh opened his testimony by explaining that he took about six minutes to summon Woodgate and Adams, who were patrolling about 500 yards away and they had then taken a further four minutes to walk another 500-600 yards to the lodging house. Gremond had gone on ahead; they met with her in the Rue Emile Zola.[54]

Sergeant Waugh repeated in court what he had already related in his pre-trial statement but under cross-examination by Gatehouse, Waugh denied noticing the sheet hanging out of the window before entering the house because 'it was a very dark night.'[55] He also said that the landlady had not drawn his attention to the handkerchief on the windowsill; in fact, he never even saw any handkerchief. With reference to the window through which the killer escaped, Waugh did not recall Defraey saying she could hear the window being opened and he emphatically denied being the person who had closed the French window.

He also recalled that 'the room was in confusion' when he and the two other military policemen abandoned the scene of the crime while they went to report to Captain Fitzpatrick. Waugh, Woodgate and Adams had left the crime scene wholly unguarded and met Ford, who had been patrolling the Rue Racine with a French gendarme. Ford abandoned his French companion and accompanied the military policemen to the Assistant Provost Marshal's office. Thereafter, Ford returned to the lodgings, where he proceeded to interrogate Virginie Gremond. Since Waugh could not speak any French he understood nothing of what was being said by any of the civilians at the scene of the crime.[56]

Jefferis asked Waugh why he did not secure the crime scene properly, eliciting the reply, 'My chief concern after seeing the body on the bed was to inform the French police and the APM.' The oversight would have been wholly reprehensible if Waugh had been a trained policeman or a professional detective. However, in civilian life he was an estate agent and his wartime experience had hitherto involved controlling soldiers under sentence in army field punishment compounds and detention centres.

He also mentioned that Gremond had brought a lamp into the room and placed it on the table that had been upended before their entry. The landlady had evidently righted the table and remained in the room during Waugh's absence and without anyone to prevent her doing so, she had tampered with the scene of crime. Circumstantial evidence suggests she had time and took the opportunity to tidy up the room, untie and bundled-up the sheet and counterpane that were dangling into the street, and before closing the French window she had noticed the khaki handkerchief on the windowsill.[57]

Before ending his testimony, Waugh was asked by the court how he could be certain about the time when he arrived at the house. He responded, 'I fixed the time at 10.30pm by my watch which I had set by the Hotel de Ville clock that day. I looked at my watch when I got to the house. It was then 10.30pm.'

Waugh finished his contribution as a witness for the prosecution by dismissing out of hand any suggestion that Gremond had spoken to him during the initial five minutes they had been together in the room. In response to an inquiry from the court, Waugh remarked, 'I did not hear Mlle Gremond say anything while I was in the room. I think I would have noticed it if Mlle Gremond had come up to me while I was at the window.[58]

Waugh's testimony rather undermined Gremond's evidence and certainly called into question exactly when and how the khaki handkerchief came to be deposited on the windowsill of the French window. Though references to the khaki handkerchief continued to figure at intervals during the trial, Waugh's evidence nullified its value as material evidence.

Lance-Corporal Woodgate endorsed much of Waugh's narrative, including the position of Tremerel's body, the upturned table and women's clothing he noticed lying in the corner of the room. He confirmed that during the five minutes he spent at the scene, the civilian witnesses conversed only with one another in French, and as for the khaki handkerchief, Woodgate said:

> I went to the window; there was nothing on the sill. If a handkerchief had been there I should have seen it. Mlle Gremond did not point out any handkerchief to me while I was in the room ... I did not shut the window. I do not think the room was in confusion.

Lance-Corporal Adams' testimony broadly corroborated Waugh's version of events: he did not see a sheet dangling from an open window as they entered the lodgings, nor did he hear any noises emanating from the room before breaking down the door. He agreed that there had been little opportunity to conduct a detailed examination during the five minutes he had spent in the room before being called away by Waugh.

Adams also confirmed Sergeant Waugh's recollection that the landlady had not shown them the khaki handkerchief: 'I saw Mlle Gremond go to the window. She did not point out anything there to any of us.' However, he did recall Virginie speaking to Waugh en route to the lodgings: 'As we were approaching the house Mlle Gremond said something to the sergeant. I did not see her pointing.'

Under cross-examination by the court, Adams described the cavalier fashion in which the French and

British police had behaved after breaking down the door. He confessed:

> When we went away, there were no police, English or French left in the house. When we came back with Corporal Ford, Sergeant Waugh brought a gendarme with him. The French gendarme only stayed a few minutes then went away.

The court also pressed Adams to explain why none of the policemen had noticed the sheet dangling down from the French window when they initially approached the lodging house. Rather lamely, Adams explained, 'The Rue Emile Zola was very dark,' though he conceded, 'There was a lamp at the corner of the two streets which was lighted.'

Having listened to witnesses about events in Le Havre, the prosecuting officer went on to draw the court's attention to the testimony of four sergeants who shared the tent in which Wickings had bedded down at No.17 Camp, Harfleur. Aside from the court's interest in establishing the time when Wickings returned to the camp on 19 December, without openly alleging the abrasions could have been inflicted by Tremerel, the prosecution was anxious to establish when the NCO's face had been scratched.

On 18 December, Wickings had mentioned to Sergeant Christopher Murray, the first of the sergeants to testify, that he had a pass for the following night.[59] On the following night, Murray went to bed just before

10.00pm. He declared: 'I was awakened later by the accused looking for his blankets. I cannot exactly say what the time was but I should say about 10.30pm. There was no light in the tent.'

Wickings was looking for some of his blankets that had gone missing; they conversed briefly and shared a bottle of stout. Murray was unable to recall exactly when he went back to sleep but he felt certain that Wickings did not leave the tent again. Wickings was up and about by 6.30am the following day but it was not until about 10.00am that Murray noticed Wickings 'had two scratches on his chin. They were scarcely noticeable. They were each about an inch and a half long,' but he maintained that the latter had 'carried out his duties in his usual manner.'

Murray had only known Wickings for about a week but his testimony appeared to provide the latter with an alibi. If he was in the tent with Murray at 10.30pm, Wickings could not have committed the killing at Le Havre.

After the court enquired whether he had noticed any scratches on Wickings' face before 20 December, Murray replied, 'I did not notice the two scratches on accused's face when I saw him the day before.' Unfortunately, the written proceedings do not disclose whether this response was a ringing declaration or an almost diffident acknowledgement that Wickings' face may have been scratched but so faintly that Murray had not spotted the abrasions.

Sergeant Robert Smyth explained that he occupied a bed next to Wickings and had turned in at 9.30pm on 19 December but was still awake half an hour later when a bugle call sounded Lights Out.[60] Smyth had then fallen asleep and was woken up by Wickings' arrival at about 11.30pm. Smyth was certain about the time because 'Somebody in the tent said "what's the time?" and a voice said "It must be half-past eleven."'

He also heard Wickings complain, 'Some of you lads must have my blankets,' and then, 'All right, I have got three.' Smyth arose early the following morning but did not pay any attention to Wickings until about 9.00am, when he recalled:

> I noticed three marks on the outside of his face. They were about 1/8th of an inch apart. Accused might have received these marks from a fall. They were indistinct marks and I would not swear that they were fresh marks. The centre one was the longest one and that was about an inch long. They were parallel with each other and running down the face. I had not noticed these scratches before this occasion.

Captain Gatehouse opened his cross-examination of Smyth by establishing that the police had initially interrogated the latter during the first week of January. Smyth then disclosed the sergeants went to bed 'sometimes by 9.00pm: we are very often all in bed by 10.00pm, seldom after.' The only confirmation he could advance about the time Wickings entered the tent was the brief exchange to which he had earlier referred. Smyth admitted:

> I did not recognize the voice of either the person who asked the time or the person who answered. I am quite certain that someone asked the time and someone answered. When the accused came into the tent, I had a blanket over my head and could not hear much. I did not hear a drink being given to Sergeant Murray.

He added, 'I have not got a watch and I don't know of anyone else in the tent who had one at that time,' drawing attention to a couple of points that were wholly unexplored in cross-examination. Smyth could have overheard a conversation between a couple of individuals standing outside or perhaps even passing by the tent. And if he had been correct about the exchange being aired within the tent, he ought to have been able to identify whether one of the speakers was Wickings because Smyth and all the other sergeants had Irish accents.

Aside from being unsure about the exact time when Wickings entered the tent, Smyth also amended his earlier testimony. When re-examined by Jefferis about the date when the NCO was initially questioned about the case, Smyth replied, 'The first time I was questioned about this case was, I believe, before Christmas. This is what I referred to in my cross-examination.' However, Smyth did not say by whom he had been questioned and no one referred to any pre-trial statement he had made, other than what had been copied down by Jefferis at least sixteen days after the murder.

With reference to his pre-trial statement, the court sought clarification from Smyth about what he meant when he had described the scratches he had seen on Wickings' face during 20 December being 'fresh'. He revised his earlier testimony, explaining, 'I said ... the scratches were fresh because they were not there on the 18th of December.'

The third (sic) tent mate to give evidence was Sergeant Mark King, whose version of events differed sharply from Smyth's.[61] King had only known Wickings for a few days before 19 December; he had gone to bed at 10.15pm and had nodded off immediately and enjoyed a sound, uninterrupted night's sleep. On waking at 6.30am, King recalled:

> I noticed the accused sitting up, getting ready to get up. He seemed to be in good spirits in his usual manner. I did not take particular notice of him. At this hour there was no light in the tent. I could not say who left the tent first, the accused or myself. I saw him again later on in the morning and did not notice anything unusual about him. I noticed nothing unusual about his appearance. I noticed on the 20th December he was wearing a muffler round his neck. I had not seen him wearing a muffler before. The weather

> was very cold and had been very cold for the preceding two days.

In response to a question about abrasions on Wickings' face, King commented, 'About 11.00am on December 20th, I noticed one or two small marks on the left or right cheek. I do not know which. They appeared to be ordinary scratches.'[62]

Jefferis then invited King to say how the scratches had been caused. It was a wholly improper question because it called on him to voice an opinion concerning something about which he had no direct knowledge. As experienced barristers, Gatehouse and Crowdy must have been fully aware of the legal transgression but neither intervened and King was permitted to speculate: 'I could not say if they had been caused by any instrument. The scratches were quite distinct. This was the first time I had noticed the scratches.'

Gatehouse opened his cross-examination of King by establishing that Wickings' comrades usually went to bed at about 10.15pm but on the night of 19 December, Sergeant King was away from camp on a pass, issued by Wickings.[63] When Gatehouse asked King if he was certain there had been a light in the tent on the morning of 20 December, the sergeant revised his earlier testimony, commenting, 'I cannot remember definitely, but we probably had a candle to get up by.'

King declared that he was on friendly terms with the defendant but he was uncertain about having breakfasted with him on 20 December. Yet he clearly recalled that, 'Accused wore the muffler around his neck and not the lower part of his face,' and also remembered Wickings mentioning an altercation involving Australian soldiers that he had witnessed in Le Havre. King then said that it was on that same morning he had given Wickings a khaki handkerchief.

On re-examination, King was quizzed about the routine procedure for issuing and surrendering passes:

> It is the custom in number 17 Camp to put in a pass through the Company Sergeant-Major. In my case, that would be the accused and he would take them to the orderly room. Lance-Corporal Barber is the acting Orderly Sergeant and I am sure the Orderly Sergeant has nothing to do with passes. At that time there was no order for Warrant Officers or Sergeants to hand in their passes and we did not hand them in on this occasion. I cannot say if the accused had a pass that day.

Finally, the association between Wickings and a khaki handkerchief re-emerged during King's final contribution to the proceedings:

> A friend at home sent me six handkerchiefs and it was one of these which I gave to the accused. I now produce four of these handkerchiefs which

> are laid before the court. These handkerchiefs have been washed. I took all six of these handkerchiefs to be similar. I gave the sixth to Sergeant Fines of the 2/7 Royal Irish Rifles.[64]

The fourth NCO who was allocated bed space in the tent with Wickings was Sergeant William Mallon.[65] On 18 December Wickings had issued a pass to Mallon but the latter decided not to leave camp. To Jefferis, Mallon explained the routine:

> When one wants a pass one gives one's name to the Orderly Sergeant, Lance Corporal Barber. It is the custom to hand in the pass when finished to the orderly Sergeant.

He also knew during the afternoon that Wickings had got a pass and was intending to visit Le Havre on the evening of 19 December. Like King, Mallon had slept through the night and was undisturbed by Wickings' arrival, and recalled:

> I woke up at 7.00am the following morning. I noticed the accused standing in the tent dressed. Accused remained in the tent for about five minutes and went out about 7.05am.

In the absence of a watch, it is difficult to appreciate what weight to attach to the differing estimates of time expressed by the four sergeants. Sunrise was not until after 8.00am and the estimates cannot all have been correct. Mallon concurred with the testimony of his fellow sergeants about Wickings' behaviour but noticed the abrasions on his face:

> I saw the accused again about 11.00am that morning. I noticed then scratches on the accused's face. I would not swear that these scratches were not there on the previous day but I did not see them.

Pressed by Jefferis, Mallon provided more details about Wickings' scratches:

> There were three scratches on the side of the accused's face. They were not half an inch long. These scratches were parallel running up and down the cheek. I do not remember the distance apart. They were distinct. I cannot say how they were caused. The scratches were on the left cheek. The skin was off.

In response to further questioning, Mallon elaborated:

> I noticed no scratches at 7.00am. There was light in the tent. I was on the opposite side of the accused and was sitting on my bed. He said something about a row with some Australians in the town.

Finally, under cross-examination by the court, Mallon said of the abrasions on Wickings' face, 'The scratches had the appearance of being fresh.'[66]

There was a sixth NCO named Sergeant Lynas who also slept in the tent and whose name featured in Smyth's written statement but who was not called on to give evidence in court. Though Smyth had denied in court that anyone in the tent possessed a timepiece, Smyth knew that Lynas possessed a watch and had referred to the fact in his written statement. Given the importance attached to establishing the time when Wickings returned to the tent, it is surprising that Lynas was not summoned to testify.[67]

Even without the benefit of hindsight, the evidence presented by the four sergeants was confused and confusing: King stated that passes were customarily handed out by the company sergeant major; Mallon maintained passes were issued by the orderly sergeant, yet it was Wickings who issued the passes on 19 December. Other discrepancies may be excused because two weeks elapsed before the sergeants made their pre-trial statements. However, it is curious that three of sergeants (excluding Mallon) with no prior cause to pay attention were able to swear that Wickings' face was unscratched prior to 20 December.

At this point in the proceedings, Lance Corporal James Barber was ushered into court to testify about the system for monitoring the supply and collection of passes at Harfleur Camp. It was his responsibility to maintain a logbook, in which he recorded details of soldiers granted leave and the times at which passes were issued and returned. However, to Jefferis, Barber disclosed:

> I have no check on the passes of sergeants returning as they are allowed out until 10.00pm and my duty finishes at 9.45pm. At that time, sergeants were not required to hand in their passes.[68]

Asked where he was at 9.45pm on the night of the murder, Barber responded:

> I should have probably been in bed in No.1 tent in 'C' Lines. It is from the same tent that I issue and receive passes. I do all my work there. The accused did not enter my tent on that evening. The next morning I noticed several passes on my table of the men who had been on pass the night before, but I did not notice one from the accused.

After Gatehouse had demanded to know why there was no entry in the log book referring to the pass Wickings had issued to Mallon, Barber admitted:

> His name does not appear in the book. I forgot to enter it. He applied just as I was entering the orderly room and I had several passes to attend to afterwards .... At that time when a sergeant had a pass, I did not usually see it again. If he had a pass in his possession and wanted the pass renewed, he could take it to the orderly room himself and have the date altered without letting me know. Therefore the book is of no value as regards sergeants. The sergeants did not show their passes on return.

Jefferis intervened, apparently attempting to salvage something of value from a revelation that was decidedly unhelpful for the prosecution. Would Barber have entered the name of an applicant for a pass into the logbook? The latter responded, 'If a sergeant put an application for a pass through me, I should have entered his name in my book.' The court demanded the NCO be more explicit; Barber confessed, 'Sergeant Mallon did not hand his pass for the 19th of December back to me.'

Barber had also voiced an excuse about being distracted and burdened with other responsibilities, but his testimony about Mallon's pass eroded the reliability of the logbook as an indicator of the time when Wickings may have returned to the camp.[69] After the hapless Barber withdrew, Jefferis invited two witnesses who had played key roles in apprehending Wickings.

The first was Barber's immediate superior, Provost Sergeant Thomas Collins, the NCO who had also followed up a hunch about Wickings being the man wanted in connection with the murder. In court, Collins stated that when he quizzed Wickings on 23 December, the latter had mentioned being 'connected with a row in the town with some Australian soldiers' and that after commenting about the incident, Wickings had said, 'I ran out.' After Collins was unable to recall any further details about the alleged incident, he withdrew and Captain Leonard Gibson, the No.17 Camp adjutant, who confirmed that Wickings had initially declared he wished to clear himself of any suspicion, took his place in court.[70]

Gibson then produced Wickings' pay book (AB64) as material evidence, and was asked by Gatehouse what else had been found in the NCO's pockets:

> There were other papers in accused's AB64 including some cards. I have no recollection of seeing any photographs but I won't swear they were not there. I cannot say what the cards were like.

Answering a brief enquiry by the court, Gibson also claimed that, 'I do not think that the accused could have had a pass without my knowing it at the time.' However, Barber's evidence had already demonstrated the contrary to be the case. Wickings could quite easily have picked up a pass and Gibson would have been none the wiser.[71]

The prosecution shifted the locus of the court's attention back to what had happened in Le Havre, and produced a succession of witnesses, including British military personnel, French police and medical men. The Assistant Provost Marshal, Captain Fitzpatrick, told the court about being summoned to the scene of the crime by Sergeant Waugh and his own discovery of the khaki handkerchief:

> I made a very careful examination of the room with the exception of the bed and its vicinity. I was very particular in examining the window ...

> and on the window ledge I picked up a khaki handkerchief ... on the outside portion of the window ledge ... I found a khaki handkerchief on the accused which I now produce, which as far as I can judge, is identical with the one I found on the window sill of No.4, Rue Racine.[72]

Fitzpatrick was invited to compare the handkerchief that had been confiscated with other belongings from Wickings and the one from the windowsill with the four handkerchiefs that had earlier been submitted as evidence by Sergeant King. The APM confessed:

> The four handkerchiefs are not similar in pattern or material to the two handkerchiefs I have produced. The material is different and the edging is quite a different size. The principal difference is the stitching.

Fitzpatrick, under cross-examination by Gatehouse about the abrasions on Wickings' face, stated:

> I particularly noticed about two scratches on the face of the accused. I particularly noticed one scratch which ran diagonally from the ear to the mouth. It was about an inch and a quarter long. As far as I can recollect, the other scratch was about half an inch long and in the vicinity of the other. I think these scratches were too jagged to have been made by a razor. They might have been caused by a pin.

Fitzpatrick went on to detail what he could remember about the room in which the murder had been committed:

> I am under the impression that the window was open but I am not certain. The sheet had been brought into the room before I arrived. The room was badly lit by a small oil lamp and we had to use two electric torches to find objects on the floor. It was dark outside.

On the khaki handkerchiefs, Fitzpatrick conceded:

> All the handkerchiefs produced are of a fairly common type. The handkerchief that I took off the accused had the appearance of having been washed but I could not say that it had been washed often.

Fitzpatrick concluded his recollection of Tremerel's room by saying that it was in disarray and that he had noticed a small box containing some letters and notebooks containing addresses. Gatehouse then moved on to ask Fitzpatrick about how long it would take for a person to walk from the Rue Racine to No.17 Camp, Harfleur. The latter responded:

> I think it would take an hour and a half at least. The last tram leaves the Hotel de Ville at 9.15pm. There is a tram for the officers, which leaves the Hotel de Ville at 10.10pm on which men travel sometimes.

Gatehouse had no more questions but he missed a point that was taken up by the prosecution, namely could Wickings have used other means to get back to camp? Fitzpatrick explained:

> If one took a taxi as far as it is allowed to go, it would take about thirty-five minutes to get from Rue Racine to No.17 Camp, Harfleur. Taxis are not allowed in the camp after 10.00pm. At about 10.45pm there are as a rule a number of taxis on the cab stand near the Hotel de Ville. They are well patronized.[73]

Fitzpatrick's cross-examination ended and he withdrew from the court. As evidence linking Wickings with the murder scene, the khaki handkerchief proved nothing; the one pocketed by Fitzpatrick could have belonged to Tremerel or another of her clients. Neither could much be made about Wickings washing his handkerchief during the three days that elapsed before his arrest.

Fitzpatrick's lack of expertise as a detective is woefully apparent from his testimony. He noticed 'about two scratches' on Wickings' face but failed to arrange for a photographic record of the abrasions. Instead of requesting Gremond to restore the electricity supply to illuminate the murder scene, he and Roberts had conducted their investigation with the aid of a couple of electric torches and an oil lamp.

Detective Sergeant Roberts opened his testimony by stating that the distance between the murder scene and the camp was 6 1/4 miles, and from the Café Jules Masurier to 4, Rue Racine was precisely 260 paces. Jefferis then broached the issue of the two descriptions. First he asked Roberts about the description Gremond had initially given to Corporal Ford. Roberts answered:

> Corporal Ford told me that he had taken a description of the accused but I did not ask him what it was. This was the first description of the accused given by Mlle Gremond to anyone, as far as I know.

Asked why he did not record and circulate the description, he replied:

> I did not think it important to take it [down?] as the man was in custody and I did not think that Ford's description would be otherwise than the description I had already obtained.

Roberts agreed that the description circulated by the French police was different to the one Gremond had furnished Ford. Had Ford ever complained about the accuracy of the police description?

> Corporal Ford should have known the description as circulated. Corporal Ford has not to my knowledge, made any remarks as to the correctness of the description circulated. If that

> description was not correct it was his duty to inform the APM.

The timing of Wickings' return to camp was a major challenge for the prosecution. Even if the latest estimate of the time at which he disturbed his fellow sergeants' sleep was accepted as accurate, on foot it would have been impossible for him to have returned to camp before midnight. However, Roberts maintained that Wickings could have trimmed about a mile off his journey by following the tramlines for 5 1/2 miles from Rue Racine to the halt at Harfleur. Alternatively, he surmised Wickings could have hitched a lift from a passing Belgian or French military vehicle or perhaps he might have caught a tram to Graville from the Quay de Southampton at 9.50pm, and walked the remainder of his way back to camp. None of Roberts' suggestions were supported by any evidence, and if his final hypothesis was correct then Wickings would have been provided with an alibi because the killer was still in Tremerel's room at 9.50pm.

The court went on to listen to a summary of the findings of the medical examination that Captain Rimmer carried out immediately after Wickings had been arrested:

> I found that he had some scratches on the right-hand corner of his mouth, three in all. They were from four to seven days old. As far as I remember these scratches were from an inch to an inch and a quarter in length, and fairly broad.

> They ran down from the corner of the mouth obliquely downwards and outwards. They ran parallel to each other. They might have been caused by a blunt instrument – but not by a sharp one. The space between the two outside scratches was from half to three quarters of an inch. There was a superficial abrasion on the knuckles of the left hand.... I should say that this had been standing for about the same length of time as the scratches. I found no evidence of active venereal disease upon the accused.

Under cross-examination by Gatehouse, Rimmer speculated about what may have caused the injuries:

> It is possible that the three marks might have been reopened about three days before, but I saw no indication of it. There was an abrasion of the skin. These marks could have been caused in a variety of ways.

The court pressed Rimmer to be more specific but all he would say was:

> There was very slight inflammation about these scratches. They were not septic. A possible cause would have been the contact between the face and a rough surface. They did not suggest the appearance of having been reopened by shaving or otherwise within forty-eight hours.

Rimmer's evidence settled very little and begged the question why Wickings was not called to account for the scratches during the medical inspection. Rimmer's speculation about what may have caused the scratches, a 'blunt instrument' or a 'rough surface' was little by way of an advance on Fitzpatrick's opinion that the scratches may have been caused by a pin. It is rather puzzling that Rimmer did not repeat in court a claim that he made in his pre-trial written statement, namely: 'It would have been possible for the scratches to have been made with fingernails of a human being.' Probably because his tests proved to be inconclusive, Rimmer also made no reference to the overcoat Wickings had surrendered when taken into custody. Rimmer had been unable to determine neither the age of some stains on the sleeve and cuffs nor could he decided whether they were composed of human or animal blood.

The final batch of witnesses was entirely composed of French officials. Maurice Ternon submitted a copy of the floor plan of the murder room and the photographs he had taken in situ of the dead woman. Police Commissioner Frambourg's testimony added very little to the conclusions he had included in his written report about the crime scene. However, he explained that he gained the mistaken impression that the dead woman had engaged in sexual intercourse because a pillow that was under her buttocks had slipped. He recalled:

> When I got into the room the marble-topped table was standing, the window was shut and a sheet and counterpane rolled up on a chair near the window.

In the wardrobe Frambourg discovered a handbag and a wooden box containing over 130 francs in cash and some jewellery. He also witnessed Captain Fitzpatrick open the French window and discover the khaki handkerchief on the sill outside, about half an hour after it had been spotted by Gremond.

After Frambourg denied having seen a dark cloak, presumably belonging to Tremerel, in the room, Gatehouse asked the commissioner about the state of the dead woman's hands. Frambourg said he had examined them and noticed 'there was a little blood from a slight scratch on one of the thumbs and no other blood on the hands.'

The court concluded by asking Frambourg whether the street lamp situated immediately outside the lodgings had been lit. Frambourg said he could not remember but added that it had been a clear night.[74]

The men who had handled Tremerel's corpse then testified: Gendarme M.J. Loyer, who conveyed the dead woman's body from the murder room to the morgue; Monsieur Le Meur, the morgue attendant; Dr Klein; and the pathologist, Dr Balard d'Herlinville.

After Le Meur formally acknowledged witnessing the autopsy, Dr Klein advanced some observations about his written report. From his preliminary inspection of the corpse, Klein concluded that Tremerel had struggled for about five or six seconds before being killed by strangulation, adding, 'I did not see any blood on the hands only at the corner of the mouth.' Klein also went on to confirm that although the head and extremities were cold he found the body otherwise still warm, indicating her death to have been very recent. Addressing the issue of sexual activity, Klein deduced:

> The sexual parts were viscous. In my opinion the position of the body and the state of the vaginal parts suggested three explanations:

1. Erotic Mania.
2. The presence of semen.
3. Mucous discharge.

> It occurred to me as probable that the woman had been 'garamouched'.[75]

Dr d'Herlinville was sworn in. He shared with the court the findings of the autopsy he had performed on Tremerel's body. He confirmed that she had eaten a meal less than an hour before the attack and agreed with Klein's conclusions about the brevity of her struggle and asphyxia as the cause of death but added some further details:

> There was an excoriation on the right thumb which might have been made by a finger nail, and an excoriation of the left elbow which might have been made by knocking against a hard object.... I examined the fingernails; they were dirty but there was nothing else peculiar.

Gatehouse did not press him to either confirm or rule out Dr Klein's speculation about oral sex but asked d'Herlinville to confirm that he had found no evidence of recent sexual activity. The pathologist responded:

> Unless the woman had washed or taken an injection [vaginal douche] in between there had been no complete sexual act recently.

At the conclusion of the d'Herlinville's evidence, the prosecution rested its case. The case for the defence opened with a formal complaint being lodged about the wretched conditions in which Wickings had been kept while in detention. Gatehouse stated:

> The accused has been in solitary confinement for three weeks, with only a rug, no chair or table and no change of clothes, which I do not consider fair or proper treatment. He should not have been allowed, in a serious case like this, to have made any statement whatever in the summary or to have cross-examined the witnesses. I am putting the accused in the witness box, at his own particular request. He has always protested his innocence. I am of the opinion that Corporal Ford

> should have been called by the prosecution as he was the first person who received a description of the murderer from Mlle Gremond and that I therefore propose to call him myself, though by doing so I shall lose the right of the last word. You will see now whether the statement he now makes agrees with the one he made at the taking of the summary.[76]

The complaint was duly noted and the court responded by offering to summon Corporal Ford to give evidence, thereby permitting the defence to retain the right of the last word. The offer was declined; Gatehouse probably calculated Wickings' case might be better served if he called on Ford to testify.

His custodians subsequently contested Gatehouse's allusion to Wickings' deprivation while in detention but other contemporary accounts suggest that the stressful conditions referred to by Gatehouse were unexceptional.[77] However, Gatehouse's objection to the breach of procedure in gathering summaries of evidence carried more immediate legal weight. He maintained that Jefferis' 'advice' to Wickings compromised the voluntary nature of the latter's pre-trial statement. The *Rules of Procedure* clearly state:

> In no case must he be authoritatively called on to account for his proceedings, or required to make any statement, or asked any questions; the

> answer to any such question will not be admissible in evidence against him.[78]

However, the rule was also subject to interpretation and the court, advised by Captain Crowdy, declared that Wickings had not been 'authoritatively called on to account for his proceedings'.[79]

Finally, Wickings had his opportunity to testify. Though the written proceedings do not reveal the extent to which Wickings was prompted by Gatehouse, at first sight the NCO's evidence appears well structured and quite comprehensive.[80] He began by recalling his military career and impressive war service:

> I first came out to France in February 1915. I have been out here for about three years off and on. When I came out I was a rifleman. I was promoted to Lance-Corporal on 18th October, 1915; Corporal on December 1st, 1915. I became Acting Sergeant but relinquished the acting rank to rejoin my own company. I once again became a Lance Corporal, in February 1916, and became Lance Sergeant in September 1917. I have been in the following engagements: St Eloi; 2nd Battle of Ypres; Loos; Delville Wood; Fleurs; Arras (Easter Monday 1917); again Arras (Infantry Hill). I have been wounded twice. The only punishment I have had in my service since the beginning of the war is one reprimand.[81]

He explained how he had obtained passes on December 18:

> I was then acting Company Sergeant Major of Number 2 Company. On that day, I put in a pass. I received my pass also those of Sergeant King and Sergeant Mallon. I gave Sergeant King his pass and also gave Sergeant Mallon his. My pass was for the 19th of December.

Again, probably with some assistance from Gatehouse, Wickings carefully presented his own account of what happened on 19 December:

> I left the camp at 4:30pm. I went to Harfleur and caught the tram to the Hotel de Ville, Havre.

He remembered entering the café at 10, Rue Jules de Masurier at approximately 6.05pm:

> I had one bottle of stout there, standing up at the counter. I was only in the café for five minutes and came straight out. About five minutes afterwards, I was stopped by a woman who asked me to go home with her.

The woman was Henriette Tremerel; she escorted him to No.4 Rue Racine and into the Gremond's kitchen. Wickings recalled:

> The kitchen was without anyone in it when we entered. Mlle Gremond entered about two minutes afterwards. Just before Mlle Gremond entered the

> woman who I went home with had three drinks in small glasses.

Gatehouse explained how his pay book came to be handled by Tremerel:

> She asked me how much service I had. I replied 'ten years'. She asked me how old I was and I replied 'twenty-seven'. She did not believe me so she asked me to let her see my pay book. I brought two pay books, one photograph and some Christmas cards out of my pocket. I showed Mme Tremerel the pay book and Christmas card now before the court and also showed her a photograph of my sister and brother-in-law. Mlle Gremond spoke to Mme Tremerel and Mme Tremerel pulled my chin round and showed her my neck and asked if that was where I had been wounded.

Wickings insisted:

> Nothing was said about a pass. I did not show Mme Tremerel four francs and say it was all I had, nor did I say 'I bring you plenty money tomorrow.' Mme Tremerel did not take the books from my pocket.

He admitted going upstairs with Tremerel and referred to being in her room:

> Mlle Tremerel showed me some letters and addresses she had been receiving from English soldiers, which were in a small box. She told me that she receives letters from British soldiers and she generally takes addresses of people who sleep with her. After I had been there for three or four minutes a private of the ASC [Army Service Corps] came into the room. This private was wearing his greatcoat, his haversack and water bottle. He appeared as if he had not had a shave for seven days.

Addressing Wickings, the intruder apologized for interrupting proceedings and:

> He then spoke French to Mlle Tremerel The private then went out. After he had gone out Mlle Tremerel told me he would be back at 7.30pm.... Tremerel did not lock the door when we went in. I then had connection with Mlle Tremerel. I did not undress, nor did she. I gave her a five franc note after the connection. I washed myself. I then went downstairs and she followed behind and we went into the kitchen. It was nearly ten minutes to seven. When we got downstairs Mlle Gremond was still there and she poured out three drinks. After Mlle Gremond had had her drink she went out. About a minute after, I paid Mme Tremerel two francs for the drinks [with] one franc note and a one franc piece. I then said 'Goodnight' and came out.

Gatehouse prompted Wickings for further details of the conversation with Tremerel in the kitchen. Wickings maintained, 'Mlle Tremerel spoke English all the time except when she spoke about my scar.'

Wickings left the lodging house and arrived back at the café about two or three minutes before 7.00pm, where he treated a French sailor to a glass of wine and was enjoying a bottle of stout when Binks entered the premises and exchanged greetings. Johnson and Hawes arrived soon afterwards and at about 7.15pm they all went into the back room and continued drinking together until 8.00pm or 8.10pm, when the café closed its doors to British military personnel. He chatted to Binks outside the café for a few minutes and walked over to the Rue de Paris, where he intended to get a tram back to Harfleur. Wickings continued:

> I waited for the tram, but no tram with the red and green light came. I then walked up to the Hotel de Ville and caught the 9.15pm tram and got off at the railway arch [on] the far side of Harfleur station. I was on the tram for a good half hour. When I got off the tram I walked to the turning where one goes to Harfleur camp. At the railway crossing is a police post. I stopped there for about three minutes. I showed my pass and lit a cigarette by the fire.

He had then gone into the camp and was on his way to visit the latrines when the Lights Out bugle call sounded. He remained in the latrines for about ten minutes before handing in his pass. He explained:

> I proceeded to the Orderly Sergeant's tent and put my pass on his table. When I put the pass in I put the pass through the door onto the table, which is near the door, without going into the tent. It cannot fall off the table as there is a ledge all round it. I then went to my own tent. This was about 10.20.

Wickings' own version of what happened after he reached his tent was far more detailed than accounts by other witnesses in the written proceedings:

> When I entered the tent no one was awake. It was dark. In my tent we are usually asleep by ten o'clock as some of us go to bed at 8.30. When I entered the tent I struck a match to find my blankets. I saw two between the tent boards and the tent wall and one which was put down as a mat in front of the door.... I went out and shouted to the storeman but I could not wake him. I then returned to my tent. This time I woke Sergeant Murray and told him I wanted to find my blankets and after I had made my bed I gave him a bottle of stout. Nobody was awake except Sergeant Murray. No one asked me the time, and no one replied. It was just 10.30 when I got to bed.

Wickings told the court that he had got up at 6.30am the following morning and breakfasted with Sergeant King; no other sergeants in his tent stirred until 6.45am. Wickings went on to account for the abrasions on his face:

> I had some scars on my face when I got up which were caused by an accident ... at 4:00pm on the 18th December I was shaving and the mirror which was attached to some equipment which gave way while hanging on the tent pole, gave me a cut and a graze. I cannot say whether it was done by a buckle of the equipment or the razor. On the 20th when I got up these grazes had fairly healed over. I shaved at 8.30am that morning and opened them up again. I went about my duties in the usual way. The scars showed up more that day because I had knocked the scab off while shaving.

Briefly returning to Rimmer's observation of abrasions on his knuckles, Wickings explained that they were simply the legacy of some old wounds and occasionally flared up every so often, although did not say how he came by them. Wickings also refuted any inference that he had taken to wearing a muffler to conceal the scratches on his cheek. He explained that had worn the muffler since 8 December because the weather had turned cold.

Wickings said that on 23 December he had listened to Captain Gibson reading out the description of a man being sought by the authorities. Because he was a good deal shorter than the height of the wanted man, until approached by Provost Sergeant Collins, Wickings had discounted himself. Because Gibson had not specified the offence allegedly committed by the wanted man, Wickings was under the impression that the authorities were investigating a confrontation involving Australian troops and civilians that he had witnessed in Le Havre. Wickings remembered:

> Sergeant Collins came to me on 23rd December and said to me 'You look pretty near the description except in height.' I said 'Do you think so?' He pointed to the scar on my neck. He asked me about a row in the town. I said I had seen some Australians with bottles in their hands in the town. He said to me 'I advise you to go and see the Adjutant.' I went and saw the Adjutant about a quarter of an hour afterwards.

Wickings concluded by declaring:

> It is untrue that I was in the house No.4 Rue Racine at 9.00pm or anywhere near that time. I am entirely innocent of the charges made against me.[82]

With assistance from Captain Gatehouse, Wickings' explanation appeared to be quite plausible but his claims were subjected to rigorous, sustained cross-examination by Jefferis. Before addressing the vexed issue of passes, the prosecuting officer demolished Gatehouse's complaint; Wickings had been properly cautioned before agreeing to make a written statement. The latter admitted that he had been cautioned:

> I think the prosecutor warned me two or three times. I was warned that anything I said might be used in evidence against me and I also think I was warned to be very careful what I said, but I am not sure.

After Jefferis put it to Wickings that he had lied about getting passes for the night of 19 December, the latter responded by accusing Lance Corporal Barber of perjury:

> Lance Corporal Barber told a lie when he stated that Sergeant Mallon put in his pass direct to him on going to the orderly room. I warned Lance Corporal Barber on the evening of the 18th that I wanted a pass for the 19th. Lance Corporal Barber took all three names down on that date ... on a slip of paper.
>
> It is not true that Lance Corporal Barber writes the names in the pass book immediately on receipt of applications for pass, he enters the name of the applicant in a book when he gives the applicant his pass. I did not draw my pass from him on the evening of the 19th ... I took three passes including my own from Lance

> Corporal Barber's table, from amongst twenty-two or twenty-four others.

It was a tactless move on Wickings' part to accuse Barber of lying. Barber did not claim to have issued the pass to Sergeant Mallon. Because the latter had not wished to take advantage of the pass, he personally returned it to Barber. The written proceedings infer that Wickings had confused Mallon's return of the pass with it being issued by Barber.

Wickings also declared that Tremerel had referred to a 'permission' because he had kept his pass in the pocket of one of his two pay books. Moreover, the pay book containing his pass had remained at all times in the pocket of his tunic and the two women could not therefore have seen the pass when he had shown them his other pay book, his postcards and photographs. Neither did he remember Tremerel exhorting him to return to camp.

Though Wickings was correct in asserting 'Everyone has to hand in their passes. If they are not handed in, it would not be known if you were in barracks or not,' he admitted being unaware that sergeants need not hand in their passes.

Jefferis worried away at Wickings' recollection of his activities in the café and the lodgings. However, it was all to no avail; Wickings recalled exactly where he had been and what he had to drink. He never went further upstairs than the first landing; in

Gremond's kitchen there was no evidence of a meal; he saw only three bottles on the table. He declared, 'Mme Gremond stated a falsehood when she said I entered immediately after supper.'

Jefferis also probed Wickings' movements after he had returned to camp but in his responses the NCO consistently adhered to his previously declared version of events. On being asked why he did not use the sergeants' latrine instead of the ones used by all ranks, Wickings replied:

> The latrines I went to were nearer to my lines than those near the sergeants' mess.
>
> There were several men in the latrines that night when I went there. I said goodnight to them when I came away.

However, Wickings was unable to produce anyone who could corroborate his movements. Notwithstanding his reference to encountering other soldiers during his nocturnal perambulation around No.17 Camp on 19 December, absolutely nobody, including Gatehouse, appears to have tried to canvass the camp for witnesses who may have seen or spoken with Wickings. That said, during his sojourn in the latrines, Wickings himself admitted, 'I did not take enough notice of anyone to recognize them.' Under Jefferis' cross-examination, Wickings again adhered to his own recollection of the sequence of events in the sergeants' tent, hunting for blankets, and waking up Murray.

On the facial marks he had sustained while shaving, Wickings said that nobody had witnessed the accident and that he had dried up the injury with alum. He contended, 'There was one scratch about an inch long and a graze. The medical officer who examined me is incorrect when he said there were three.' As for the evidence presented by King, Murray, Mallon, and Smyth, Wickings insisted that they were all mistaken:

> Sergeant Smyth did not see me after 3.00pm on the afternoon of the 18th December. I was never in the company of Sergeants Murray, Mallon, or King since the 16th December by day. I remember seeing Sergeant King for a few seconds on the evening of the 18th December.

The NCOs did not spot the facial abrasions, Wickings contended, because when he was in their company it had been too dark for them to see clearly.

Wickings appeared to be crumbling under Jefferis' relentless cross-examination, and it was decidedly tactless of him to maintain prosecution witnesses were either liars or wholly mistaken about what they had seen. Wickings blundered on:

> The statement of Mlle Gueroult referring to the absence of scratches on my face is untrue. She never saw me between six and seven that evening. The statements of Riflemen Binks, Hawes, and Johnson that they did not see the scratches is due to the fact that the scratches were very

> hard to see unless you looked directly at them. Their statements are incorrect. They [i.e. the scratches] were then a day old but the alum had dried them up lovely, even the graze.

He pleaded:

> I cannot bring any sergeant or man to prove that I had scratches on my face prior to the evening of the 19th as I am a stranger to the camp and I do not know many sergeants. It is an employment base depot and is constantly changing. I joined the camp about a week prior to the 19th of December.

Jefferis carried on pressing Wickings, and the NCO continued to insist that the prosecution witnesses were liars and the French police were mistaken. Thus:

> I recollect that in December last the weather was not very warm. Sergeant King's statement is inaccurate in regard to my wearing of a muffler before the 20th as I wore a cap comforter around my neck since December 8th. In the description of the wanted man that was read out to me the height was 5′ 8″ or 5′ 9″ otherwise it was nearly my description. The description mentioned a scar on the face and I have none.

However, Wickings had a scar on his neck, as had been noted by Mme Gremond. Jefferis ended his cross-examination by quizzing the NCO about the alleged row involving the Australians. According to Sergeant Collins, when referring to the altercation, Wickings had said that he 'ran out.' Wickings argued that Collins had been mistaken, if only because the altercation he had witnessed took place in the street.

When Gatehouse rose to re-examine Wickings, there was precious little that could be salvaged from Jefferis' erosion of Wickings' defence. There followed a desultory exchange of questions, prompting a rather disjointed series of statements by Wickings:

> It was dark in the latrines that night. My height is 5 feet 4 inches. The evidence I have given today is substantially the same as that which I gave when the summary was taken.

It was left up to the court to ask the obvious question. If Wickings was to be believed then what caused Virginie Gremond to fabricate a deadly yarn? Wickings confessed:

> I can suggest no reason for Mlle Gremond's statement that I was at her house at about 9.00pm. All I can say is that the statement is false.

With that, Wickings stepped down and Gatehouse called the only defence witness, Lance Corporal Ford.[83] After being invited to recall the night of the murder, Ford said:

> On December 19th, I arrived at 4, Rue Racine with Sergeant Waugh at about 10.30pm. I went in and had a conversation with Mlle Gremond. I speak enough French to make myself understood. I asked for a description of the man who had been in the house. She replied: *'Il est grand commes vous, blesse dans la gorge et dans la figure la* (pointing with her finger to the right side of her nose) *une petit moustache, trois galons, il est sergeant.'*[84] I looked at the windowsill where the sheet was hanging down. Had there been a khaki handkerchief there I think I should have noticed it.

Though there is no record of the following two questions posed by Gatehouse, Ford's inclination to give evidence at the court martial appears to have been a contentious issue, though whether for the prosecution or the defence remains unclear. Nevertheless, Ford answered, 'It is not true that I was eager to give evidence at this trial,' and 'my height is 5 feet 10 inches in boots.'

Under cross-examination by Jeffries, Ford maintained that he had drafted neither a written statement nor a report, other than communicating Gremond's description of 'Arthur' to Sergeant Waugh on 19 December. Ford said he was ignorant of any alternative description of the wanted man and in response to a final question from Jefferis, Ford swore:

'I did not know the accused before the murder. I have never visited the accused in his cell.'

Jefferis' attempt to infer that there may have been some measure of collusion between Wickings and Ford was decidedly optimistic. Moreover, there were striking differences between Gremond's immediate recollection of 'Arthur' and Wickings. The latter was six inches shorter than the man Gremond had described; Wickings was clean-shaven and although he had a scar on his neck, he did not also have a scar on his nose.

There were no more witnesses. Neither Gatehouse nor Jefferis gave a closing address, opting instead to submit arguments. Gatehouse also sought leave of the court to have Wickings examined by a medical board to determine whether or not he was sane. The move may have been prompted by his genuine concern about Wickings' evident loss of self-control under cross-examination by Jefferis; it could equally have been a ploy to see whether battle fatigue and his war wounds might figure in mitigation of sentence. Unfortunately for Wickings, Gatehouse's request may have been interpreted negatively by the officers of the court as a virtual admission of the defendant's guilt.

The defence of insanity is raised when it is clear that the accused actually committed the offence but was legally insane at the time and could not have formed the necessary intent to kill. To prove this, Wickings would have to show that he was suffering from a mental disease that prevented him from knowing that what he did was wrong. However, Wickings had maintained his innocence from the very start, when he had entered a plea of not guilty and he stuck to his story throughout the trial.

Jefferis' closing argument began with a reference to Wickings having been properly cautioned before making his pre-trial written statement. He then dealt with the strongest link in the defence case; the testimony of Lance Corporal Ford:

> I don't think it is necessary for me to deal at length with the question of calling Lance Corporal Ford. The only point is the fact that the Assistant Provost Marshal saw the woman Gremond personally only one hour or so after the crime was committed and obtained the description of the man wanted, first hand.
>
> The prosecution quite appreciates the good character and service of the accused but unfortunately this cannot be taken into consideration by the court when deciding the issue.
>
> As regards the question of passes it is quite obvious there is no supervision in the camp and therefore I submit that sergeants could return at any time providing that they were not seen by the police. The APM has told the court that there

is at least one way into the camp without being noticed by the police.

As far as the prosecution is concerned, the accused can be given the benefit of the doubt as to whether or not he was at the house of the murder shortly after six o'clock, but I wish to call the particular notice of the court to the following point:

During the examination-in-chief of Mlle Gremond the defending counsel requested the court to insert in the proceedings the following words of Mme Tremerel: 'This little fellow was with me at 6.'

I consider this remark is the most damning of the whole case for I submit it proves most conclusively that the accused must have visited the house a second time.

If the court is troubled with the question of motive I must point out that the only person alive who knows what took place in the room during the half hour preceding the murder is the murderer, and in that time the motive could have originated.

I must also bring to the notice of the court the fact that the accused has adopted a system of endeavouring to disprove the statements of all the material witnesses, as a defence and yet not one witness has been brought to substantiate his statement.

With regard to the scratches, the accused states that they were caused either by a razor or by a buckle from some equipment. I suggest that they could not possibly be caused by a buckle as no buckle contains three pins. You have heard what the medical officer also stated 'that the scratches could not be caused by a sharp instrument.'

It will be remembered by the court that seven or eight witnesses have come before them to say that no scratches were seen on his face prior to the time of the murder. If only one or even two witnesses came forward to say this, perhaps the court would be quite justified in giving the accused the benefit of the doubt, but not when there are quite large numbers of witnesses. Even the accused's particular friend Sergeant King says they were not on his face at 4:20pm on 19th December.

It was Sergeant King – (the man so often in the company of the accused) who says he wore no muffler prior to the date of the murder, despite the fact that the weather was severely cold, and immediately after this date he always wore one.

These are the only points that I wish to impress on the court. The fact of whether he could have returned to camp by any conveyance need not be referred to by me as all the Members of the Court are in a position to decide by their own knowledge.

I feel sure that I am quite justified in leaving the case in the hands of the court without occupying your valuable time any further as the whole of the facts are known as well by you as myself and I am aware of the fact that it is the evidence, and the evidence alone which decides the issue.[85]

Gatehouse submitted ten pages of foolscap paper on which he had scribbled his final argument. Although in note form, the points he made are generally comprehensible and his critique of prosecution witnesses' testimony lent support to Wickings' contention, namely that he was with the deceased woman at 6.00pm and not at 9.00pm on 19 December.

The principal points for the prosecution are contained in the evidence of the first four French witnesses of whom Mlle Gremond is of course the most important and in the evidence as to the scratches [and] the handkerchief.

To all intents and purposes the case rests on Gremond's evidence. I propose to go through the evidence of the witnesses as they appear in the

Summary and deal with most of them one by one.

1st witness Mlle Gueroult is produced to prove the presence of the accused in the café, 10 Rue Jules Masurier between 6.00 and 7.00pm on the night of December 19th. I submit that she fails.

She says that the accused entered about 6.00pm. That three other British soldiers came in about ten minutes later and that they all went into a back room together.

She says that he stayed till the café closed: but judge her evidence by that of the next three witnesses. They all say that they came in about 7.00pm and went into the back room about ten minutes later. If that is true what becomes of Mlle Gueroult's evidence apart from a statement by Mme Tremerel I shall refer to later. They say he had no scratches on his face then: but they were not questioned till some days afterwards.

They all say they left about 8.00pm and Binks had a talk outside the café with the accused before they parted.

Mlle Gremond says he came in at nine or a little later and went upstairs, mistook the landing and was called down my Mme Tremerel.

Mlle Gremond says that Tremerel said, 'This little fellow came to see me at six o'clock this evening.' This statement I suggest was made by Gremond to account for the fact he was there at 6.00pm showing that he was aware of the fact that he was with her then. The statement [of Tremerel] I suggest was never made at all.

If the accused had visited the deceased that night would he have been likely to come back? He would have known her room and could not have mistaken the landing.

She says Mlle Tremerel said 'will you sleep with me?' He said 'Yes'. This contradicts evidence she gave in Summary. How could the accused know when he made his statement that both Gremond and Tremerel would not be able to show they were elsewhere between 6.00 and 7.00 unless he was with them between those hours?

She says she heard knocks on the ceiling about 9.45pm. Three minutes trying to get in, during which she heard the voice of the accused in French with a jeering accent.

Police came at 10.30pm. She says she saw the light put out in the room and told the police. This they all deny.

The man must have been in the room when they arrived. What was he doing all that time? See also [the] evidence of [the] police as to [the] sheet not being seen and evidence of Defraey that she heard someone in the room.

She [Gremond] says [the] body was cold at [the] extremities when they got in. [She] saw the handkerchief on the sill and pointed [it] out to the police. This they deny.

She denies [having a] conversation with Ford as to the moustache. She could not recognize him. She was so excited. Room in confusion as though someone had been searching for something.

Can her evidence be believed? Was the handkerchief left on the sill by the murderer or put on the sill by someone else who shut the window[?]

I suggest that Mlle Gremond, who is fond of her friend, and is convinced that a British soldier murdered her, is trying to fix the crime on a British soldier whose identity she can establish. Perhaps her excited state has upset the balance of her mind and she believes [she can identify the killer].

Defraey says while Gremond [was] away it sounded as though everything in the room were being knocked over as though someone were ransacking it. The answer of the man in the room was in English. Heard a window being opened while the police were there. Gremond was about fifteen minutes at door before she went for the police. Deceased had a long dark [coat?]. How did accused know it if he had not seen her in it?

Lemoine says that the man was of average height. She cannot speak [as] to his features. She identified Mills not from [his] features but from build and height, 5ft 8 1/2 [inches].

The police all say no sheet was hanging from the window when they arrived. Waugh fixes the time of 10.30pm by his watch. They all deny that Mme Gremond pointed out the handkerchief and say they would have seen it if it had been there. They went to the window.

Evidence of Murray, King, Smyth, and Mallon proves nothing in point of time for the prosecution. Murray says he thinks the time the accused came in was about 10:30pm. None of them noticed scratches to his face when they got up on 20th December. The accused mentioned a row with some Australians on that day. Mallon says he cannot swear the scratches were not there on the previous day.

Barber's evidence shows that the passes book was carelessly kept.

Collins: Admits that accused mentioned a row with some Australians.

Capt. Gibson: Cannot remember whether a photo and two Xmas cards were produced by the accused.

Captain Fitzpatrick: Says the light was bad and that he had difficulty seeing the handkerchief but the police say they would have seen it if it had been there.

Roberts: Says he has had a search made for [a] taxi driver who drove a sergeant on that night and no such man can be found.

Capt. Rimmer: Says scratches were four to seven days old and could have been caused in a variety of ways.

Frambourg: Says that the condition of the vaginal parts was consistent with erotic mania. [There was] nothing to show there had been a struggle. Condition suggested an unnatural practice. Not a common English one.

Dr Klein: No blood on hands.

Dr d'Herlinville: No semen. Nails were dirty but I noticed nothing else about them.

General observations on the case: Was the accused [out] on pass that night? No evidence that he was not.

Scratches: No evidence the deceased scratched the murderer. No blood on her hands or skin on her nails. Slight struggle only. Evidence of witnesses who say they did not notice the scratches on 19th December [is] negative and unreliable. The accused could have said they were made on the 20th. Muffler suggestion dealt with.

Handkerchiefs: The question is not so much whether he left a handkerchief but whether he left it on the windowsill.

Did King give accused the handkerchief which was taken from him. The accused must have known the handkerchief would be compared. He may be mistaken. The handkerchiefs are all of a common type.

How came the handkerchief on the windowsill: ***Too*** obvious a clue not to arouse suspicion of its genuineness.

The position of the body is consistent with the theory that sexual connection had or was about to take place. How explained? Pillow under the buttocks and legs wide apart. The opinion of the medical men was that she was strangled where she lay.

How came the table to be overturned and the knocks on the floor heard? The chemise was neatly rolled up.

Times: Last tram 9.15pm. The distance [to Harfleur Camp] is 6 miles, uphill all the way. The murderer could not have left the house till after 10.30pm. The latest anyone ever suggests for the time of the accused's return is 11.30pm.

Trams run until 9.15pm for men. [A] search for a taxi driver has failed and according to the prosecution the accused had only four francs, which presumably he gave to the woman, according to their theory.

Doctrine of Probabilities

Would the accused have carefully identified himself and then committed the crime?

His general character should be taken into consideration.

What was his conduct on returning to camp[?] A guilty man would have destroyed [the] postcard and photographs; anything which could identify him with the crime. They were all found in his possession.

Why was not the description circulated put in by the police if it mentioned a man of 5′ 8 1/2″?

Defence

The prisoner gave his evidence. How did he give it – like an innocent or guilty man?

You may think he was too pat with his times: but consider he has been brooding over this case trying to fix dates and times with certainty. Was he seriously corrected in cross-examination?

Isn't his evidence now the same as that he gave on the summary? He tells you how he got the scratches.[86]

Gatehouse concluded his notes by adding a few disjointed sentences about Ford's evidence. There was inevitably a good deal of repetition in what Gatehouse had to say, and as an experienced court martial officer he would have known that only an optimist would presume that he had done enough to cultivate reasonable doubt in the minds of the officers sitting in judgement.

If Gatehouse entertained any hopes of an acquittal they were dashed on 10 February when the court concluded that Wickings was guilty. Three days later the written proceedings were forwarded to Brigadier General John Nicholson, the Officer Commanding Le Havre Base, who recommended the sentence be carried out; on 15 February, Major General Joseph Asser, the Inspector General, Lines of Communication, agreed.[87]

On 17 February, Captain Crowdy, the Court Martial Officer, forwarded a memorandum to the Deputy Assistant Adjutant General, HQ, Lines of Communication Area, in which he revealed the grounds on which it was decided that Wickings was the man who had murdered Henriette Tremerel.

Crowdy wrote:

> 2 (a) The court was not satisfied that the words *'petite moustache'* were actually used by Mlle Gremond. The knowledge of French possessed by Lance Corporal Ford, to judge by his accent and the evidence, was not sufficient to enable the court to rely upon the accuracy of his hearing. Mlle Gremond said she had mentioned *'moustache'* saying *'sans moustache'* or *'pas de moustache'* which latter Lance Corporal Ford may have mistaken for *'petite moustache'*.

(b) The accused is a light-haired man and it is quite possible that a mistake might be made as to his having a slight moustache or not. Assuming that Mlle Gremond had been under the false impression that he had, the other and more noticeable traits attributed by her to the person wanted corresponded too closely with those of the accused for a mistake as to whether he had a slight fair moustache, or not, to impeach the general accuracy of the description.[88]

3) My remembrance as to the prosecutor's address is that he did not speak of any specific description having been furnished other than that given to Lance Corporal Ford, but the counsel for the accused spoke of this as being the first description, and my impression is that a description was stated by Mlle Gremond in her evidence to have been given by her to the police other than Lance Corporal Ford. Also that the Commissionaire of Police – Frambourg – stated that Mlle Gremond had on the night in question, described the man who was wanted to him. The APM of Havre was not asked as to whether he received any description from Mlle Gremond by the prosecutor and the court did not question him on this head knowing that he has not much knowledge of French.

The court was not affected by any statement as to the evidence of other descriptions than that

> given by Lance Corporal Ford, but dealt with the evidence of that NCO and its bearing on the grounds given above and attached more importance, on the question of identity, to the consensus of the evidence that the person with the woman on the night of the murder was English, the corroboration of his being a sergeant, the absence of any evidence of motive on the part of Mlle Gremond for implicating or exculpating any particular English Sergeant, and, above all, the certitude of her identification at the parade.[89]

A court martial was the finder of fact and arbiter of law. Its Members were able to appraise Ford's demeanour in the witness box and the credibility of his evidence but they were not empowered to make assumptions factually unsupported by evidence. Ford was never questioned about his fluency and comprehension of French but the court wholly improperly concluded (solely on the basis of his accent) that his knowledge of the language and communication skills were inadequate.

Both the court and Jefferis had plenty of opportunities to conduct a proper evaluation of Ford's grasp of French but never challenged his linguistic ability. Thus, Crowdy's rejection of Ford's evidence on the tenuous grounds that the NCO must have misunderstood what Gremond had said was effectively a ploy that marginalized exculpatory evidence. Nor was any evidence produced during the trial or in the written summaries to support Crowdy's assertion that Gremond had provided Commissioner Frambourg with a description of the killer.

Crowdy conceded that Captain Fitzpatrick was not asked whether he spoke French because the court already knew that he could not. However, Jefferis had confidently stated that: 'The only fact is that the Assistant Provost Marshal saw the woman Gremond personally only an hour or so after the crime was committed and obtained the description of the man wanted, first hand.' The means by which Fitzpatrick elicited the description from Gremond remains unexplained.

The courts martial officer's musings about the moustache are also unsatisfactory. Gremond was less than consistent about the wanted man having or perhaps not having a moustache. In his attempt to resolve the conundrum, Crowdy postulated that because Wickings had light hair, Gremond may have formed the mistaken impression that he had a 'slight fair moustache'. However, there was not a scrap of evidential support submitted during the trial to support Crowdy's speculation and, effectively, partisan support for the prosecution.

On 25 February Wickings appeared before a medical board composed of Army 'nerve specialists', who ruled that at the time of the murder and thereafter he was 'sane and capable of appreciating the nature and quality of his actions.'[90] Their report was attached to the written proceedings, forwarded to the Adjutant General and on 3 March Field Marshal Haig confirmed the death sentence passed on Wickings.

It is doubtful whether Haig had time in which to read more than a typed, single-paged summary of the case, nor did the Commander-in-Chief append any explanation for endorsing a death sentence. However, his decision to have Wickings executed would have been informed by developments extending beyond Le Havre.

Historians chronicling Haig's disastrous Passchendaele offensive ignore the simultaneous eruption of strikes and mutinies by discontented military labourers and British troops in ports and bases on the Lines of Communication in Northern France. Throughout the summer at Calais, Dunkirk, Étaples and elsewhere, these incidents unsettled local French civilians, whose complaints were relayed to the BEF by French police commissioners. The disorder was quelled and the French authorities were assured that soldiers' misbehaviour would be curbed.[91] Thus the death sentence passed on Wickings provided British consular and BEF liaison staff with a suitable opportunity to add substance to their expressions of reassurance.

The BEF did not usually invite comment about the exemplary punishment of military criminals but Tremerel's death had featured in the local press. Contre-Amiral Charles Didelot, the French military governor of Le Havre, expressed his opinions about Wicking's punishment via an unsolicited letter to the French military mission.[92] The original text may have been more nuanced than the English translation but the grounds on which he requested Wickings be spared also draw attention to a wider and no less disturbing discourse about patriarchy. Didelot wrote:

> The English Sergeant [sic] WILKENS has been condemned to death by a court martial at HAVRE having been convicted of the murder of one, TREMEREL, a prostitute living at HAVRE.
>
> The Consular General at HAVRE has notified me officially that if the accused is found Guilty the punishment would be more severe because the victim was a Frenchwoman. Nevertheless, she was little worthy of interest. This woman, who formerly held a certain position, had fallen into the lowest debauchery, and [was] contaminated physically as well as morally. She was convicted of theft in April 1915.
>
> It appears that the commutation of the capital penalty passes upon WILKENS will be not only accepted but approved by the population of HAVRE.
>
> The proceedings of trial are probably at this moment with GHQ, and if you consider, as I do, that an intervention might be made in favour of

> Sergeant WILKENS, I request you to be good enough to make it in time for this action to have a useful effect.[93]

Wickings also wrote two or more letters that were forwarded with his meagre belongings to his family in Southsea; he donated his cap badge to one of his guards and bequeathed his small collection of farthings to a friend. Then at 6.04am on 7 March 1918 he was shot dead by a firing squad under the command of Captain Fitzpatrick.[94]

Did Arthur Wickings kill Henrietta Tremerel? There are too many inconsistencies in the evidence to say for certain that he did. The prosecution case was entirely circumstantial and rested largely on the testimony of Gremond who, as Gatehouse pointed out, may have entertained an ulterior motive for pointing the finger at Wickings.

There was no forensic evidence linking Wickings to the crime. It was never proved that the handkerchief belonged to him, or that Tremerel caused the scratches on his face; no skin or other tissue was found under her fingernails. No bloodstains were found in the room, yet Captain Rimmer testified that Wickings' wounds would have bled freely. The stains alleged to have been found on Wickings' greatcoat were never proved to have been human blood and the garment itself was not produced as evidence.

Wickings never confessed. Might the murderer have been another soldier, as he insisted? The police did not think so, because no effort was made to trace the soldier who Wickings claimed to have interrupted convivial intimacies in Tremerel's boudoir.

History does not record what happened subsequently to Mlle Gueroult, Mlle Gremond and other residents of No.4 Rue Racine. The neighbourhood was totally obliterated by Allied bombing in 1944; the lodgers are all long dead, and buried with them is the truth of what happened on the night of 19 December 1917.

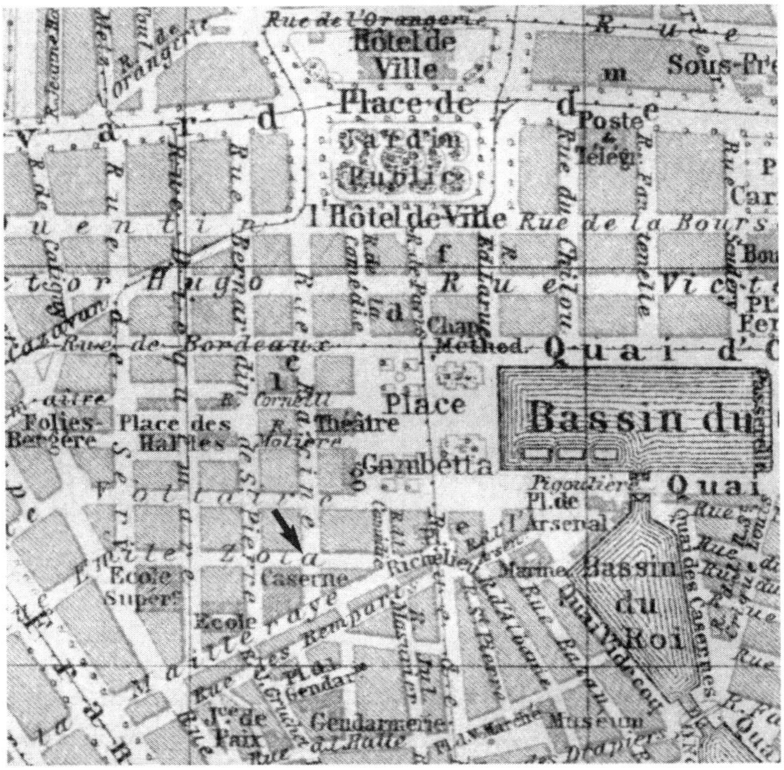

No. 4 Rue Racine.

Meanwhile, Virginie dashed to the Rue des Remparts, where she encountered a military policeman, Sergeant

Ralph Waugh, ANZAC Provost Corps. It took him just over five minutes to summon a couple of other military policemen who were patrolling nearby before they began to make their way to the lodging house. Roughly fifteen minutes elapsed before the three policemen reached the first floor landing, where Waugh loudly identified himself and demanded the door be opened. Eliciting no response, he ordered one of the policemen, Corporal Harry Woodgate, to batter open the door. Woodgate did his best but he later reckoned that it took him about him five or ten minutes to break in. While the door was being forced open, Mme Defraey, who had remained on the landing, thought she heard footsteps from within the room and the sound of a window being opened.[9]

Just as the door finally gave way, Bergilez reported that on the Rue Emile Zola side of Henriette's room one set of French windows had been opened, from which there dangled a bed sheet.[10] When the three policemen finally entered the room, followed by Virginie, who was carrying a lighted oil lamp, they found the semi-naked corpse of Henriette Tremerel, sprawled on her bed. They also saw that a counterpane and bed sheet had been tied to the iron safety rail of the open French windows and had evidently been used by her killer to slip down to the Rue Emile Zola and make good his escape.[11]

The British and French authorities were both alerted; witnesses were interviewed; the crime scene was examined and a search began for Henriette's killer.

Waugh ordered Lance Corporal Charles Ford, a French-speaking British military policeman to gather witness statements.[12] Victor Frambourg, the local Commissioner of Police, and the local police surgeon, Dr Klein, conducted a preliminary examination of Henriette's corpse and her room. Klein noted:

> The deceased was lying on her back and lying across the bed, the head nearest the wall and bent slightly to the left, and turned slightly backwards. The legs were stiff and wide apart. The chemise (the only garment on the body) was turned up above the waist and was neither torn nor stained. Under the buttocks was a pillow, the greater portion of which lay forward under the legs. The body was still warm, with exception of the head, the forearms and the legs. The face was purple; the eyes were bloodshot, especially the left one. The mouth was slightly open and a slight flow of congealed blood had exuded onto the left cheek and chin. At the front of the neck, at the level of the larynx, was a large purple-red abrasion, extending to the chin. Next to this large abrasion there were scratches on either side of the larynx, undoubtedly caused by the murderer's nails. There were four or five of these scratches about 2/5ths of an inch long on either side of the larynx. On feeling the larynx I found the cartilages very loose. They cracked under my fingers. They had therefore been broken, which fully accounted for the slight trickling of blood at the mouth.

> There was also on the inside of the right thumb a small scratch which may have been a nail scratch; the skin was torn and hanging on by a strip. All the scratches and abrasions were received before death. No traces of struggle or violence were visible on the chest or abdomen, thighs or legs.[13]

Frambourg's report endorsed what Klein had written about the cause of death but added some further details about the crime scene. He noted:

> The size of the room is 15 feet by 12 feet 6 inches. There are two windows facing Rue Racine and two facing Rue Emile Zola. On entering the room I found the bed on my right situated East and West. On the bed the body of Mme Tremerel was lying. The body was only clothed in a chemise which was neatly rolled up above the hips. The legs were wide apart and the feet hanging over the edge of the bed. The right arm of the body was resting on a pillow and the right hand was folded in a perfectly natural position and lying by the fold of the chemise. The left arm was bent bringing the left hand up towards the neck. The whole attitude of the body gave one the impression that there was no struggle and that sexual connection has recently taken place....

Frambourg also concluded that the dead women's belongings, including her jewellery, had not been disturbed:

> The furniture in the room when I arrived was tidy except that a bookcase was on the floor. On opening the wardrobe I noticed that everything appeared to be tidy inside. There was a small jewel case in the wardrobe containing 130 francs in an envelope and in a small purse 75 centimes in copper and two five-franc pieces. There was also four rings and two small brooches and a watch (gold) in the jewel case. There was a handbag in the wardrobe containing 21 francs and 95 centimes in notes and coin.[14]

The British investigation, headed by Captain Thomas Fitzpatrick, the Assistant Provost Marshal, Le Havre, and Detective Sergeant William Roberts, was rather limited, principally because it was 11.30pm when they arrived at the lodging house, and Frambourg and Klein were already conducting their own investigation.[15] Virginie drew Fitzpatrick's attention to a khaki handkerchief on the windowsill of the open French window; surmising that it might have belonged to the murderer, he pocketed the item. Otherwise Fitzpatrick, lacking either investigative training or experience, was content to let the French police carry on photographing the room and conducting their forensic investigation.

However, Virginie had already tampered with the contents of the room and the killer's apparent escape route yielded no further clues. Fingerprinting was not a forensic resource then enjoyed by French regional police forces, and Frambourg's powers of deduction were inconclusive and his initial conclusions were wrong.[16] Thus, he speculated that the murderer's hobnailed boots being scraped against the masonry caused some scratches he noticed on the exterior wall immediately beneath the French window.[17] However, his hypothesis about what had happened to Henriette was partially contradicted by an autopsy report that concluded she had been asphyxiated after a brief struggle but stated there were no traces of semen on her corpse.[18]

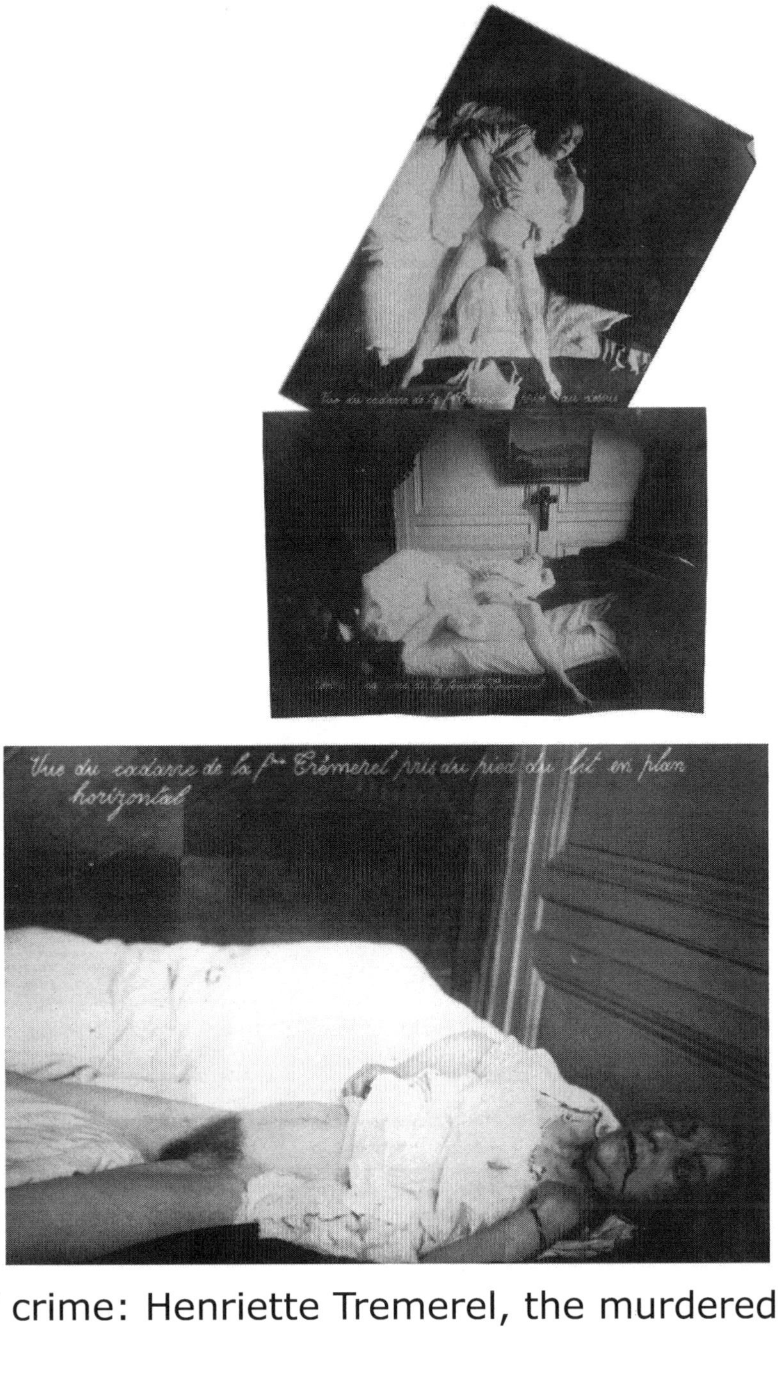

Scene of crime: Henriette Tremerel, the murdered woman.

British efforts to trace the killer advanced on 23 December, when all NCOs at the Employment Base Depot, No.17 Camp, Harfleur, were paraded by the

Adjutant and listened to him read out a description of the suspect.[19] One of the assembled NCOs, Provost Sergeant Thomas Collins, spotted another sergeant who resembled the wanted man, and discreetly followed him after the parade was dismissed.[20] The sergeant arrived outside No.2 Tent, D Lines, No.17 Camp; Collins confronted him, and enquired, ‘Do you know anything about this affair in town?’ Collins recalled that the sergeant replied, ‘Yes, there was a row there with some Australian soldiers and I ran out.’ Acting on Collins’ advice, the sergeant reported to the Adjutant, identified himself as Lance Sergeant Arthur Wickings, 9th Battalion Rifle Brigade, and was detained in the guardroom.

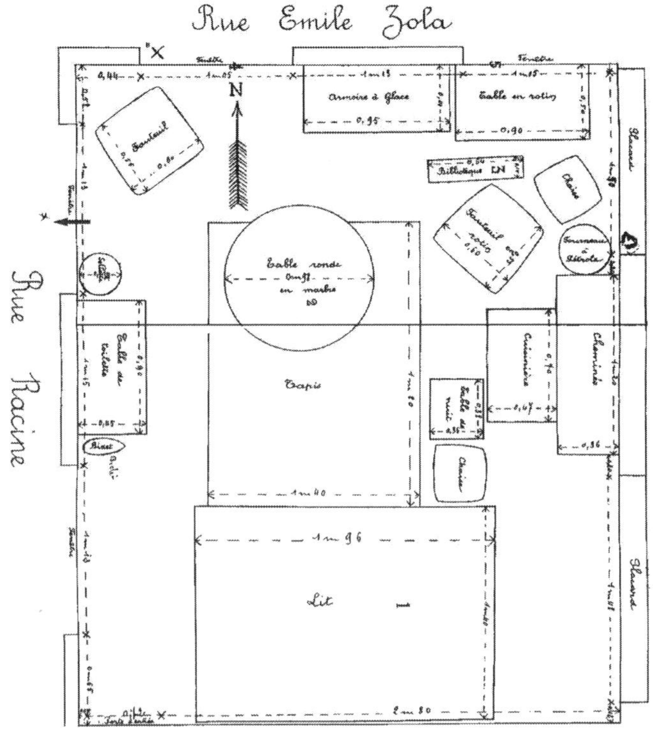

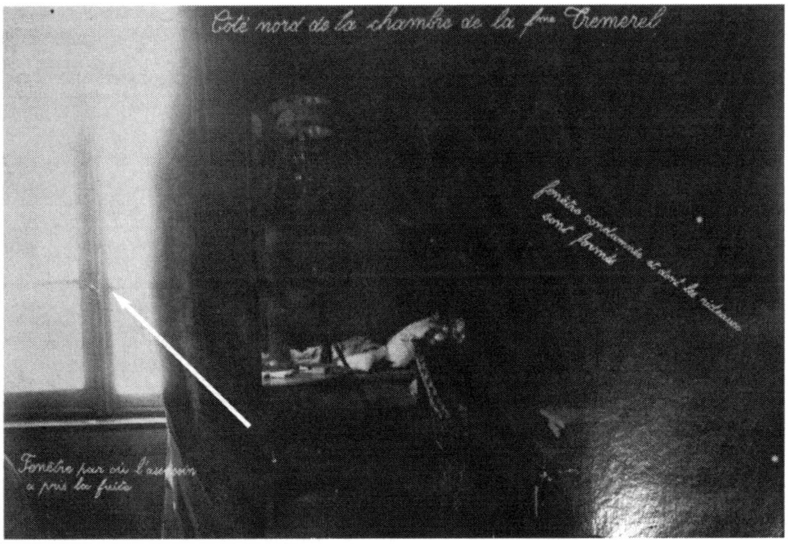

French windows through which the murderer made his escape into the Rue Racine. West side of the room.

Dressing table flanked by French windows. West side of the room.

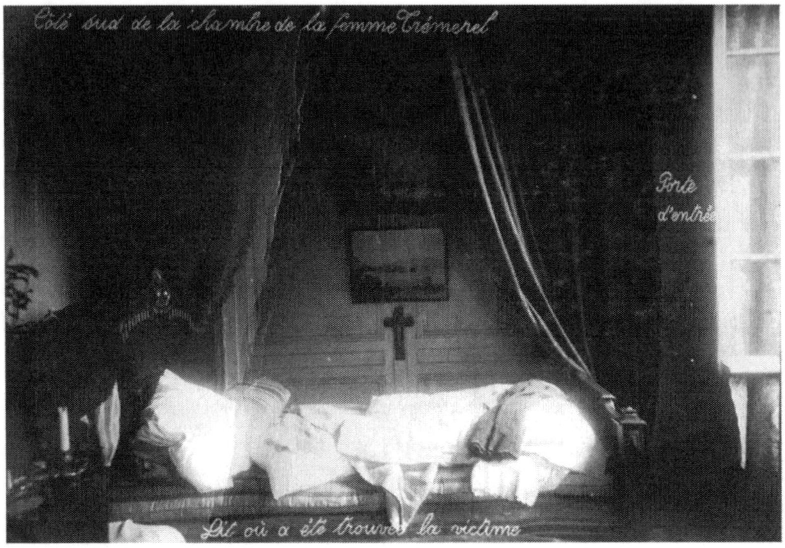

The victim's bed; entrance door on the right. South side of the room.

CHAPTER 10

Accused Was Drunk

Sunrise on Saturday 13 April 1918 found 38-year-old Private John Skone and some comrades from 2nd Battalion, Welsh Regiment, in the reserve line trenches near Gorre, a fortified hamlet situated about 4 kilometres to the east of Bethune.[1] Though sentries were required to stay in their posts, it was possible for the remainder of the section to relax after they had all been ordered 'stand down'. The morning's rum ration was issued between 6.30am and 7.00am and while NCOs busied themselves arranging for the delivery of breakfast, the men under their command relaxed for a while, chatting with one another, smoking, snoozing and carrying out minor chores.

About five minutes after downing his rum ration, Private Skone approached an NCO and requested permission to leave the trench in order to get some cloth with which to make a helmet cover. The NCO agreed and Skone made his way along a communication trench to a nearby building where he encountered some chums from his company. The latter were in the process of enjoying the contents of some wine bottles they had looted from a local citizen's cellar and Skone joined in the drinking session, forgetting about both the cloth for his helmet cover and the passage of time.

When he finally returned to the trench it was about 9.20am; he was drunk and in trouble. An NCO remonstrated with him and ordered his arrest. Skone responded by firing a shot with his rifle that killed Lance Serjeant Edwin Williams, a 42-year-old married man from Pontypridd.[2] After discarding the gun Skone was escorted away to the guardroom. He was kept under close arrest until 28 April, when a field general court martial was convened to try him at Hersin-Coupigny, a small coal-mining town.

Some of the officers assigned to take part in the trial were impressively well qualified and could draw on a wealth of legal experience. The President of the Court was Major Grenville Battcock, Loyal North Lancashire Regiment, the Members of the Court consisted of Captain Murdo Mackenzie, Cameron Highlanders and 2nd Lieutenant George Goldie, Loyal North Lancashire Regiment, assisted by Captain Hugh Beazley, General List, a court martial officer who was also a qualified barrister. The prosecuting officer was Lieutenant Claude Lewis, Adjutant 2nd Battalion Welsh Regiment, and in presenting his defence, Skone was assisted by Captain Louis Hoare, Durham Light Infantry, who was also a barrister.[3]

Skone pleaded not guilty to two charges: murder, and a second, alternative charge of manslaughter. The case for the prosecution was pretty straightforward and since the fatal incident had taken place in a very short time, it did not take long for eyewitnesses to recount what they had seen.

The first soldier to testify for the prosecution was Corporal Thomas Lynch, who witnessed the shooting and had also been ordered to arrest Skone. Lynch began by confirming that Skone's absence had been reported at 8.20am and that he was drunk when he returned at 9.20am. Lynch went on to recall:

> Sergeant Williams asked the accused where he had been. I did not hear the accused's reply. Sergeant Williams ordered me to place accused under arrest. I got out of the trench to do so. As I was getting out, I saw accused point his rifle at, and take delibera0te aim at Sergeant Williams, who was about ten yards away. I went towards accused. Before I reached him, accused had pressed the trigger. I saw Sergeant Williams fall. When I reached accused and got hold of him, accused immediately threw his rifle on the ground. I placed accused under arrest, and escorted him to Company HQ, a distance of 600 yards. Accused came without any trouble. Accused staggered a little. Accused was drunk.[4]

Under cross-examination by Hoare, Lynch added few further details. He explained that Williams had barely finished issuing the order for Skone's arrest when the latter raised his rifle, operated the bolt to charge the breech and deliberately took aim. Although initially startled by Skone's actions, Lynch reacted by rushing to intervene but failed to prevent the fatal shot being discharged.

In response to cross-examination by the court, Lynch recalled that after the shooting Skone had remained silent and was led away, leaving his discarded rifle behind on the ground.

In his testimony, the next witness, Lance Corporal William Smith, added a few more details about the killing:

> I saw Sergeant Williams go to Corporal Lynch and order Corporal Lynch to take the accused to the guardroom. Sergeant Williams and Corporal Lynch were on top of the trench. The accused was in the trench at the time. I saw the accused take a rifle and stagger from the trench to within ten paces of Sergeant Williams. Accused then stopped in a firing position. Accused then came to the aiming position. Accused was about to fire when Sergeant Williams turned round and said: 'Don't be a bloody fool.' Accused said something. A shot was fired. I was looking at Sergeant Williams at the time. Sergeant Williams fell. Afterwards, accused went away with Corporal Lynch.[5]

Under cross-examination by Lewis, Smith added, 'I saw the accused charge the breech.'

Captain Hoare's cross-examination was brief; he established that the trench had been dry and that

Smith had not examined the discarded rifle. In response to a query by the court, Smith confirmed he had not heard shots being fired from anywhere else at the time.

The following witness was Private Herbert Scrase, who had been on sentry duty near the crime scene. He recalled:

> I heard Sergeant Williams order Corporal Lynch to place the accused under arrest for absence. A few minutes later, I saw the accused with his rifle at the aim. I saw nothing previous on the part of the accused. The rifle was fired. Accused threw the rifle on the floor. Sergeant Williams fell, dead.[6]

Hoare did not cross-examine Scrase, even though there was an important discrepancy between his testimony and what Lynch and Smith had stated. Scrase maintained that a few minutes elapsed between Williams ordering Skone's arrest and the latter aiming his rifle at the sergeant. However, Lynch had testified that there had been virtually no delay between Williams' order and Skone's lethal reaction. If Scrase was correct, Williams' death may be construed as a premeditated, murderous reaction by Skone; if Lynch was correct, then it could be argued that Skone had acted on impulse.

The final witness for the prosecution was the battalion's medical officer, Captain Reginald Morrell, RAMC.[7] His evidence was brief:

> On 13.4.18, I went across to the trenches in the reserve area. I found the body of Sergeant Williams. The body was still warm. Sergeant Williams was dead. Death had taken place within half an hour of my seeing the body. The cause of death was a bullet wound in the middle of the back of the neck. Such a wound would cause death.

Captain Hoare declined to cross-examine Morrell and the case for the prosecution closed.

The defence relied heavily on Skone's generally good record of service and the adverse impact of illness and emotional stress on his behaviour. After being sworn, Skone began by explaining that he was thirty-eight years old and submitted documentary proof of his twelve years' unblemished service as a stoker in the Royal Navy. He explained:

> I joined the army in October 1914.... I have been in France since November 1914, except that I was wounded in Festubert and went to hospital in England. I was with the South Wales Bord[erers] then. In April 1915 I transferred to the Welch Regiment. I was wounded at Loos and at Passchendaele. I did not leave the regiment from the Passchendaele wound. My health lately has

been poor. I have been depressed with family troubles. I went sick on 11.4.18 [but] did duty. I bore Sergeant Williams no ill-will. We were as friendly as two brothers. I have two entries on my conduct sheet. Seven days' Field Punishment No.1 is my biggest sentence yet.

On the morning of 13.4.18, after stand down I asked leave to leave the trench. Corporal Lynch knew I had gone. I went with the intention to obtain material for [a] head cover. I had [my] rum issue at stand down, five minutes before I left the trench.

I went to the nearest building. I met a few of the company; my company. They were drinking wine found in the cellar. I joined them and drank red and white wine. I left them when I felt the wine going to my head. I thought I would get back before being in a bad state.

I got to the trench all right. I had been there about five minutes [when] my head went bad. I do not remember then what happened. I do not remember seeing Sergeant Williams or hearing him talk. I did not realize that Sergeant Williams was dead till I got to the guardroom.

Skone concluded by saying that he had suffered from two or three bouts of malaria. Somewhat inexplicably, Hoare neglected the opportunity to ask Skone whether he had experienced an attack of malaria shortly before he had killed Williams. It was generally agreed that Skone was drunk but if he had also been suffering from a malarial attack, illness-induced mental confusion could have been exaggerated by alcohol. Instead, Hoare simply drew the court's attention to Skone's mentally depressed state.

After a final question from the prosecution secured from Skone an admission that he had failed to bring back the cloth for his helmet cover, the court withdrew to consider its verdict. On re-opening, the court was told Skone's disciplinary record: on 23 February 1918, when he had made 'improper remarks' within earshot of a couple of NCOs Skone was punished with a week's Field Punishment No.1; on 8 April he had 'fallen out without permission' and been subsequently punished by his battalion commander with five days' Field Punishment No.2. The second sentence had barely been completed when he shot Williams.

Before the court again withdrew to deliberate about the sentence Hoare was invited to enter a plea on Skone's behalf. The written proceedings record Hoare's response:

> The court can find manslaughter not murder. [The] accused's character is good. I do not say that he was so drunk as in itself so as to reduce [the charge] to manslaughter. His health and depression [are] relevant. It may be that the rifle went off by clumsiness rather than by shooting.

> His drunkenness, depression and general state of health suggest manslaughter. [It was] a short impulsive act. Recommendation [to mercy] on grounds [of previous good] service.

Hoare's contention that the fatal shot was discharged because of Skone's clumsiness does not bear scrutiny. Skone, though inebriated, was observed engaging in a textbook load-aim-fire drill, and there was no supporting evidence produced to confirm he had slipped or stumbled, thereby causing the rifle to be discharged accidentally. Perhaps more plausibly, Hoare could have tried to argue that Skone's attention was distracted by Corporal Lynch running in his direction or shouting. Alternatively, he could have sought to maintain that Skone originally intended to merely frighten with near miss rather than to shoot to kill Williams. If so, such hypotheses were never recorded in the written proceedings.

When he shot Williams, might Skone have been temporarily insane? If so, the burden of proof rested with the defence but it could not have been supported solely by Skone's own testimony. Hoare could only have mounted a defence of insanity if he could call on expert testimony, which he failed to procure or produce.

Skone had contracted malaria during his naval service and while undergoing his spell of Field Punishment No.2, he had reported sick but was ordered back to duty. It may have been a malarial twinge but did not involve a full-blown fever. Although Skone recalled that he felt his 'head going' on returning to the trench, he failed to impress either Morrell or, perhaps more importantly, Hoare that his 'head going' may have been linked in some way with the disease, perhaps significantly enough to have prevented him appreciating the 'nature and quality of the act he was doing'.[8]

In addition to unspecified 'family troubles', Hoare could have made a case for Skone being unhinged by battle stress. After all, Skone had been involved in very bloody fighting; he had been wounded three times and resumed combat duty after convalescence. He had an unblemished disciplinary record between October 1914 and February 1918 and the subsequent deterioration in his conduct and perhaps an increase in his consumption of alcohol thereafter could quite plausibly have been linked with battle stress. However, neither Hoare nor anyone else bothered to establish how much alcohol was consumed by Skone on 13 April.

Hoare alluded to Skone's years of unblemished service and associated battle injuries but did not call expert medical testimony to robustly advance a submission that the defendant's action may have been influenced thereby. Of course, contemporary medical understanding had not greatly advanced in effectively remedying severe nervous conditions that were commonly termed 'shell shock'. However, the exercise of palliative measures and creation of dedicated treatment facilities during 1917 by the BEF represented a more universal recognition of the incidence of NYD(N).[9]

Leaving aside whether these excuses could have been invoked and developed by Hoare, due account needs to be taken of the fact that Hoare had access to little of the support he would have been able to summon as a practising barrister. It is also very doubtful whether he would have had much time in which to prepare for Skone's trial. Though the *Manual of Military Law* stipulated he had for seven days 'every facility' to communicate with his client, in practice a Prisoner's Friend did not usually have more than a few hours in which to gather evidence and prepare a case. Moreover, once a court martial had been convened the proceedings could not be delayed on the grounds that the defence was unprepared.

Hoare might have tried to secure more time in which to prepare for Skone's trial by seeking an adjournment to gather further material evidence, citing the *Manual of Military Law:*

> When a court is once assembled and the accused has been arraigned, the court should continue the trial from day to day and sit for a reasonable period on every day unless it appears to the court that an adjournment is necessary for the ends of justice, or that such a continuance is impracticable.[10]

It is doubtful whether such a move might have been successful but Hoare would have had little to lose by requesting an adjournment. Even if it were refused, at least the issue would be on record as a point that merited consideration by the confirming officers.

The written proceedings do not suggest that Hoare's advocacy was particularly robust. After all, Skone's life was at stake, raising and developing the aforementioned issues was more than a matter of Hoare toying with legal semantics. Unfortunately for defendants convicted of a capital offence, the *Manual of Military Law* made no provision for a conviction being quashed because the Prisoner's Friend was ineffective.

Hoare failed to convince the court that Skone had acted on impulse; the soldier was found guilty on the more serious count of murder and sentenced to death. However, the court expressed some recognition of Hoare's efforts and simultaneously acknowledged what Skone had to say in his own defence in an addendum: 'The court recommend him to mercy on the grounds of previous good service.'[11]

Unfortunately for Skone, the confirming officers were universally unimpressed by the recommendation. Thus, Brigadier General Herbert Morant remarked, 'I do not consider that the circumstances of this case present sufficient grounds for recommendation to mercy'; Major General Strickland wrote, 'I can see no justification for recommending that the sentence be not carried out. I therefore recommend that the sentence be carried out'; Lieutenant General Holland added, 'There seems to have been absolutely no justification for the crime'; and General Horne concluded, 'I cannot see any reason why the sentence should not be carried out. The case appears to be quite clear – deliberate murder – I recommend that the death penalty be executed.' On 6 May Field Marshal Sir Douglas Haig added his confirmation of the death sentence passed on Private Skone.[12]

Rather unusually, the bureaucratic instructions detailing how, when and by whom Skone was to be killed were retained in his court martial dossier. To Brigadier General Morant, Major Joseph Westley, the Deputy Assistant Adjutant General, despatched the following note:

> The APM will visit you and make all necessary arrangements for the execution.
>
> The sentence will be promulgated and AFA3 completed. The AF will be handed to the APM at the time of execution.
>
> A firing party of 1 officer and 10 ORs other ranks will be provided by the 2nd Battn. Welsh Regt. The officer will personally load rifles, 9 with ball and one with blank, or failing that, unloaded, and give executive word to fire.

SCF [Senior Chaplain to the Forces] will be informed of hour of promulgation in order that a chaplain may be with the condemned man after promulgation.

A grave will be dug and all arrangements necessary for the removal of the body, and burial will be made by OC, 2nd Bn. Welsh Regt.

The APM will hand over the prisoner to a guard of the 2nd Battn. Welsh Regt. immediately before promulgation.

A medical officer will be present at the execution and will present the necessary death certificate. He will be available from the promulgation until execution.

The APM will report as soon as possible after the execution in the particulars required in S.S. 4120 Sect. 67.

Promulgation and execution will take place as soon as possible and will not await the unit coming out of the line.

It is proposed to carry out the promulgation on the evening of the 9th at Details Camp, COUPIGNY & the execution in the same neighbourhood at dawn on the 10th.[13]

The APM, 1st Division, Captain John Conway Lloyd, who had been the Mayor of Brecon before the war, supervised the execution and Captain Morrell certified that Skone died at 5.14am on 10 May 1918. His remains were buried in Hersin Communal Cemetery, where his headstone records his forename as James and the register refers to his widowed mother as next of kin.[14]

There is nothing immediately discernible in Skone's background or family history to suggest that before enlisting as a soldier he was any more predisposed to commit murder than hundreds of thousands of other working class men who served in the British Army during the First World War. However, his training as an infantryman and successful observance of combat etiquette demanded that he kill as many of the enemy as he could.

During his war service, after having been plied with rum before going into an assault, he doubtlessly killed many men and became accustomed to the association between being inebriated and eliminating the enemy. Unless he enjoyed killing, the rum ration issued before an attack served to erode any residual distaste he may have entertained about slaughtering fellow human beings.

In the drink-addled brain of a well-trained, experienced killer like Skone, the Lance Sergeant's admonishment and the prospect of incarceration would have sufficed to transform Williams into the enemy. Being drunk was not an excuse for killing the NCO. However senior officers' wilful disinclination to acknowledge the part drink played in the murder was in some respects, no less inexcusable.

CHAPTER 11

A Good Turn

It has always been a matter of some regret to revolutionary anarchists that more soldiers do not shoot their officers. When a Tommy did so during the First World War, anecdotal evidence suggests that most acted discreetly. A few, caring not a whit for their own survival, did not bother with subtlety in execution nor did they choose to explain their motivation or express remorse for their actions. Others, like Sapper Robert Bell, detached themselves from responsibility for their action by declaring it to have been the result of an accident.

Robert Bell laboured with his widower father in a colliery at Aberaman in the Rhondda Valley during 1911, though both were originally from Brandon, County Durham. After the 1910 'Block Strike' and subsequent lockout imposed by the Powell Duffryn Steam Coal Company, it was rather unusual at the time for a pair of Geordie miners to find work as colliers in Aberaman. No matter whether they were strike-breaking scabs or locked-out miners, 26-year-old Robert Bell would certainly have been well acquainted with direct action and the use of force to resolve grievances long before he joined the Royal Engineers as a Kitchener volunteer on 9 January 1915.[1]

Sapper Bell's enlistment with the 123rd Field Company, Royal Engineers, was also a little unusual because the formation was predominantly composed of skilled craftsmen who had originally enlisted with the 13th Battalion Welsh Regiment in Cardiff.

In the absence of any service records to account for his wartime experiences, there is no reason to suppose that Bell's military career was much different to that of the other sappers serving with No.4 Section. He would have been in action during the biggest and bloodiest battles of the First World War, on the Somme during 1916 and the Passchendaele debacle in 1917. Nor does he appear to have been a particularly ill-behaved soldier; Bell's disciplinary record featured only three entries. His name had been entered in the company (mis)conduct book for an unspecified offence during October 1915; after having been absent overnight, on 3 March 1916 he was fined seven days' pay and put last on the roster for leave; for being drunk in his billet on 16 May he had also been admonished on 29 May by Lieutenant Colonel George Knox, the officer commanding Royal Engineers, 38th (Welsh) Division.[2]

The German Spring 1918 Offensive compelled a general withdrawal by the British Army, but the onward advance slackened and had halted during early April. General Fanshawe, the 3rd Army Commander had held 38th Division in reserve but the crisis had still imposed a great strain on the division's support units. The Pioneers and Engineers had been kept busy establishing defensive emplacements, and almost endlessly digging trenches and dugouts for protection against enemy air raids. It is easy to appreciate that tired soldiers could be tetchy about nitpicking routine kit inspections but it was also vitally important to ensure that every soldier's weapons, ammunition and gas masks were well maintained and ready for immediate use. Exactly such a kit inspection was scheduled for No.4 Section for 4.00pm on 17 April but shortly after midday Robert Bell had been granted permission to hunt for game with his rifle.

Of course, standing orders prohibited the looting of farms, wine cellars or civilian larders and also using service rifles for shooting birds and rabbits. During the retreat, however, scavenging and foraging was almost universal and Robert Bell's donation to the officers' mess of some of the fruits of his hunting prowess ensured that no one in authority objected.[3] It was springtime and the countryside around Senlis where the company was encamped there were partridges and hares to be potted as well as domestic poultry and animals from abandoned farms.

Bell arrived back from his hunting expedition and joined his section, drawn up in two ranks on the parade ground. Before conducting the rifle and kit inspection, the inspecting officer, Second Lieutenant Wynell Hastings Lloyd, noticed Bell was improperly dressed and ticked him off for not wearing the regulation puttees. The sapper was ordered off the parade ground and told to put on the puttees; he went to a nearby dugout and for about ten minutes Lieutenant Lloyd continued to direct the inspection.

A bullet then drilled a couple of holes through Lloyd's skull, killing him instantly; the men on parade scattered. The NCO who had been carrying out the inspection rushed over to the dugout, where he found Bell and a recently fired rifle. The sapper did not offer any resistance, and after a couple of minutes a couple more NCOs arrived, Bell was escorted away and Lloyd's body was carried off the parade ground.[4]

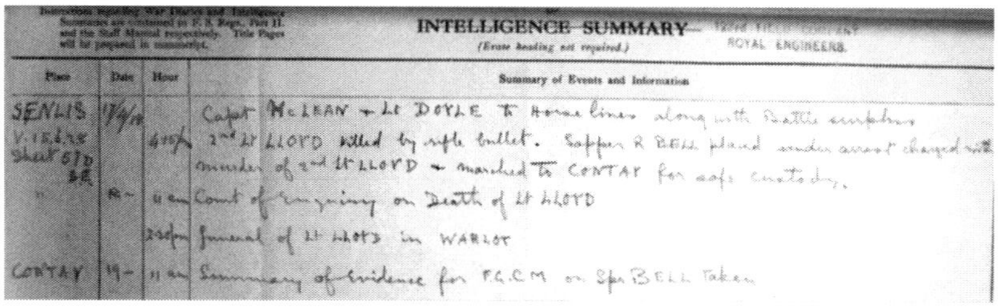
INTELLIGENCE SUMMARY
(Erase heading not required.)
ROYAL ENGINEERS

Place	Date	Hour	Summary of Events and Information
SENLIS	17/4/18		Capt McLEAN & Lt DOYLE to Horse lines along with Battle [illegible]
V.15.b.8 Sheet 57D SE		4.15pm	2nd Lt LLOYD killed by rifle bullet. Sapper R BELL placed under arrest charged with murder of 2nd Lt LLOYD & marched to CONTAY for safe custody.
"	18	11am	Court of Enquiry on Death of Lt LLOYD
		2.30pm	Funeral of Lt LLOYD in WARLOY
CONTAY	19	11am	Summary of Evidence for F.G.C.M on Spr BELL taken

An investigation ensued and on 4 May a field general court martial was convened to try Sapper Robert Bell for the murder of Lieutenant Lloyd. The President was Major Richard Williams, Welsh Regiment, who was assisted in his deliberations by two officers serving with the Royal Welsh Fusiliers, Major Frederick McLellan and 2nd Lieutenant Evan Evans. The Court Martial Officer, Captain Douglas Cecil Stuart, Border Regiment, and the Prisoner's Friend, Lieutenant Claude Meeson, Machine Gun Corps, were both qualified solicitors in civilian life.[5]

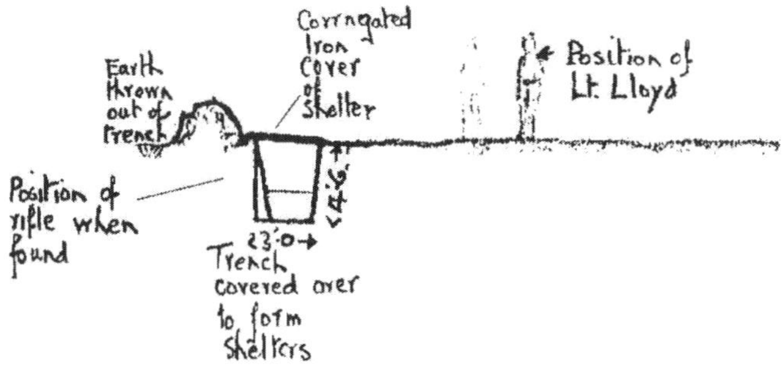

Major John Wood, the Officer Commanding 123rd Company, Royal Engineers, conducted the prosecution, which opened with testimony from Sapper Edward Pears.[6] Pears literally presented the view of a soldier in the ranks because that was where he had been situated at 4.00pm on 17 April. He recalled:

> An order had been given for the examination of arms, ammunition, and gas masks. The Section fell in facing the trench .... Lt. Lloyd of our section came on parade. An order was given to port arms and Lt. Lloyd examined the arms and emergency rations. The accused was a member of my section. While on parade I stood about three yards from him. I was standing in the first rank. I think the accused also stood in the front rank. After the emergency rations had been examined Lt. Lloyd went to the right end of the parade. Immediately Lt. Lloyd came on parade and spoke to the accused and I heard the word 'puttees' spoken. I saw the accused walk off the parade. The accused was not on parade during the inspection. After the emergency rations had been examined and Lt. Lloyd had walked down to his right flank,

> I heard a shot fired and saw Lt. Lloyd on the ground. The parade broke up. Lt. Lloyd was about eight yards from me. The parade was immediately ordered to fall in again. Just after the examination of emergency rations I saw a muzzle of a rifle sticking out of the trench which was in front of us, the rifle was to my right front.

Under cross-examination by Meeson, Pears revealed:

> I heard a conversation when in the ranks between Lt. Lloyd and the accused. The only word I distinctly caught was 'puttees'. If there had been any high speaking I should have heard it. From the time I saw the rifle sticking up over the trench and the firing of the shot may have been a minute. I did not have my eyes on the rifle at the time when the shot was fired. I saw no man with the rifle, I only saw the rifle.

In response to questioning by the court, Pears added, 'When we fell in the second time, we fell in facing the same way. I saw blood on the ground. I saw the accused arrested.'[7]

The second witness was Lance Corporal Rowland Ordish, who submitted in evidence a couple of sketches of the parade ground and dugout.[8] He explained:

> The measurements shown are accurate. The shelter marked in red to 'Position of Lt. Lloyd' is four yards. The position of Lt. Lloyd was indicated to me and I made the measurement accordingly. The position of the section was roughly indicated to me and I made that measurement accordingly.

In response to a query by Meeson, Ordish added, 'Cpl. Prior pointed out the position of Lt. Lloyd and the position of the section.'[9]

According to Ordish's sketches, the trench was 4 1/2 feet (1.37 metres) deep and 3 feet wide (0.9 metres). On the south side, earth had been piled up to form a rudimentary parapet. The distance from the spot where the section had paraded to the shelter was 48 feet (14.6 metres) and the distance from the trench to where Lloyd's body was found was 16 feet (4.9 metres).

In carrying out the kit inspection Lieutenant Lloyd had been assisted by Corporal Reuben Prior, who had also helped Ordish in drafting the latter's scene of crime sketches.[10] Prior was not only present when Lloyd perished but he was also the man who had sprinted into the trench and arrested Bell. When delivering his narrative account of the fatal incident Prior's testimony was clearly and cogently expressed:

> At 3.40pm on 17 April I warned everyone to be fully dressed for parade at 3.50pm. Lt. Lloyd came on parade. I fell the section in. Lt. Lloyd noticed the accused had not got his puttees on. I fell accused out and brought him in front of Lt. Lloyd. The accused was asked why he hadn't any puttees on. He replied that the puttees hurt his legs. Lt. Lloyd dismissed [the excuse?] and told him to put his puttees on. Mr. Lloyd then carried on with the inspection of rifles, ammunition, [and] iron rations. After the iron rations had been inspected, the gas NCO inspected the front rank. I inspected the rear rank. The section was paraded in two ranks for these inspections. The accused, before he was sent off parade, was in the first rank. While inspecting the rear rank I heard a shot. I turned round and saw Lt. Lloyd fall. I rushed up to him, but found I could do nothing for him, as he was dead as far as I could tell. I looked in front of me right and left of me, but I could see nobody except the accused in the trench. The accused was directly in front of me when I looked in the trench.[11]

Referring to Ordish's sketch plan, Prior went on to say:

> I was at point 'P' with my back facing the trench 'O'. I turned round when I heard the shot. I saw

> Lt. Lloyd standing and beginning to fall at point 'B' which was about four yards from point 'O'. Accused was standing in the trench at point 'L'. The accused had no rifle in his hand.

Although he did not witness Bell actually fire the fatal shot, when Prior subsequently entered the trench, he noticed:

> There was a rifle in the trench two feet away from him, which was leaning against the parapet. The rifle was not pointing in the direction of Lt. Lloyd. It was turned with the magazine upwards. I did not examine it. I arrested the accused ... I placed a guard on the accused. Someone handed me his rifle, which was in the trench and I handed it over to the Sergeant-Major. I am of the opinion that the shot came from the direction of the trench.

Cross-examined by Meeson, Prior confirmed he had been standing next to Lloyd when the officer had spoken with Bell about the puttees, and added:

> When the shot was fired my back was turned to the trench. I turned around immediately. When I turned I did not see a rifle sticking up nor did I see the accused immediately.

Prior, again in response to questions by Meeson, admitted that he had known about Bell's absence from camp but was rather coy in disclosing his knowledge of the latter's hunting activities:

> The accused came to me at 12.30pm on 17 April and asked me if he could go for a walk. I gave him permission. I'm not aware accused went out shooting game. I do know he shot a hare a week previously on coming back from work. I did not see the accused go out on the afternoon of that day. I saw accused return at 3.30pm ... I can't say if accused had his rifle with him when he returned.

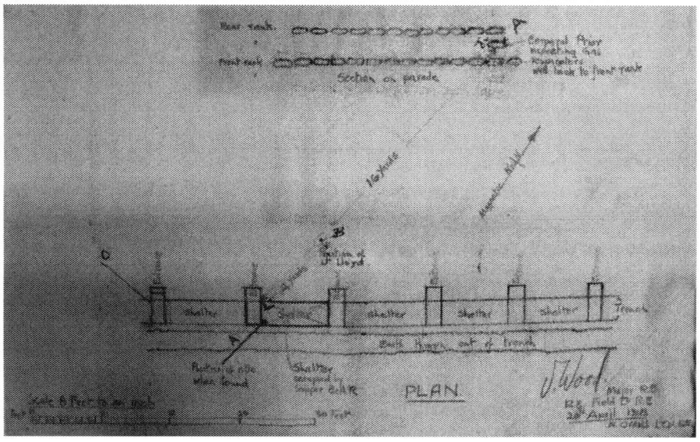

Prior also said that Bell was 'not upset as far as I noticed when I got to him in the trench.'

The court then briefly cross-examined Prior, turning attention to the alleged murder weapon. The NCO stated:

> There was no one else in the bay of the trench where the accused was. The accused had his rifle on parade when he fell in for rifle inspection. The

> accused took his rifle off parade when he went for his puttees. I gave orders personally that all rifles were to be cleaned before the parade. The accused I think was not present when I ordered the rifles to be cleaned as he had gone out.[12]

Other than a brief exchange between Lieutenant Lloyd and Bell no witness had thus far alluded to any motive that Bell may have had to harm Lieutenant Lloyd. The remaining three witnesses for the prosecution dwelt on their own reaction to the shooting and roles in restoring order or taking Bell into custody. In his testimony, the next witness to give evidence, Company Sergeant Major Foster focussed on procedure and process:

> At 4.15pm on the 17 April 1918, I was working in my dugout about sixty-five paces from where Number 4 Section ... had fallen in. I heard a rifle fired. I at once ordered Sergeant Ferris to come with me and we went across to where Number 4 section was paraded. When I heard the shot fired, I looked up and saw Lt. Lloyd falling down. He was about four yards from the trench. Point 'Q' on plan 'X' would be approximately my position. On reaching Lt. Lloyd I saw he was dead. I saw the accused placed between two sentries with fixed bayonets. I searched him at once. I found on him, some money, books, and in his right hand pocket I found two clips of ammunition, five rounds in each. I then fell Number 4 Section in

> as they had scattered. I then went down to the officer's tent and came back to take the accused's number from Corporal Prior. I then proceeded back to the officer's tent and as I was about one yard in front of the accused, the accused said to me: 'You know me Sergeant Major.' I replied: 'Of course I do.' The accused then said: 'When I set out to accomplish a thing I do it, there it is.' That is all the accused said to me. I first saw his rifle just after I searched the accused. It was then leaning up against the side of the trench. I got out of the trench into which I had got and took the rifle [as/up?] to examine [it]. On examination I found an empty cartridge case in the breech and two live rounds in the magazine. The cut-off was open and the dust cap open. I produce the rifle to the court.[13]

The officers of the court examined the weapon; Foster continued:

> I don't know whose rifle it is, as I don't keep a record of them. I did not look down the barrel. I partly withdrew the empty case and then replaced it. I saw the body of Lt. Lloyd. The bullet had apparently entered the back of the head slightly above and back of the left ear. It came out somewhere over the left eye.

To Meeson, Foster disclosed, 'The rifle has been in my charge since the affair occurred. I have not cleaned it at all.' About Bell, he commented, 'I did not ask the accused any questions. I have known the accused for about three years. I don't know if the accused had any trouble with Lt. Lloyd. So far as I know, the accused had no ill-feeling towards Lt. Lloyd.'[14]

His immediate subordinate, Sergeant William Ferris, followed Foster as a witness.[15] Ferris said little but his reference to a comment he had allegedly overheard being made by Bell was the strongest evidence that the killing had been a wilful act:

> On 17 April at about 4.10pm I was working with CSM Foster, in a dugout. No.4 Section was parading about 60 yards away. I heard a shot fired. I saw a crowd gather round someone on the ground. I ran over to see what it was about. When I got there I saw the accused with two sentries on him. I was ordered by the CSM to hold the accused's hands while he searched the accused. When the search was finished I let the accused's hands go. The CSM then left him. I stood behind Bell, the accused when he said: 'I've done the section a good turn. You'll think of Bob Bell in years to come.'[16]

If verified, these two sentences could be construed as an admission by Bell that he had deliberately shot Lieutenant Lloyd. However, Ferris did not say to whom the alleged remarks had been addressed and neither had any other witness reported hearing Bell utter the remarks. If he had spoken loudly and clearly enough for Ferris to hear, Bell's admission should also have been overheard by the two soldiers who had been ordered to be his armed escort. To carry any weight, the prosecution needed to produce corroboration. Meeson sought further clarification from Ferris in response to which the latter conceded, 'The accused did not say this to me. I was standing behind him. He never said anything more in my presence.'

The final prosecution witness was a United States Army medical officer, Captain Joseph Gold:

> On 17 April I examined an officer. He was dead. He had a wound in the forehead. I only made a cursory examination owing to the fact that he was dead. There was blood on the side of the head, the hair was matted and I did not examine the body minutely. Major Wood, RE, was present when I made the examination.[17]

There was no cross-examination by the defence; the prosecution rested.

Sapper Bell took the stand and made a statement in his own defence but refused to take the oath or make a solemn declaration. Exactly why he demurred remains unclear but as a consequence he could not be cross-examined. However, it also meant that no matter how compelling might have been the grounds he advanced, the court would be under little obligation to give any weight to his evidence. It took Bell only a few minutes to air a semi-detached explanation that inferred Lloyd's death had been entirely accidental:

> At 12.30pm on 17 April 1918 I received permission from Corporal Prior to take a walk. I went taking my rifle with me with the intention of getting a hare or a partridge. I failed to get a shot at a hare and returned to camp, in order to be in time for the inspection. I went on parade and was immediately called off by the officer to put my puttees on. I went to the trench with the intention of doing so. After an interval of ten minutes I couldn't find my puttees anywhere so I attempted to get out of the trench and rejoin the section. In jumping up I slipped, the rifle flying forward and exploding immediately. I had forgotten to abstract the round which I had put in in the early part of the afternoon, and that was the cause of the unfortunate result. It has always been my practice out in France to go out shooting game and the previous week I had shot a hare and a brace of partridges for the officers' mess.

If it had been a freakish accident then Bell was almost as much a victim as Lloyd. However, no corroborative evidence had been presented to support the proposition that Lloyd's death was accidental. If Bell had taken the oath, Meeson might have been afforded the opportunity to engage in cross-examination, and perhaps coaxed a refutation of the damaging remarks attributed to him by Sergeant Ferris and Company Sergeant Major Foster.

The only other defence witness was Sapper Walter Short.[18] His contribution confirmed Bell had been engaged in shooting game but cast no further light on the killing of Lieutenant. Lloyd:

> The accused had to my knowledge gone out shooting game. On several occasions he has brought game home. I saw the accused come back on 17 April. He had with him a small black rabbit. The rabbit had been shot.

After all of the witnesses had been heard, Meeson summed up the case for the defence and tried to persuade the court to return a verdict of manslaughter. In common with many other capital cases, the final submission by the Prisoner's Friend was reduced to a series of scribbled points that were tacked onto the end of the written proceedings:

1. No one actually saw the shot fired.
2. No one heard any words between the accused and the deceased officer. No motive for the crime. Suggest it was an accident.
3. Accused's statement as to gaming borne out by prosecution and witness for defence.
4. Also, that court must be convinced that this is a case of such gross negligence or intention to

shoot the deceased before they can find a verdict against the accused.

5. I submit that at most, a verdict of manslaughter can be returned.[19]

There was no response from Wood, and the court adjourned to consider its findings. The evidence against Bell was strong and his defence was pitifully weak because Meeson had very little evidence with which to work. His submission failed to impress the court and Robert Bell was found guilty of murder.

Major Wood informed the court about Bell's disciplinary record and declared that the convicted man had always worked well in his section. In mitigation, Bell told the court that he was twenty-nine years old, unmarried and had been in France since December 1915. Unfortunately for Bell, Wood's positive endorsement of his value as a sapper was not enough for the court to eschew awarding a death sentence, unencumbered by any recommendation to mercy.

In reviewing the trial, Meeson was quite correct in pointing out that the prosecution had failed to produce evidence of a motive for the crime. There was no evidence of any ill feeling between Lloyd and Bell before the shooting and according to testimony by Pears and Prior, the lieutenant had simply ordered Bell to go and don puttees. Lloyd was not reported to have been particularly miffed or upset, neither is there any indication that Lloyd intended to punish Bell. In complying with Lloyd's order, Bell did not grumble or hesitate to obey. If the killing was deliberate, what had caused Bell to commit murder?

Meeson had vainly attempted to secure a verdict of manslaughter but did the facts presented in court suggest that such a verdict would have been proper? The court should certainly have examined the defence claim that the killing had been unintentional. Bell could have been telling the truth and if so, provision for returning a verdict of manslaughter featured in the *Manual of Military Law* (1914), which stated:

> It may be taken generally, that in all cases where a killing cannot be justified, if it does not amount to murder, it is manslaughter, and a person charged with murder can be convicted of manslaughter. For instance, an act of negligence or other unlawful act which results in death, if the act is not such that a reasonable man must have known that it would be likely to cause death or injury to someone, would render the person guilty of manslaughter, not of murder.[20]

Of course, climbing out of a trench with an unsafe, loaded and cocked rifle was negligent and potentially likely to cause death or serious injury. However, Bell had been shooting game during the afternoon, a fact undisputed by the prosecution, and his rifle may have been charged and cocked, ready for a quick potshot. Not much may be construed from the magazine cut-off being open but there was no statement or discussion about the weapon's safety catch. The design of the

Lee-Enfield rifle was such that when the safety catch was engaged, the bolt and the cocking piece were locked. Even if the gun had been cocked, it could not have been fired without the safety catch being released and the trigger being pulled. In the event, other than circumstantial evidence, the remarks allegedly made by Bell sufficed to convince the court that he had wilfully murdered Lloyd.

Although it would almost certainly not have saved him from execution, at no point did Bell display any emotion or express remorse for what he claimed to have been a tragic accident. Why therefore did Bell kill Lloyd? Was he deranged and seized by a sudden and overpowering urge to shoot Lloyd? If so, English law does not recognize the notion that a person might be overcome with an irresistible impulse to commit an unlawful act because at the time they were under a mental impairment such as they could not control their actions. Instead, English courts determined insanity by applying the McNaughten Rules, whereby a defendant of whom it was proven could not differentiate between right and wrong because of mental disease, was deemed insane.

Because Bell's service and medical records have not survived, it is not possible to establish whether he may have previously suffered from battle stress. However, the cumulative nervous strain of the preceding month's fighting could have eroded Bell's capacity for rational thinking, and Lloyd's order may have proved to be the final straw. The nature of the killing must have caused Meeson to consider whether Bell had been insane when he shot Lloyd but because the defence held that the killing had been an accident, there were no grounds on which the Prisoner's Friend could have pressed for the sapper to be examined by a Medical Board.

After he had been condemned to death, arrangements could have been made for Bell's sanity to be assessed. According to Field Marshal Haig:

> When a man has been sentenced to death, if at any time doubt has been raised as to his responsibility for his actions, or if the suggestion has been advanced that he has suffered from shell shock ... orders are issued for him to be examined by a medical board which expresses an opinion as to his sanity, and as to whether or not he should be held responsible for his actions. One of the members of the board is always a medical officer of neurological experience. The sentence of death is not carried out in the case of such a man unless the medical board expresses the positive opinion that he is to be held responsible for his actions.[21]

However, the procedure was certainly not entertained by Major General Charles Blackader, the Officer Commanding 38th Division. He endorsed the decision to execute Bell, stating, 'I cannot see any mitigating circumstances and consider that the sentence should be carried out.'[22] The other confirming officers agreed and Field Marshal Haig confirmed the sentence on 16 May. Sapper Robert Bell was executed near Herissart at 4.12am on 22 May 1918 by a firing squad under the command of Captain Claude Tully, Assistant Provost Marshal, 38th Division.[23]

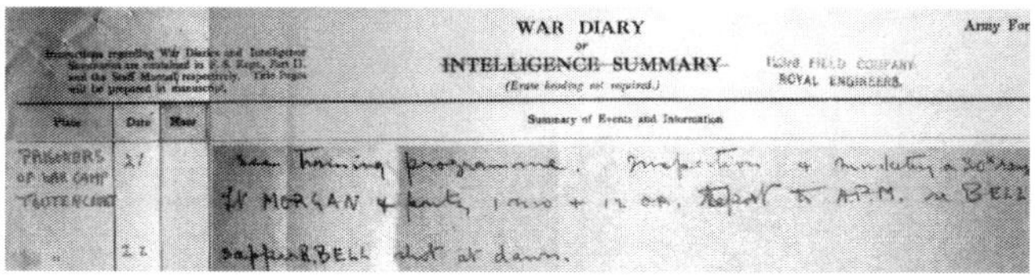
WAR DIARY
or
~~INTELLIGENCE SUMMARY~~
(Erase heading not required.)

ROYAL ENGINEERS.

Army For

Place	Date	Hour	Summary of Events and Information
PRISONERS OF WAR CAMP	21		See Training programme. Inspection + [illegible]
			Lt MORGAN + party, 1 NCO + 12 O.R. Report to A.P.M. re BELL
"	22		Sapper R. BELL shot at dawn.

CHAPTER 12

Something Unexplained

Second Lieutenant John Henry Paterson was the only British officer executed for murder during the First World War. His crime attracted minimal publicity and the British Government kept details secret until the early 1980s, when Judge Anthony Babington was granted permission to examine the written proceedings. However, the highly confidential terms of access prevented Babington from naming either Paterson or any of the other executed men. Thus, Paterson was referred to as Second Lieutenant P_____ when Babington's research was eventually published. In his book about the British Army's courts martial system, *For the Sake of Example,* Babington summarized the trial but concluded, 'There is something puzzling about this case – something unexplained. The facts emerge in a misty sequence, orderly and precise, but at the end the enigmatic quality remains.'[1]

Babington never elaborated on what he reckoned to have been 'unexplained' about the case but an abbreviated account of Paterson's military career can easily be reconstructed from his attestation papers, service records, medical reports and assorted correspondence. While the ensuing resume of times, dates and movements of Private John Paterson does not explain everything, there is little to suggest that there was anything unique or even particularly unusual about his enlistment or experiences as a Tommy in the trenches.

Paterson was a clerical worker living in West Ham when war was declared but did not join the 17th Battalion, Middlesex Regiment until early April 1915. The formation was created in response to an Army recruiting stunt conjured up by the Conservative MP, William Joynson Hicks, and attracted enormous publicity, especially when the entire first team and many supporters of Clapton Orient Football Club enlisted en masse. Although Paterson was also associated with the club, his name did not figure anywhere in press reports about the 'Footballers' Battalion'.[2]

Paterson's preliminary training and service in the United Kingdom was conducted in various locations and was wholly unblemished until the battalion was posted to Perham Down on Salisbury Plain in August 1915, where he was confined to barracks for a week after returning a few hours late from leave. During September he was again confined to barracks for three days for making an 'improper remark' to a warrant officer, and subsequently attracted a further week's confinement to barracks for talking on parade. These petty offences did not interfere with his completion of the final stages of field training as an infantryman and proficiency as a signaller. When the battalion was mobilized for service with the BEF, Paterson was included in the advance party that embarked at Southampton on 16 November.[3]

After a brief stay in Bethune, the battalion spent December and January at the front near Annequin, where Paterson and his comrades became acquainted with the infelicities of trench warfare and casualties began to mount. Four dead and thirty-three wounded, by the standards of the time, was not particularly heavy, but non-combat related injuries also levied a toll on the battalion. The latter included Paterson, who was disabled with a swollen foot for over a fortnight during February. It was scant relief from enemy gas attacks, shelling and being bitten by lice but worse was to come on 1 June, when forty-seven (sic) Footballers were killed or wounded as a consequence of an abortive raid on enemy positions at Souchez.[4]

On 27 July, the Footballers' Battalion played its part in the Battle of the Somme. From the commencement of its attack on Delville Wood, the battalion was harassed by small arms and machine guns before being virtually shredded by enemy artillery fire. In two days a quarter of the battalion was killed or wounded.[5] Paterson sustained a gunshot wound in the neck and was admitted to No.21 Casualty Clearing Station; he was also diagnosed as suffering from shell shock and evacuated to Boulogne, where he remained until the end of August.[6]

By the time he was fit enough to rejoin the Footballers, further casualties had thinned its ranks but on 13 November the battalion was assigned to take part in the bloody coda to the Battle of the Somme, the attack on the Redan Ridge. In his celebratory account the journalist-cum-historian Everard Wyrall referred to the Footballers going into action cheerfully, singing and playing mouth organs as they advanced through fog, over ground carpeted with the rotting remains of British soldiers felled in earlier attacks. However, any sense of jollification experienced by Private Paterson was swiftly knocked out of him when he was again wounded and evacuated with a 'Cont[used].Head'.[7]

The head injury must have been quite serious because he was dispatched to No.20 General Hospital, Camiers, where he remained until 20 December. After convalescing at No.41 Infantry Base Depot, Étaples, Paterson was considered physically robust enough to be attached to No.2 Training Camp, part of Étaples Camp's infamous Bullring. Paterson's sojourn in France came to an end on 3 March, when he was shipped back to the United Kingdom, posted to the regimental depot for three months and then sent to Gailes Camp, Ayrshire, for training as an officer.[8]

After successfully completing nine weeks' training with No.10 Officer Cadet Battalion, on 27 September he was commissioned as Second Lieutenant with the Essex Regiment and returned to France on 16 November. By the end of the month he again found himself on the Somme battlefield, back in action with 1st Battalion Essex Regiment, 29th Division, as it was being beaten back by a massive German counterattack at Bourlon Wood. Sorely raked by enemy artillery and aerial strafing, 29th Division was compelled to retreat and a couple of other British divisions were decimated, and Paterson was lucky to escape being wounded for a third time or killed.[9]

He spent the remainder of the winter on duty at a number of locations in and around the Pas de Calais and Western Flanders. On 17 December he was in Calais; during early January and early February he was posted to St Omer, and for most of March he was stationed near Abeele. By 4 February 1918, when his battalion was transferred to 112th Brigade, 37th Division, there was nothing in Paterson's service record to suggest that the military authorities were at all remiss in selecting him to lead men into battle.[10]

The afternoon of 26 March found Paterson at Maida Camp, near Kruistraathoek, on the southern flank of the Ypres Salient, roughly 4 kilometres behind the firing line. It was the fifth day of General Ludendorff's *Kaiserschlacht;* the British Army was being pushed back and preparing to withdraw from Albert, and in anticipation of an extension of the enemy onslaught, the ring of trenches and defence works around Ypres were improved and reinforced. Paterson's personal contribution to these preparations involved conducting a working party of soldiers from Maida Camp to the 37th Division's forward trenches at Zillebeke.[11]

Enemy artillery fire never entirely ceased in the vicinity but the party's progress was uninterrupted by shelling. Yet after about half an hour Paterson ordered a halt because, he explained, it was *too early;* approaching the front line in broad daylight would have been unnecessarily hazardous. The soldiers were therefore ordered to fall out and wait until nightfall, and in the meantime Paterson took advantage of the opportunity to use the officers' latrine in a nearby camp. He rejoined the party before 7.00pm, as dusk was falling, and the march resumed but it was a bright moonlit night, and Paterson ordered a further pause at Shrapnel Corner. To Sergeant Sidney Appleton, the senior NCO, Paterson said he needed to recover a pocket book and orders that he had left behind in the officers' latrine. He left Appleton in charge of the party and retraced his way along the track to the camp and vanished.[12]

Appleton initially thought that Paterson may have been wounded or killed but it swiftly became clear to the military authorities that the missing subaltern was very much alive. He had made his way to St Omer, where he remained for about a week before travelling to Calais, where he stayed for most of the following three months. Exactly where Paterson resided in Calais remains open to conjecture but he supported himself financially by drawing substantial advances on his pay from Army cashiers and cashing fraudulent cheques at French banks.[13] During June his photo portrait and description were circulated in the United Kingdom and featured in the *Police Gazette* but Paterson never left France, and he was finally spotted on 3 July, crossing the Canal de Calais at the Pont-de-Coulogne.

Two military police detectives, Sergeant Harold Collison and Lance Corporal Stockton, who were monitoring the eponymous bridge and a nearby railway line, saw Paterson and a young lady casually perambulating across a footbridge.[14] The detectives, who were disguised as artillerymen, followed the couple and intercepted them on the outskirts of the village of Coulogne. On being challenged about his identity, Paterson asserted he was 'Second Lieutenant Barford, 1st Essex Regiment' but was unable to produce any documentary evidence to support his claim. He therefore invited the detectives to accompany him to the British military camp at Beaumarais, where he promised they would be able to confirm his identity.[15]

Paterson and his female companion, followed by the two detectives, meandered along in the general direction of the Rue de Dunkirk, where Paterson paused. He then disclosed his true identity to Sergeant Collison and begged for half an hour's grace, time in which to share tea with his girlfriend at her family home. Since the house was nearby, Collison agreed.

The couple entered the house at about 7.30pm and the two detectives remained outside, where they kept an eye on the house. After a couple of hours Paterson emerged to assure Stockton that he had no intention of escaping and claimed that Collison was happy to wait a while longer. Shortly before sunset, Collison's patience evaporated; he approached the gate to a yard immediately adjacent to the house and sent a summons via the girlfriend's mother, telling Paterson to come outside.[16]

The latter responded immediately; he went out and spoke for a few minutes with Collison. He then produced a revolver and fired two shots: the first shot wounded Paterson in the groin; the second struck the NCO in the chest. Mortally wounded, Collison collapsed, Stockton ran away and Paterson escaped, hobbling along with his girlfriend's assistance.[17]

On 9 July a court of enquiry formally concluded that Collison had been slain by Paterson, for whom a search was already being energetically conducted in France and the United Kingdom. Eventually, Commissioner Eugene Mollex, a French secret policeman attached to the British 2nd Army Headquarters, traced Paterson's whereabouts. Aided by a tip-off, Mollex and a couple of his colleagues kept watch on a house in St Omer and nabbed Paterson when he turned up on the doorstep at 11.00pm on 22 July.[18]

It took more than a month to make the necessary arrangements to try Paterson but on 11 September he was eventually tried by a general court martial convened in Boulogne. The gathering was presided over by Brigadier General Francis Lumley, Commandant of No.4 Rest Camp, and the Members consisted of Lieutenant Colonel Hugh Rice, Major William Hickson, Major Thomas Paget-Tomlinson and Captain Nicholas Leadbitter. The court was advised by a judge advocate, Major Ernest Green, and Captain Walter Blake Odgers conducted the prosecution. A highly experienced criminal barrister, Lieutenant Ernest Walsh, defended Paterson.[19]

Paterson was indicted on one count of murder, one count of desertion, and five counts of forgery. It was agreed to hear the murder charge separately but with reference to the other capital charge, desertion, the court refused to accept Paterson's admission of guilt and entered on his behalf a formal plea of not guilty. The court accepted Paterson's guilty plea to all the forgery charges, and without further ado the President directed the Prosecution to proceed with the murder charge.[20]

The first witness to be sworn in was Sergeant Appleton, whose entire testimony directly addressed the charge of desertion, not murder, but no one objected to him testifying. The NCO briefly confirmed when and where he had last seen Paterson, detailing the latter's abandonment of the working party near Shrapnel Corner. After he had concluded, in response to a question from Walsh, Appleton added, 'Things were pretty quiet. There were only half a dozen shells over all the evening.'[21]

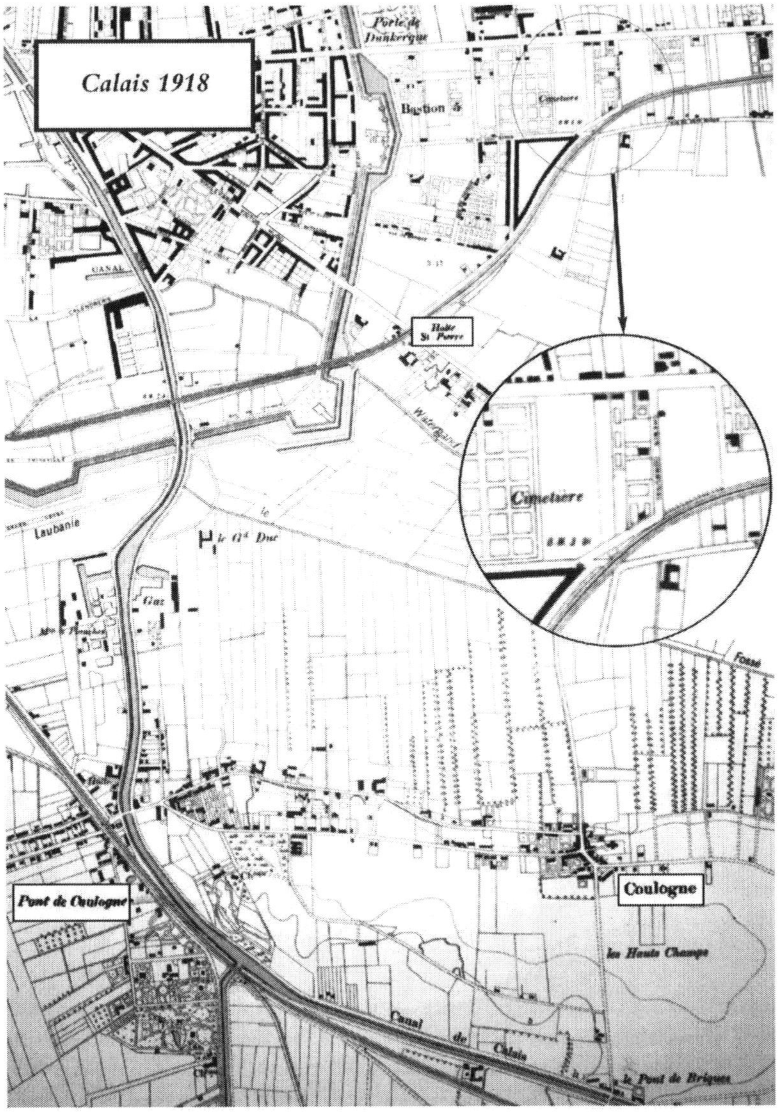

Fatal encounter: Sgt. Collison and L. Cpl. Stockton confront Lt. Paterson and Augustine Duquenoy.

The second witness was Lance Corporal Stockton, who identified Paterson's female companion as Mlle Augustine Duquenoy and recounted in court the sequence of events up to the point when the subaltern had revealed his true identity to Collison. He did not initially expand on Collison's decision to grant permission to a self-confessed absentee time in which to enjoy tea with his girlfriend's family. Instead, Stockton narrated at some length what happened outside the house.

He explained that the Duquenoy family home was surrounded by trees and located 'between the Dunkirk road and the railway, close to where the new railway line crosses the road. The new railway line sweeps round from the road to the back of the house.'[22]

He explained:

> Detective Sergeant Collison and I then took up a position: I was on the railway embankment and the sergeant was on the other side of the house in the lane leading up from the Dunkirk road to the house, and we kept watch in these positions ... at 8.45pm the accused came down the garden close to where I was and said to me 'I hope you don't think I am running away. I am having a talk with the girls in the house.'

Stockton declared that he did not mind but asked if Collison had been consulted, and was told, 'Yes, I've explained to the sergeant and it is alright,' before Paterson went back into the house.

From his elevated position, about 18 metres away from the house, Stockton had an unobstructed view across a small garden and could see into the yard of the house. He saw Paterson and Collison meet together and responded when summoned by the latter:

> I ... went down the embankment and turned down the garden path towards the yard. When I was two or three paces from the yard gate, I heard a revolver shot. At that time the accused and Detective Sergeant Collison were 12 yards away and I could see quite clearly. I heard Sergeant Collison say, 'What's that' as I got to the yard gate I saw the accused point a revolver at Detective Sergeant Collison and saw him fire. I saw the flash. I saw Sergeant Collison stagger. The accused then rushed towards me. He still had the revolver and I heard a third shot. I ran down the garden path, as I was not armed.... When I got to the railway embankment, I turned round and saw that the accused was not following me. I then called to two soldiers whom I saw on the road ... they followed me back to the yard. I there found a Frenchman holding Sergeant Collison in a sitting position.... He was bleeding from the mouth and nose. I got some water. I think Detective Sergeant Collison was then dead.[23]

Paterson's defending officer, Lieutenant Walsh, briefly cross-examined Stockton about the latter's prewar experience as a railway police detective. While observing the Duquenoy house, Stockton told Walsh:

> I could see Detective Sergeant Collison in the lane from the railway embankment. There are broken

> parts in the fence which permitted me to see Collison in the lane.

Walsh turned his attention to the number of shots that Paterson was alleged to have discharged. Stockton insisted that in all, three shots had been fired.

> I gave my statement on the Monday morning following the event, which was five days after. This was not the first time I said there was a third shot as I said so in my report to the APM. I told Sergeant-Major Bennett that I had heard a third shot.

Taxed by Walsh about the accuracy of his recollection, Stockton insisted:

> I am not aware that I am the only person who said there were three shots ... I felt positively sure there was a third shot. I did not see the flash or hear the bullet. I was about 8 to 12 yards away.

Pressed for further details, Stockton recalled:

> I did not see the revolver when I heard the first shot but I saw the flash of the second shot. I did not see the revolver when I heard the first shot. I was in view of the accused over the garden fence which was about 3 to 3 1/2 feet high. I did not see the flash of the first shot because I did not see the revolver. I think he took it from his

> pocket.... I was by the gate when the third shot went off. I ran down the path. I started running just as the third shot was fired. I had turned round. I did not see the revolver levelled at me. I saw the accused rush towards the garden gate before I turned.[24]

Stockton also took the opportunity to distance himself from responsibility for deferring Paterson's arrest:

> I had no conversation with Detective-Sergeant Collison about allowing the officer to remain in the house. My instructions were to arrest the accused. I did not think Detective Sergeant Collison was doing the right thing by allowing the accused to go into the house but Collison was in charge. I thought it blameworthy.

He conceded that Paterson had also 'spoken very nicely' to Collison and the latter had reciprocated by treating Paterson with respect. Moreover, Stockton added, 'It was Collison's practice to go about armed when on dangerous work, and one might expect that he would be armed.'

2nd Lieutenant John Paterson.

Again, in response to questions by Walsh, Stockton explained in great detail how Paterson killed Collison:

> The second shot killed the sergeant. I was then in the gateway of the yard. Collison was then to my right front with his left front towards me. He was not opposite to [the] door. He was to the right of the door of the house. I did not see the accused come out of the door when he joined

> Sergeant Collison in the yard. Collison was standing between me and the officer in an oblique direction. Collison was between 1 & 2 yards from the officer (accused) when the first shot went off. Collison did not then make a dash for the accused. He took a side pace to the left and looked down, apparently to see where the shot had come from. He did not come between me and the accused. I first saw the accused's right hand when he pointed the revolver at Collison. He deliberately pointed the revolver at Collison and took deliberate aim. I did not see accused take it from his pocket as his right hand when down at his side would not be in my view. I did not see his right arm when the first shot was fired. I am quite sure I saw accused deliberately point the revolver at Collison. I did not see him [sic] raised his arm. The movement of the sergeant made no difference to my view. He would have to have moved another yard to have made a difference. I had no doubt in my mind when the accused's arm was pointing at Collison that accused intended to shoot Collison.[25]

It was compelling evidence. Stockton admitted:

> I did not rush to Collison's assistance as it was done in the twinkle of an eye and it would have been certain death for me, as I was unarmed and I ran away as it was the safest thing to do. It has not occurred to me that I might be in serious

> disgrace for running away. I have never exaggerated my evidence to excuse myself. It has never entered my head, how, for the same reason I have invented the story of the third shot. I heard the third shot.

In response to a couple or so questions from Captain Odgers, Stockton said there was hardly any interval between the first and second shots being discharged. He also claimed that Paterson, with revolver in hand, had rushed towards the garden gate. The court also solicited confirmation from Stockton that he had an unobstructed view of Paterson and Collison when the gun was fired. Partially contradicting his earlier testimony, Stockton responded:

> I could see clearly the whole of accused and Collison when the first shot was fired. Accused had the revolver in his right hand pointing to his front as he rushed towards the gate.[26]

Stockton's evidence certainly damned Paterson as a killer but the detective's evidence was also tainted by a whiff of self-exoneration.

Paterson's female companion, 22-year-old Mlle Augustine Duquenoy, appeared to give evidence for the prosecution with the assistance of an interpreter. From the written proceedings, what she had to relate was delivered in a series of rather stilted sentences and rather uncertainly translated. However, she prefaced her evidence by generally confirming the sequence of events that had already been aired by Stockton. Duquenoy continued:

> I went with accused to my father's house.... We arrived at the house at about 7.30pm. The sergeant and the corporal stopped outside and the accused went outside and spoke to the sergeant at about 8.30pm. Accused then came in and had some tea. He went out again about 8.40pm. Before going out he said to me, 'If they do not leave I will fire at them.' He then had a revolver.... And when accused went out of the house he had it in his right pocket. I saw the accused speaking to the sergeant for about ten minutes. They were standing close together. I did not notice the position in which the accused was standing. His right hand was in his right-hand pocket. I then heard a shot. I was then in the house. I only heard one shot. I then came outside the house screaming. I then saw the sergeant on the ground. The accused was then at the garden gate [speaking to the corporal]. The accused still had the revolver in his hand. The corporal was running away down the garden towards the railway.[27]

Mlle Duquenoy then presented the court with an explanation of her role in Paterson's flight from the scene of the crime:

> The accused then took the hat off my head in order to make me go with him. He put the

> revolver back in his pocket. I then went with the accused down the railway to where it crosses the Dunkirk road and then by Petit Courgain to Calais. The accused and I arrived at the Café Belge near the station at Calais about 11.00pm where we spent the night. I then noticed that accused was wounded in the leg near the private parts. I asked why he did it and he said, 'I did not mean to kill him. He is only wounded.'

After asserting that Paterson had not fired a third shot at Stockton, Odgers pressed her to say more about Paterson's sojourn in Calais. She recalled:

> We stayed at the Café Belge the whole of the next day and the following night. Neither I nor the accused left the café while staying there and we had our meals in our room. We left the café two days after at 9.00am and I then left him and I did not see him again.[28]

In response to cross-examination by Walsh, Duquenoy declared:

> I first gave a statement at the request of the French police. I understand English well and speak it a little. I gave the statement in French to a Frenchman. I don't understand the expression 'fucking bastard' used in my statement.[29]

In the text of her pre-trial statement, she alleged that, while in the kitchen of the Duquenoy family house, Paterson had threatened to use his revolver to intimidate Stockton and Collison, and had directly referred to the latter as a 'fucking bastard'.[30] When quizzed about the number of shots Paterson fired, she maintained that there had only been two. Both had been fired while she was inside the house and though she had not heard the first one very well, she had reacted immediately and made for the door to the yard. By the time she emerged from the house, Collison was already lying on the ground in the yard. She added:

> The yard is not very large and the officer was then in the yard. I did not then see the corporal before he went down the garden path. There was no third shot.... It was not possible for there to have been a third shot without my hearing it.[31]

Neither her parents nor her sister, she maintained, had ever referred to the discharge of a third shot.

Walsh was remarkably incurious about her sojourn with Paterson at the Café Belge. Yet in her pretrial statement, she claimed to have been kidnapped by Paterson:

> The officer then took my hat, still holding the revolver in his hand, so that I should have to go with him. I did not want to go but he forced me at the point of a revolver.[32]

Neither was Walsh apparently interested in finding out why Duquenoy had not attempted to escape or summon assistance. In court, she clearly had a substantial motive for trying to emphasize the involuntary nature of her role in Paterson's escape from the scene of the shooting. Walsh cannot have overlooked the possibility that she could have been telling a pack of lies about being kidnapped. When re-examined by Captain Odgers, she changed her story:

> I saw the sergeant fall to the ground. He was standing up when I first saw him. When I heard the second shot I saw the sergeant fall. I was then at the door which was open. It was hearing the first shot which made me go towards the door. I have never heard anyone using the term 'fucking bastard'.[33]

In response to further questions by the court, Augustine Duquenoy commented in greater detail about Paterson's self-inflicted wound:

> There was a hole in accused's breeches where the wound was and also in the pocket of his coat. When I went to the door after the first shot I saw the accused with the revolver in his hand. He was putting it back into his pocket. The wound on accused's leg was deep. It took an hour 1 1/2 hours on foot to walk from my house to the Café Belge.[34]

Assisted by the interpreter, Mlle Neomi Duquenoy, Augustine's sister, was the next witness to testify. She formally identified Paterson and confirmed that he was the officer who had been in her house on the night of 3 July and recalled:

> I saw a sergeant walking about in the lane leading from our house to the main road. I saw the accused later talking to the sergeant about 8.50pm. They were then in the lane. I went to draw some water from the well and went back into the house. My child was crying and I went to get it out of the cradle. The accused then came in for some tea and my sister and accused had tea together. I poured it out. The accused and my sister went out of the house at about 9.00pm. I went back to my room and heard a shot which was not very distinct. I then heard another shot very well. I then went to the door and saw a British soldier lying on the ground. I did not see the accused or the corporal of police. I did not see the accused again that night.[35]

Cross-examined briefly by Walsh, Neomi concurred with her sister's recollection and swore that she also had heard only two shots fired.

Before the court rose at the end of the day's proceedings, it heard evidence from two medical witnesses. Lieutenant John Allen, RAMC, the orderly medical officer at Beaumarais Camp, recalled being summoned to examine the deceased detective at the

Duquenoy house on 3 July.[36] Captain Arthur Pryce, RAMC, the pathologist who examined Collison's corpse on 5 July, informed the court about Collison's injuries:

> Death was caused by a gunshot wound to the chest. The bullet entered close to the right nipple and was found under the skin of the left sixth rib. In its course it had passed through both lungs and the heart.

Under cross-examination by Walsh, Pryce added:

> The bullet entered the body near the right nipple towards the side going a little downwards and a little backwards. I think that the revolver must have been aimed at the side of the man. It could not have been aimed at the front of the chest.[37]

The testimony of a succession of witnesses who gave evidence on 12 September, albeit not in chronological order, mostly addressed developments that had taken place after Collison's death. Thus Private Edward Roper told the court that he had been sitting in a café in Beaumarais, 'between the Dunkirk Road and the Railway' when he heard a shot. His curiosity aroused, Roper left the café and went to the Duquenoy's cottage, where he found the Duquenoy sisters' father and Collison's corpse. He mentioned in court that en route he had briefly encountered Stockton but did not disclose what had been said to him by the police detective.[38]

Special Commissaire Eugene Mollex, one of the French officers who had finally apprehended Paterson, told the court about Paterson's arrest, though not the means by which his whereabouts had been traced to St Omer. He submitted in evidence some items confiscated from Paterson, including a British officer's Advance Book and a revolver, loaded with one cartridge. Mollex also disclosed that under interrogation Paterson had expressed personal regret on learning that Collison had died.[39]

Private John Campbell, an Argyll & Sutherland Highlander who recalled seeing a couple proceeding away from the house, observed Paterson's departure from the Duquenoy's house. He told the court:

> [Paterson] had his cap in his right hand.... He was in a bent position going along the railway.... The girl had no hat on. She had hold of the officer's right arm with her two hands. She was a pace in front of the accused.[40]

Private Jack Landau's evidence and responses to cross-examination by the court revealed nothing about Paterson's lethal behaviour but what they had to relate directly contradicted Stockton's version of events. Landau had heard a shot and a cry, presumably Augustine's, while crossing the lane near the Duquenoy's house and had tried to stop Stockton running away. Landau recalled:

> I thought he had done something wrong. He was very excited and agitated. He told me that an officer had shot a sergeant. He did not say that there had been more than one shot. He did not suggest that the officer had fired a third shot. He did not say that he himself had been shot at. He asked me if I had a rifle ... I turned round directly I heard the shot. The corporal was then running towards me down the railway line between the railway line and the yard. Had he been running down the [garden] path I could not have seen him.[41]

Since the first shot had been muffled, it must have been the second discharge that Landau would have heard. If so, Stockton must already have been running away when the second shot was fired and could not therefore have seen Paterson pointing his revolver at Collison.

Stockton was recalled to testify, and Walsh asked him why neither he nor Collison had been armed. The detective explained:

> Every policeman carries a revolver while on duty. I was not carrying one that day as I was on a duty which made it dangerous to carry a revolver. I carried one the day before and the day after. My orders were to carry a revolver and Sergeant Collison would have the same orders.

He told the Prosecuting Officer:

> Some have the big Smith & Wesson revolver but I had the small Webley. I had never seen Sergeant Collison with anything but the big service revolver. No one but policemen at the base wear revolvers at the hip as far as I am aware. Both Sergeant Collison and I were wearing artillery badges to conceal that we were police. It did not occur to me that the arresting of an absentee officer would be a particularly dangerous duty.

In response to further cross-examination by the court, Stockton added:

> I have had orders to carry my revolver when on ordinary police duty, but when on detective duty we are given a free hand. I was working on the railways and I had to get underneath the couplings and that is why I did not carry a revolver.[42]

He stepped down and the case for the prosecution was concluded. The case for the defence involved only one witness, Paterson himself. He stated:

> I am twenty-eight years of age. Before the war I was trading in West Africa and returned to England in February 1914. I enlisted in April 1915 in the 17th Battalion Middlesex Regiment. I came out to France in December 1915. I was out here in the ranks till March 1917. I have been twice wounded. I was wounded first on the Somme in 1916 and again that year in November at

Beaumont Hamel. I went to a cadet school. I was gazetted in September 1917 and came out to France again on November 16th, 1917. I came out as a draft and was attached to the 1st Essex Regiment from the end of November 1917 until the 26th of March 1918. I had never been in any trouble with my regiment till the latter date. I knew Miss Duquenoy before the 3rd July 1918. It was a habit of mine to carry a revolver. I made it a matter of habit when in Africa. I bought it because it was more handy than the service revolver. The evidence of Stockton as to my interview with Sergeant Collison in the street and their watching the house is substantially correct. I never was minded to pick a quarrel with either Collison or Stockton. They had treated me kindly, I had told the sergeant who I was; I was under the impression that I was being arrested for desertion. Nothing occurred between 7.30pm and 9.20pm to arouse the anger of myself or Collison or Stockton. I came out of the house at 9.20pm as Sergeant Collison came into the courtyard to make him think I intended to go with him just then. We stood chatting while Sergeant Collison called for the corporal [Stockton] who was on the railway embankment. My revolver was in my right hand breeches pocket. I did not have my hand upon it when I first went out but afterwards I placed both hands in my pockets.

Since the case for the defence hinged on Paterson's claim that his revolver had been discharged accidentally, Walsh enquired about the reliability of the pistol, an Imperial No.2. Paterson explained:

> The revolver goes off very easily and the safety catch worked loose and could be easily shifted. I was talking to Collison and I told him he had better call the corporal. The corporal was about six yards from me inside the yard. I put my hand in my pocket and it went off and I shot myself in the groin. I then pulled the revolver out of my pocket and I had pulled it clear of my pocket when the revolver went off again. After the first shot, the sergeant said, What's that?' and seemed to make a grab. My impression was that he was surprised and startled. He made no apparent attempt to close with me. There was no reason why I should fire off the second shot. It was [went?] off like a mousetrap.

He also described what happened in the immediate aftermath of the shooting.

> I could then see Corporal Stockton. Sergeant Collison was slightly to my left front and the corporal was about six yards away more to my left from where the first shot was fired. Sergeant Collison may have taken a pace away in the direction of the corporal. At no time before the second shot was fired did Collison come in a position which was facing me.

Paterson went on to explain his motives for brandishing the gun:

> I pulled out the revolver in some mad-brained scheme to scare these fellows off. I had often in fun done the same thing abroad. I do not mean I was doing this in fun. It occurred to me that if I pointed the revolver the two men would run as I did not wish to be taken that night. It is not true that I took deliberate aim at the sergeant. I was never minded to shoot the sergeant. It was not a reasonable proposition to expect to get away after firing a revolver so close to a main road.

Paterson concluded his evidence by reflecting:

> I realized the position in which I was. I did not know that I had killed the sergeant. I could have sworn that I hadn't killed him, owing to the position of my arm. I did not brandish the revolver towards Stockton while he was at the gate. It was still in my hand. I did not fire a third shot towards him. If I had I could have hit him, as I'm a good shot, I was less than 11 yards from him. I did not fire a third shot at all. I think there were four cartridges in my revolver on that evening. I had discharged one round between the 2nd July and the 3rd July leaving one round in my revolver. I left one round in my revolver for myself. I discharged the other one because an accident had already occurred. I ejected the third cartridge I did not discharge it.[43]

Captain Odgers then began a rigorous cross-examination of Paterson, who immediately accepted full responsibility for the killing:

> I admit that Sergeant Collison met his death as the result of a revolver shot fired by me. My defence is that it was accidental.

Initially, Paterson explained to Odgers, he had been under the impression that Collison and Stockton were unarmed. However, after settling down for tea in the Duquenoy house he had revised his opinion and surmised that the two detectives may have been carrying pistols. He continued:

> My revolver was in my breeches pocket, possibly quarter of an hour before the shooting. I had taken it out of my back hip pocket at about nine o'clock that night in order to examine it and put it in my front pocket after examining the safety catch. It was less dangerous [than?] in the hip pocket. I placed it in my front pocket because it was easier to pull out. It may have passed through my mind to unload the revolver when I examined it. I had the revolver when going for a walk that afternoon in my hip pocket. I knew the safety catch was likely to slip off or it may have worked off in my pocket. About 9.00pm, before leaving the house I said to Mlle Duquenoy that I was going to clear them off and would take my revolver.

Paterson told the court that after shooting Collison:

> I moved towards the gate to see if the corporal was hiding there. My revolver was in my hand. Mlle Duquenoy then came and took me by the hand. I did not go back into the house but I looked in as my cane was there, but I did not go in as I had no time. I did not intend to give myself up that night.

In response to further questions from Odgers, Paterson tried to explain how Collison had been killed entirely by accident. He explained:

> Collison is about my height. The revolver must have been fired down. The sergeant appeared to duck and that is why the bullet struck him where it did, as he was in a lower position. There may have been five bullets in my revolver that afternoon. I swear I did not fire three shots in the yard. I take it that the revolver stopped going off because I ceased to press the trigger. I had no intention of firing it. I pressed the trigger accidentally.

During the course of his responses to Odgers' inquisition, Paterson recalled that Augustine Duquenoy had taken him by the hand and they had fled to a hotel, where they stayed for a couple of nights. She had dressed his wound and Paterson had assured her that he had only wounded Collison.

Although Paterson's recovery was not of immediate relevance, presumably in response to an enquiry from Walsh, about his own wound Paterson commented:

> I did not go to any hospital in Calais. I first saw a doctor when I was arrested after I came to Boulogne and I have since been examined by other doctors who saw the wound in my leg. The wound was unattended by a medical man for about four weeks.

Although he had already confessed that he had intended to use the revolver to intimidate the police detectives, the court again questioned Paterson about his motives, eliciting the following response:

> My original intention was to produce the revolver with the intention of intimidating the police, but when it went off in my pocket it upset my calculations and I pulled it out and it went off again. My intention of frightening the police wasn't carried out.

He concluded his defence by explaining, 'I went away owing to the girl's influence and not wishing to bring her into the case.'

The closing argument by the prosecutor was relatively brief. The written proceedings noted Odgers claiming:

> There is only one question for the decision of the court. The presumption is exceedingly strong that the shooting was committed with the intention of

> escaping arrest. On accused's [own] statement he went out with the intention of flourishing the revolver to frighten the police away. The accused says that the first shot was a surprise but after that he deliberately took the revolver out of his pocket with his finger on the trigger and says that it went off. The accused knew that the sergeant was there to arrest him and on his own statement he did not mean to be arrested that night. Counsel submitted that he put the revolver in his front pocket with the intention of firing it from a concealed position and by mistake he wounded himself. If the court is satisfied that there was not a third shot, they might feel that such reliance cannot be placed on the story of Stockton ... but even in that case Stockton may simply have made a mistake. He definitely says that he saw the accused fire the revolver at Collison. Counsel submitted that the story told by Stockton was a true story....[44]

In response, Lieutenant Walsh argued for Paterson's action to be treated as manslaughter and maintained that Stockton had lied. The written proceedings recorded what the Defending Counsel's contention:

> There are three verdicts possible (1) Murder (2) Manslaughter (3) Not guilty. Counsel submitted that where the weapon and the action of the accused would necessarily cause death, that was murder; but if the weapon used and the action

> of the accused would not necessarily cause death, it would be manslaughter. If the court does not accept the word of the accused in its entirety, I think accused was minded to threaten the police by the production of a revolver, and if, in the course of his action, he produces a revolver to frighten them and it goes off, then he may be guilty of manslaughter not murder. Counsel submitted that Stockton had the strongest motive for telling a lie. If accused fired a third shot he must have fired it deliberately at Stockton and could not be heard to say that he had not fired at the sergeant deliberately.

Finally, the Judge Advocate addressed the court. Summing up, Major Green said:

> It having been admitted by the accused that Detective Sergeant Collison died as the result of a revolver shot fired by the accused, the court has to consider the circumstances under which that shot was fired. Lance Corporal Stockton is the only witness for the prosecution who actually saw the shot fired, although, immediately after the sergeant fell, Mlle A. Duquenoy came out of the house and states that she then saw accused by the yard gate with the revolver in his hand, and Corporal Stockton was running down the garden path. Stockton swears that [the] accused deliberately pointed the revolver at Sergeant Collison and took deliberate aim, and the accused

had sworn that he put his hand in his pocket and the first shot went off by accident and wounded him and that he then pulled the revolver out of his pocket and it went off by accident a second time and shot the Sergeant, also that he pressed the trigger accidentally. The court must consider all the circumstances, especially [the] accused's statement to Mlle Duquenoy before he left the house and his statement that he pulled out the revolver under some mad brain scheme of scaring these fellows away. The court must also consider whether, after the first shot, the accused must have known that the safety catch was not at safety when he pulled the revolver from his pocket. The court must either accept the evidence of Stockton or of the accused as to the second shot.

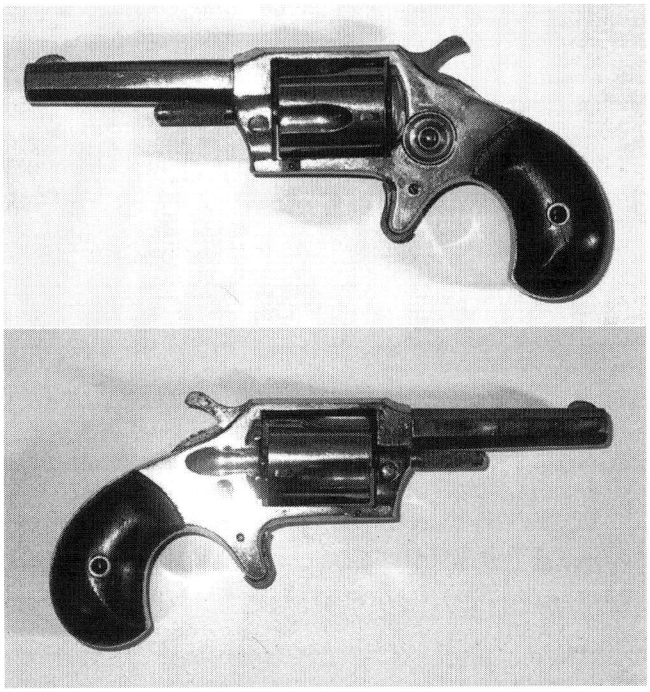

An Imperial No.2 revolver, 1915 model.

The Judge Advocate dealt with the evidence concerning the third shot but the written transcript of the trial does record in detail exactly what he said before moving on to formally remind the court about the legal distinction between manslaughter and murder. If the court was not fully satisfied about their verdict Major Green maintained that Paterson should be given the benefit of the doubt.[45]

The court rose and retired to deliberate for a while and concluded that Paterson was guilty of murder. It then re-convened to hear evidence concerning the remaining charges, to which Paterson had pleaded guilty. The court accepted his plea with reference to the cheque fraud charges but desertion was a capital offence, and the court was required by the Army to enter a formal plea of not guilty.

The prosecution called only four witnesses: Sergeant Appleton and Corporal Sword, who testified about the departure and duration of Paterson's absence, and Corporal Stockton and Commissionaire Mollex, who gave evidence about Paterson's arrest.[46] Their testimony was brief and referred in passing to the killing of Collison. The witnesses were not cross-examined by Lieutenant Walsh; the prosecutor waived the opportunity to deliver a closing address, and there was no summing up by the Judge Advocate. The court found Paterson guilty of desertion and sentenced him to death.

Field Marshal Sir Douglas Haig confirmed the sentence and on Tuesday, 24 September, Lieutenant John Henry Paterson was executed by firing squad at Boulogne. The ritual killing was choreographed by Major Eusabius Andrewes, Deputy Assistant Provost Marshal, Boulogne, and the medical officer who signed the death certificate recorded that Paterson's death at 6.27 1/2 am had been instantaneous.[47]

With reference to Paterson's court martial, everything appears cut and dried. Collison was murdered by Paterson, an act unmitigated by any claim on the latter's part that he had been disorientated or temporarily deranged by having accidentally wounded himself in the groin before discharging the second, fatal, shot. Declaring by way of a defence that the pistol had a faulty safety catch was flimsy distraction from the killer's clear intent to threaten to shoot the two detectives, whether they were themselves armed or unarmed. However, a number of other associated issues may account for the lingering sense of mystery to which Babington alluded in his summary of the case.

Exactly what covert duty the two detectives were undertaking at the Pont-de-Coulogne has never been established. However, Collison's identification of the wanted man appears to have been fortuitous, which may go some way to account for the detective's ultimately fatal procrastination. Posthumous criticism of the career policeman's misplaced deference to Paterson's commissioned status fails to take due account of Paterson's unchallenging demeanour and disarmingly polite responses to the detective's questions. There was nothing mysterious about Stockton's behaviour; when pressed to explain his conduct, he candidly admitted that being unarmed, he had run away because he did not wish to be shot by Paterson. That said, Stockton therefore had good reason to reinforce the impression that Paterson was a cold-blooded killer.[48]

Even after allowing for flaws in the translation of her statements, the personal status and testimony of Augustine Duquenoy remains ambiguous and unsatisfactory. Given her role in assisting Paterson to escape from the crime scene, she was an accessory to murder yet she was not charged with any criminal offence. French and British interrogation failed to disclose details about her relationship with Paterson, even though he alluded in court to having 'known' her before 3 July. There even remains an intriguing possibility that Augustine may even have been aware of his whereabouts after 5 July, when they parted company at the Café Belge.[49]

If they were lovers then Augustine was truly a femme fatale because she doomed Paterson in court with her references to him checking his revolver and declaring his intention to use the weapon to threaten Collison and Stockton. Her decision to appear as a key witness for the prosecution could be attributed to a combination of rational self-interest and understandable fickleness in her affections. She excused her role in Paterson's escape from the Duquenoy home by maintaining that he had intimidated her with his revolver. Her allegation reinforced the impression that notwithstanding his groin injury, Paterson was a calculating, gun-toting desperado, coercing a vulnerable young woman. The extent of Augustine's vulnerability was never explored but she was twenty-two years old and like her sister, apparently an unmarried mother with an infant child. The location of the Duquenoy home hints at their economic disadvantage, if not actually impoverishment, and the poorly executed signatures that Augustine and Neomi Duquenoy penned at the foot of their pre-trial statements suggests both sisters may have also been barely literate.[50] These points of vulnerability may have been exploited by

Paterson but could no less easily have been influential in Augustine's ill-explored and therefore mysterious relationship with the French police and British military authorities.

The emotional damage wrought by Collison's death and the War Office created a mystery about Paterson's demise that was ignored by Babington and has hitherto been ill addressed in other accounts.[51] The trauma experienced by the Duquenoy family would have been eclipsed by the anguish of a couple of grieving widows: Louisa Collison, the murdered detective's wife, and Alice, Lieutenant Paterson's 40-year-old spouse.

Alice Willett, a sewing machinist, had married Second Lieutenant *James* Henry Paterson at West Ham Registry Office on 12 November 1917.[52] They had lived in connubial bliss for only a couple of nights before he was posted back to France and they were compelled to sustain their marriage by correspondence. However, after 26 March 1918, her letters began to be returned; Alice became worried and was already upset before 18 April, when a War Office telegram notified her that her husband had been posted missing. In July, the authorities informed her that he was no longer missing but since her letters were still being returned, Alice began lobbying the Essex regimental depot and the War Office.

During October, after being officially notified that her husband had 'died on service in France on 24

September, 1918,' she entreated the War Office to disclose further details about his fate:

> Owing to the absence of any details respecting his death excepting the one message which you kindly forwarded to me, I feel that I must ask if you can convey to me the principles by which he met his death and to whether he left any message for me as I am in that unfortunate position of knowing nothing whatsoever. Forgive the trouble I may cause you but I am nearly broken-hearted to know nothing of him. The whole case seems to me very confusing further words I cannot state.[53]

Alice's brother-in-law also begged the authorities for information:

> She [Mrs Paterson] being quite unable to bear this awful strain any longer, what with the anxiety of no news coupled with the fact of no financial assistance coming to her from her husband and last but not least, being unable to do business herself owing to continuance of ill-health.[54]

The official response to these entreaties took the form of a letter that was less than wholly transparent:

> In reply to your letter of November 20th, 1918 asking that you may be given the principles by which your late husband met his death, it was hoped that, as you had not ere this referred to

> this office letter which conveyed to you the news that he died in France upon September 24th, 1918, you would not ask for any details. However as you do now ask it is with extreme grief that I am directed to tell you that he was shot at 6.27am on that date consequent upon a sentence of death passed upon him by a General Court Martial and confirmed by the Field Marshal Commanding the British Forces in the Field. He was found guilty of desertion and other crimes. In conveying to you the above solemn sad facts I am directed to offer to you yourself the deepest sympathy in your great sorrow.[55]

Alice Paterson never discovered from the War Office the full extent of her husband's murderous misdeeds and was spared having to settle his unpaid debts, which included an overdrawn account with bankers Cox & Co. and an outstanding bill for an officer's uniform supplied by an Edinburgh outfitter during late 1917.[56] Nevertheless, his execution must have caused her to question why her beloved had, without any explanation, broken her heart and besmirched the good reputation of his regiment by running away. Alice seems to have known little about his family and when required by the War Office to state her late husband's birthplace, she wrote: 'Bow (I believe).'[57]

As with other details about her husband's life, it was almost correct because James was born in Stepney during 1887, the youngest son of Joseph and Matilda

Sarah Peterson. His father was a jobbing builder and his three older brothers worked as painters and decorators, but James attended Forest Gate Commercial & Civil Service College, where he was awarded a teaching certificate. If he ever secured a teaching appointment it may have been only for a comparatively short time because by 1911, James Peterson was employed as a commercial clerk in Mile End, working for Nathan Sampson & Co., boot and shoe retailers.[58]

For reasons that remain unexplained, when James Paterson enlisted at West Africa House in Holborn during April 1915, he identified himself as John Henry Paterson, a storekeeper, aged twenty-five years and ten months. During his court martial, Paterson added that his storekeeping activities entailed working in West Africa, where he had become accustomed to carrying a pistol. He was never quizzed about these claims and, in the absence of documentary corroboration and with the benefit of hindsight, such inexactitudes undermine the reliability of anything Paterson had to say during his trial. Even so, prior to 26 March 1918, he had been a good soldier and the London Metropolitan Police reported that he had never been charged or convicted of any civil offences.[59]

Paterson never hinted about the reason why he decided to recklessly abandon the men under his command. However, the location and circumstantial evidence does not suggest that his desertion was premeditated and his medical history admits speculation about battle trauma having played a part in prompting him to go absent. Yet Paterson never raised the issue in his own defence and soldiers went absent at the front for many reasons, not all of which were combat-related. In Paterson's case, two developments may have caused him to desert: the burden of indebtedness and near suicidal disenchantment at the prospect of being mutilated or killed in action.

At the time he deserted, Paterson was heavily in debt and liable to have been censured by a court martial and probably cashiered like many other subalterns with modest incomes who lived beyond their means. On being awarded his commission at Gailes Camp, Paterson had kitted himself out with lieutenant's uniform and accoutrements from Anderson & Sons in Edinburgh. His purchases on account had not been settled and he was being pressed to pay £52 4/8d but even before paying his regimental mess bills, Paterson's weekly income as a subaltern was only £5 and neither his wife, widowed mother or immediate relatives were wealthy enough to bail him out. It appears beyond coincidence that during his travels as a fugitive, he adopted the surname 'Anderson' when cashing cheques that sustained him financially.[60]

Other than as a general colloquial reference to symptoms of combat-related stress, reference to shell shock had ceased to figure in medical diagnosis by British Army medical officers long before Paterson deserted. Nor is there any indication that even had a medical board examined him that Paterson would have been classified as suffering from NYDN (i.e. Not Yet Diagnosed, Nerves). However, after being wounded and subjected to enemy artillery bombardment, as well as having spent almost three months on duty behind the lines, he would have been understandably apprehensive at the prospect of returning to the front line while a major enemy offensive was in progress.

Because he was a recently-commissioned 'temporary gentlemen' who had been afforded little opportunity to engage socially with his fellow officers, any expression of weakness would not have been viewed sympathetically, neither could he have shared his fears with the men under his command. Paterson had not attended a public school or gone to university so he could not call for assistance from an influential old boys' network and, in any case, surrendering his commission and returning to the ranks would not have guaranteed more than a temporary relief from trench warfare.

As a veteran he knew all too well that in taking the path that led away from the trenches at Zillebeke he was effectively committing suicide. During his court martial, he claimed, 'I left one round in my revolver for myself,' and had he not been suddenly been immobilized by French police officers, Paterson may very well have saved the Army time and further trouble by shooting himself.

Conclusion: Worthy is the Lamb that was Slain

It would be surprising if everyone who has examined these cases does not share the reservations expressed in the body of this book. However, it is possible to advance a few reasonably uncontentious conclusions about the murderers and their crimes.

The defendants were all working class men, mostly mature, trained, professional killers and not callow youths bamboozled by patriotic flummery or unwilling conscripts. Paterson was the only one who enjoyed more than an elementary education and there is little to suggest that collectively they were particularly articulate or adept at self-advocacy. With the exception of Price and Moore, their records of service were generally free of criminal convictions and custodial sentences but in at least eight cases, there was unequivocal evidence that the defendants had been drinking or were drunk when they committed their offences. In terms of their general social characteristics, there is little that sets them apart from most of their victims or the mass of their contemporaries serving as infantrymen on the Western Front.

Except for the murder of Henriette Tremerel, the killings were all-military affairs in which the murderers used rifles to slaughter comrades from their own or immediately adjacent military formations. Their weapons of choice were unexceptional and there was no subterfuge about the manner in which they committed their crimes. Notwithstanding hints to the contrary, in the cases of Price, Bell and possibly Moore, there is no verifiable evidence to imply that their lethal conduct was aided or abetted by other soldiers. In general, the killings were abhorred and customary formal and informally expressed commiserations were communicated to a victim's family. However, as the Morgan family correspondence demonstrates, comradely condolences could also be despatched to an executed man's family.

General courts martial tried Chisholm, Paterson and probably Morgan and Price; all the other hearings involved field general courts martial, usually with a courts martial officer in attendance. Only Chisholm and Knight, and possibly also Morgan and Price, were faced with having to defend themselves without assistance from a Prisoner's Friend. Even so, critical re-examination of these murder cases yields further support to established criticism of the legal frailties of the wartime courts martial that sentenced men to death for desertion and cowardice.

A convening officer was required to choose the commissioned officers selected to conduct the trials and identify the prosecutor and court martial officer in the pro forma schedule of proceedings. As is evident from notes about their respective backgrounds, between these officers and a defendant there existed a social crevasse and an associated miasma of class justice, undispersed by the appointment of an upper-crust barrister to act as a Prisoner's Friend. Nor may such criticism be relieved by acknowledging a whiff of injustice to be readily detectable in the vicinity of the bench, bar and criminal courts of England.

The officers staffing the courts martial that sentenced soldiers to death for murder manifested little or no interest in identifying what caused defendants to kill their comrades. In case after case, officers focussed their attention narrowly on the immediate situation in which the homicidal act had taken place, and in practice the primary function of the hearing appears to have been to confirm a defendant's guilt. In assessing motives for pulling the trigger, little account was taken by the courts martial of a defendant's drunken, distressed or deranged mental state at the time an offence was committed. Making due allowance for Paterson's reference to committing suicide, even had regulations permitted otherwise there is no evidence that the other defendants would have opted to plead guilty.

In addition to the socially restricted profile of officers staffing the courts martial, institutional considerations also influenced the confirmatory process. Unreservedly accepting the dictum, 'The object of military law is to maintain discipline among the troops,' most confirming officers appear to have dwelt on inappropriate soldierly conduct rather than the act of the killing of another human being.[1] In other cases, a convicted murderer's fate was decided by a scanty assessment of his character, based on personal behaviour and, rather ironically, his record as a fighting man.

Allowing for the occasional recommendation to mercy, at no point did almost anyone involved in the confirmatory process consider what might have been the consequences of commuting a death sentence awarded for murder to a term of imprisonment. Exemplified by comments from Lieutenant General Sir Henry Wilson and Major General Sir Reginald Barnes, such considerations were clearly not beyond the imagination or intelligence of confirming officers.[2] Moreover, the discrimination evident in the pattern of convictions and punishments awarded officer-defendants who were court-martialled during the war showed considerable leniency, and even the majority of soldiers who were sentenced to death for desertion did not face a firing squad.[3]

Ultimately, the execution of all murderers was a consistently exercised choice, if not an openly declared policy, sanctioned by Field Marshal Sir John French and Field Marshal Sir Douglas Haig. They personally endorsed culling the proverbial black sheep from amongst the flocks herded into the trenches – and are consequently no less worthy of being dubbed comrades of Cain than the men whose deaths they ordained.

Notes

Introduction

[1] Babington, A., (1983).

[2] Putkowski & J. Sykes, Authors' Statement (1989).

[3] Moore (1974); Gill & Dallas (1975); (1985), pp.39-44.

[4] e.g. http://complaints.pccwatch.co.uk/case/3357 / (2001).

[5] Corns & Hughes-Wilson, p.371.

[6] The authors' assertion appears at odds with procedural advice stated in MML (1914) 61, p.46, namely, 'The court must never forget that the principle of English law is, that the accused person is innocent until proved guilty to be guilty ... the burden of proof lies on the prosecution.'

[7] Ibid.

[8] Hanna, p.110.

[9] See: www.shotatdawn.info/index.html; Walker, pp.179-203; Putkowski (2008), pp.17-26.

[10] On the authoritarian behaviour of British Army officers, see Oram (2003), pp.39-65.

[11] See Appendix 3: Crime and Punishment: British Army Courts Martial, August 1914-November 1918.

[12] In 1908 the right of appeal was granted to defendants found guilty of murder and sentenced to death by a criminal court.

[13] Pte. No. G7775 William Damper: Army Record of Service: Ms Letter: Mary Damper, Cathedral Walk, Cork to Royal Engineers, Chatham, rec'd in Registry, 11.10.16; See Ch.6: *The Missing Kilt.* Further information about the couple may be derived from the English C19th Census returns, and *Dampier* in the Irish Census returns for 1901 and 1911.

Chapter 1

[1] Hughie Job Hayes, b. 1881, Hounslow, Middx; educ. Duke of York's R.M. Sch., 1892; No.5848, Welsh Regt., 1896. Served: India; South Africa; Egypt; disch. 9.8.14; recalled to colours; C.S.M., No.5019, 2nd Bn. Welsh Regt.; to BEF, 13.8.14; DOW, 21.1.15.

[2] Robert Graves, pp.93-4.

[3] WO 95/1281, War Diary: 2nd Bn. Welsh Regt., 18.5.15 records Graves' arrival during the evening with a draft of fellow officers from 3rd Bn. R.W.F.. See also: Dunn, pp.125-6; 130-2; 134.

[4] Record of Service: William Price, b. Ystradyfodwg, Glamorganshire, 1873; Collier; Pte. No.2932, 2nd Bn. Welsh Regt., 1891; India, 1891-1903; L/Cpl. No.12942; to BEF, 30.11.14.

[5] 1911 Census: William Price, b. Pentre Ystrad; rag collector (patient), College Hospital, Pontypridd.

[6] Record of Service: Richard Morgan; 1911 Census; Morgan Family.

[7] WO 95/1281, War Diary, 2nd Bn. Welsh Regt., 31.10.15-2,11.15 records the Commanding Officer and over half the battalion were killed wounded or missing during the fighting around Gheluvelt. See also encl. letter: Marden to Edmonds, 14.11.32.

[8] Marden, p.332. See also Blackburne, p.32.

[9] Ibid., War Diary (op. cit.), 30.12.14 noted that men getting stuck fast in the mud were rendered immobile for hours.

[10] Ms. letter: Richard Morgan to Wife, 20.1.15. Saunders Papers.

[11] When the trial took place, the 2nd Bn. Welch Regt. was billeted in at Labeuvrière, a village 8km east of Bethune; Lillers is a small town situated circa 11km north-west of Bethune.

[12] Henry Cecil Lowther, b. Ampthill, Beds., 1869; 2/Lt. Scots Guards, 1888; Lt., 1892; Capt.,

1899; Staff Capt. & DAAG, 1901; Bde. Maj., 1902; Mil. Att., 1905; Mil. Sec., to Duke of Connaught 1911; O.C., 1st Guards Bde., 1913. Archer Geoffrey Lyttleton, b. 1884; educ. Haileybury, 1897 and Trinity Coll., Cambridge, 1906; 2/Lt., Welsh Regt., 1906; Lt., 1908; Adjt., 1910-13; Capt., 1913; Staff Capt., 3rd Brigade, 1.11.14.

[13] Blackburne, op. cit., p.40.

[14] If Graves resume (op. cit., p.94) is correct about the location, it seems quite likely that the execution took place at the Carmelite Convent, Bethune. 'Stick it, Welsh' was alleged to have been the final exhortation uttered by Captain Haggard, 2nd Bn. Welsh Regt., DOW 15.9.14. For a contrasting reaction by a French observer attending a British military execution, see Putkowski & Sykes (1992 edn.), pp.250-1.

[15] i.e. Jane and Richard Morgan, Coal Miner, 33 Consort Street, Mountain Ash, Glamorganshire. Richard was their eldest son.

[16] Ms. letter: Pte. No.12379 T. Day to Mrs & Mr John Morgan, 26.4.15, Saunders Papers; Thomas Charles Day, b. Llanwonno, Glam., 1874; Pte. No.12379, 2nd Bn. Welsh Regt.; to BEF, 29.11.14. Day, a married man, lived at 1, Consort Street, Miskin, Mountain Ash.

[17] Ms. Letter: Pte. Rees Bevan, A Coy., 2nd Bn. Welsh Regt. to Mr & Mrs John Morgan, n.d. (circa April 1915). Rees Davies Bevan, b. Miskin, Glam., 1883; Collier; Pte. No.7145, 2 Bn. Welsh Regt., 9.6.02; South Africa; India; to BEF, 9.11.14. Bevan's family were near neighbours of Mr & Mrs Morgan.

Chapter 2

[1] On the typical composition and wartime activities of a Fortress Company, RE, see: Sambrook, iv-v; pp.18-26; 44; 90-7; 109-118.

[2] Acting Corporal No.14780 Alexander Chisholm, b. Newcastle-on-Tyne, 1884; Fitter, Steam Engines; 2nd Cpl., Royal Engineers, Colchester, 1911; 20th Fortress Coy., RE; to BEF, October 1914.

[3] Robert Lewis, b. Whitchurch, Glamorganshire, 1871; Carpenter (wagon), 1901; Wagon Carpenter (railways) 1911. L/Cpl. No.348, 1st Glamorgan Fortress Coy., RE; to BEF, 30.12.14.

[4] WO 71/415, GCM, Statement: William Hart Hann, b. Cardiff, 1894; Plumber; Pte. No.463, 1st Glamorgan Fortress Coy. RE 1911; L/Cpl. to BEF, 30.12.14. Lewis was either wrong or being wilfully mischievous because the movement order was associated with the deployment of troops and the Battle of Frezenberg Ridge. See: WO

95/328, War Diary, 20th Fortress Coy., RE., 8-13.5.15.

[5] Ibid.

[6] Ibid., Statement: Freeman. Thomas H. Freeman, b. Swansea, 1886; Joiner; 2nd Cpl. No.4914, 20th Fortress Coy., RE; to BEF 21.3.15.

[7] Ibid., Testimony: Charles. Charles. Richard Charles, b. 1885, Ireland;L & LM, 1909; LRCPI & LM, 1909; FRCSI, 1912; Surgeon, Ipswich Hosp., 1913; Lt., RAMC, 2.9.14; to BEF, 7.11.14. Subsequently became a world famous expert on abdominal gunshot wounds (Obit., BMJ, 1:708, 14.3.64).

[8] GCM: Evidence against Acting Corporal No.14780, Alexander Chisholm, 20th Fortress Coy., RE. Alexander Gavin Stevenson, b. South Shields, 1871; 2/Lt., RE, 1891; Lt., 1894; Capt., 1901; Maj., 1910; to BEF, 14.8.14.

[9] Ibid., GCM, Schedule: Francis William Towsey, b. 1864; Lt., West Yorks. Regt., 1885; Capt., 1892; Maj., 1894; Adjt., 1892-1903; Maj., 1904; Lt. Col., 1914; to BEF, 9.9.14. William Claudius Casson Ash, b. London, 1870; 2/Lt., Middx. Regt., 1892; Lt., 1895; Capt., 1900; Adjt., Militia 1902-7; Maj., 1909; to BEF, 21.11.14. Harman Barnes Potter, b. 1882; Gold Coast Regiment; 2/Lt., East Kent Regt., 1901; Lt., 1904; Capt., 1912; to BEF, 12.8.14. Francis Alexander

Chetwood Hamilton, b. 1875; Militia; 2/Lt., Scottish Rifles, 1897; Lt., 1899; Capt., 1903; to BEF, 15.8.14. Captain John Victor Macartney, b. Ireland, 1887; educ. St Edmund's Coll., Herts.; 2/Lt., 2nd Bn. Leinster Regt., 1906; Lt., 1908; West African Frontier Force, 1911-12; to BEF, 12.9.14. Edward Burryau Luard, b. Hastings, 1870; educ. Clifton Coll.; 2/Lt., K.S.L.I., 1891; Lt., 1894; Capt., 1900; Adjt., Militia, 1902-5; Maj., 1910; to BEF, 10.9.14. William Henry Astley de la Pryme, b. Kensington, 1880; educ. Christ's Coll., Cambridge Univ.; 2/Lt., Warw. Regt., 1901; Adjt., 1903-6; Lt., 1903; Lt., W. Yorks., 1908; Capt., 1910; Adjt., 1912; to BEF, 3.9.14.

[10] Ibid., Testimony: Charles, op. cit.

[11] Ibid., Testimony: Freeman, op. cit.

[12] Ibid.

[13] Ibid., Testimony: Harris. Sapper No.19911 Harry A. Harris, 20th Fortress Coy. RE; to BEF, 15.8.14.

[14] Ibid.

[15] Ibid., Testimony: Williamson. Dvr. No.1112, George L. Williamson, RFA; to BEF, 22.8.14; 3rd Corps. HQ, Staff.

[16] Ibid.

[17] Ibid., Testimony: Hann.

[18] Ibid.

[19] Ibid.

[20] GCM, Testimony: Griffiths. Norman Griffiths, b. Cardiff, 1891; Shipwright; Sapper No.510, 1st Glamorgan Fortress Coy., RE; to BEF 30.12.14.

[21] Ibid.

[22] Charles Scott, b. West Norwood, Surrey, 1882; Royal North West Mounted Police, Canada; Cape Mounted Rifles and Cape Mounted Police, South Africa; Sgt. No.6028, Canadian Military Mounted Police, enl. 25.11.14; att. 1st Bde., HQ., BEF.

[23] Ibid., Testimony: Scott. See also MML, ch, VI: sec.49, pp.68-9; secs.71-82, pp.73-75.

[24] Ibid., Testimony: Whittaker. Dvr No.399 William H. Whittaker, ASC; to BEF, 24.3.15; att. RAMC (T).

[25] Ibid., Testimony: Kennedy. David John Kennedy, b. Cardiff, 1897; Carpenter; Sapper No.704, RE, 8.6.14; 1st Glamorgan Fortress Coy., RE; to BEF 30.12.14.

[26] Ibid., Defence Testimony: Chisholm.

[27] Ibid., Griffiths.

[28] Ibid., Schedule.

[29] Ibid., Stevenson, op. cit.

[30] Ibid., Schedule: John Sackville Richard Tufton, b. West Ashford, 1873; educ. Eton; JP, DL, Westmorland, 1894; 2/Lt, Life Guards, 1894-6; JP, Kent, 1897; Lt., 3rd Sussex Regt., 1900; Hon. Maj., 1908; Maj., 1913; to BEF, 27.2.15.

[31] MML (1914), Ch.VII, secs.52-3, p.99.

[32] GCM, Statement: Cox. William H. Cox, b. Cardiff, 1890; Plumber; Sapper No.725, 1st Glamorgan Fortress Coy., RE; to BEF, 30.12.14.

[33] Ibid., Statement: Ballard. George Edwin Ballard, b. Whitechapel, London, 1882; Brick-maker; No.28649, Gunner, RHA, 1902; Army Reserve, 1910; No.698, Sgt., Mounted Military Police, 5.8.14; to BEF, 11.8.14; 3rd Corps HQ.

[34] The significance of Chisholm's reference to French civilians was never explored but investigations may have subsequently been initiated by the local Gendarmerie.

[35] The 1911 Census confirms that Chisholm was married with a young family. After his death, his widow, Janet Chisholm, emigrated to Moline, Canada. Lewis was also married (x2? to Mary), although his children had all left school by 1915.

Chapter 3

[1] WO 71/437 FGCM: Pte. No.15437 Charles William Knight, 10th Bn. RWF, b. Fulham, 1885; Van Guard/Carman (1901); Parents: John Knight, Plasterer & Eliza Knight, Charwoman, 25, Tilton St., Fulham, London (1920).

[2] WO 95/1436 War Diary: 10th Bn., RWF, Sept. – Oct. 1915. Eecke was situated about six kilometres behind the front line trenches.

[3] Letter: P. Leonard to Leonard Family, 5.11.15, cited in Leonard & Leonard-Johnson, p.15.

[4] Ibid., pp.65, 215, refers to soup, omlettes, chips and three sous per cup of coffee being sold by residents to troops.

[5] FGCM, Schedule: Ernest St. George Pratt b. 1863; Lt., DLI, 1884; Capt. 1894; Brev. Maj., 1900; Maj., 1903; Col., 1913; Asst. Dir., WO, 28.7.13-20.7.15; T/Brig. Gen., 76th Bde., 21.7.15. If 'military exigencies or other circumstances' prevented the taking of a summary, a trial could proceed without one. MML (1914) Rules of Procedure, para. 114[C], p.633.

[6] Ibid., Percy Wilson Brown, b. 1876; 2/Lt., Gordon Highlanders, 1896; Lt., 1898; Capt., 1901; T/Lt. Col., 12.7.15. Charles Oswald Nicholson Williams, b. India, 1863; Lancs. Militia;

T/Capt., 8th Bn. KORL, 12.10.14; T/Maj., 23.11.14; to BEF, 27.9.15; KIA, 2.12.15. George Alexander Smith, b. Aberdeen, 1872; Solicitor; 2/Lt., 1st (Vol.) Bn. Gordon Highlanders, 1901; Capt., 4th Bn. Gordon Highlanders, 18.9.1908; Maj., 1913; to BEF, 19.2.15.

[7] Ibid., William Thomas Lyons, b. Belfast 1881; Corresponding Clerk (Bank); T/2Lt., 10th Bn. RWF, 5.11.14; T/Capt. 20.7.15; Adjt., 5.9.15; to BEF, 27.9.15.

[8] Ibid., Testimony: Richards. Pte. No.15617 Thomas E. Richards, 10th Bn. RWF; to BEF, 27.9.15.

[9] Ibid., Testimony: Grundy. Sgt. No.15458 Herbert H. Grundy, 10th Bn. Royal Welsh Fus.. No. Pte. No.15461 Alfred Edwards, 10th Bn. RWF, b. Ponkey, Denbighshire, 1893; Labourer (Brickworks); to BEF, 27.9.15; Pte. No.24637 Alfred Bernard Poffley, b. Reading, Painter; enl. 3rd Bn. RWF, 12.5.15; 10th Bn., RWF.

[10] Ibid., Testimony: Freeman. Major Edward Freeman, b. Isleworth, Middx., 1875; 1st (Vols.) Bn. RWF., Capt., 1900; T/Capt., 10th Battalion, RWF, 9.9.14; T/Maj., 25.9.15.

[11] Ibid., Testimony: Grellier. Bernard Grellier, b. Epsom, 1886. LDS, RCS (Eng.), 1910; MRCS, LRCP (London), 1913; Asst. Dental Surgeon, Royal Dental Hosp.; RAMC (SR), 9.9.14; Lt.,

19.9.14; Capt., 1.4.15. During 1913, Grellier gained non-dental experience as a house surgeon and casualty officer at Charing Cross Hospital.

[12] Ibid., Testimony: Parsons. Pte. No.24406 Frank Parsons, 10th Bn. RWF; to BEF, 27.9.15.

[13] FGCM, Testimony: Defence: Knight. It is possible that the medicine was antipyrine, a common prescription for headache.

[14] Ibid., After Finding.

[15] Ibid., Beresford Ash to Pratt (op.cit.), 7.11.15. William Randal Hamilton Beresford-Ash, b. 1859, Ashbrook, Co. Londonderry; 2/Lt., RWF, 1879; Lt. Col., 1st Bn. RWF, 1904; Brev. Lt. Col., 1907; retd., 1908; DL, Co. Londonderry; C.O., 10th Bn. RWF, 13.10.14.

[16] Ibid., Pratt, 76th Bde. to HQ, 3rd Div., 7.11.15.

[17] Ibid., Haldane, 3rd Div. HQ to 2nd Army 'A', 10.11.15. James Aylmer Lowthorpe Haldane, b. 1862, 2/Lt., Gordon Highlanders, 1882; Waziristan, 1894; Chitral, 1895; Tirah 1897; ADC to C-in-C East Indies 1898; S.Africa, 1899; Mil. Att. (Japanese Army) 1904; Army HQ Staff., 1906-1909; Brig Gen, 1909; O.C., 10th Bde, 1912; O.C., 3 Div.

[18] Although military law did not provide for any appeal against the verdict of a court martial,

a confirming authority could decline to confirm the sentence and direct the court to re-assemble to review its prior findings. Rules of Procedure, para. 52(A), MML (1914, p.604.

[19] FGCM, op. cit., Plumer, HQ, 2nd Army to Mellor, D.J.A.G., 11.11.15. James Gilbert Shaw Mellor, b. 1872: educ., Trinity, Cambridge Univ., BA, 1893; LLB, 1894; Barrister (Inner Temple), 1896; S.Africa, 1900; DJAG, 1911; Maj. (Brig. Gen.), Res. of Offs., 8.8.14.

[20] Borlase Edward Wyndham Childs, b. 1876; 2nd Bn. DCLI, 1900; Lt., 1904; Adjt., 1907; Capt., Royal Irish Regt., 1910; Staff Capt., W.O.; Maj., 1912. John Bartholomew Wroughton, b. 1874; 2/Lt., Ox. L.I., 1891; 2/Lt., Sussex Regt., 1893; Lt., 1896; Capt., 1900; Adjt., Vols.1902; Maj., 1911; Staff Capt., 1912; DAA & QMG, 5.8.14-31.1.15; T/Lt. Col. & A.A.G., 1.2.15.

[21] FGCM, op. cit., Wroughton to G.O.C., 3rd Div.; Maj. John Laurence Buxton, DAA & QMG, 3rd Div. to H.Q., 76th Bde., 14.11.15.

[22] Martin Patrick Grainge Leonard, b. Wigton, 1889; educ. Rossall Sch. and Oriel College, Oxford Univ., 1912; Dean (C of E) 1913; Rev., St. Wilfred's, Newton Heath, Manch.; Capt. (TF) & Chaplain (4th Class), 9.10.14; 8th Bn. KORL.

[23] Letter: P. Leonard to Leonard Family, 5.11.15, Leonard & Leonard-Johnson, op. cit., p.16.

[24] Ibid., Letter: P. Leonard to Leonard Family, 12.11.15, p.18.

[25] Ibid., Letter: P. Leonard to Leonard Family, 17.11.15, p.20.

[26] FGCM, op. cit., Grellier to C.O., 10th RWF, 15.11.15. Pte. Alfred Poffley returned to duty and saw service in Egypt and Palestine before being demobilized after the war ended. He resumed his job as a painter but the wounds he sustained permanently affected his right leg. He died in 1942.

[27] CWGC Register, Le Grand Hazard Military Cemetery: Charles William Knight, Pte. 15437, Plot 3 Row B. Grave 9.

[28] Email: Miller to Putkowski, 21.5.11, citing Osler, pp.1083-4.

[29] Email: Foxhall to Putkowski, 19.5.11. See also: Gowers; Berkovic & Crompton, pp.3-4. The authors are grateful to Dr Katherine Foxhall, Wellcome Trust Post-Doctoral Fellow, King's College, London and Dr Geoffrey Miller MBBS, MRCP (Lond.) for references and their valuable insights about Knight's symptoms.

Chapter 4

[1] James Pick, b. Inverkeithing, Fife, 1885; Coal Miner, Bannockburn; Dvr. No. T2/11207, 197th Coy., ASC, 24th Div.; to BEF, 1.9.15; A/Farrier Staff Sgt.

[2] 197th Coy., ASC was also designated 4th Coy, ASC, 24th Divisional Train.

[3] WO 95/2203, War Diary: 197th Company ASC, 24th Division, 3.1.16. The company moved from Steenvoorde to Zealand Farm, midway between Busseboom and Poperinghe on 3.1.16. On German artillery and aerial bombardment in the vicinity, see WO 95/4042, War Diary, Town Major: Poperinghe, Dec. 1915-Feb. 1916.

[4] WO 71/446 FGCM: Driver. T. Moore, Testimony: Kenny. Thomas Kenny, b. 1894; Lorryman; enl. Dvr. No.T4/040822, 197th Coy., ASC, 6.1.15; to BEF, 1.9.15.

[5] Testimony: Kenny, ibid.

[6] Testimony: Thompson. John Pickering Thompson, b. Andover, Hants, 1883; Farmer; Texas Light Horse (5 years); East Kent Yeomanry (3 years); Legion of Frontiersmen; Pte. No.2389, 10th (Public Sch.) Bn. R. Fus., 15.9.14; 2/Lt., ASC, 2.11.14; to 197th Coy., ASC, 24th Div., 2.12.14; T/Capt., 23.1.15.

[7] Robert Bagshaw. b. Manchester, 1885; Van driver; Dvr.T3/029311, No.4 Horse Transport, ASC, 16.11.14; L/Cpl., 12.12.14; To 197th Coy., ASC, 28.7.15; A/CSM, 22.8.15; to BEF 1.9.15; CSM, 23.2.16.

[8] Testimony: Hanley. Dvr. No. T2/14550 Frederick Hanley, 197th Coy., ASC; to BEF, 31.8.15.

[9] FGCM, Schedule. The order to convene the FGCM was signed on 16.2.16 by Maj. Gen. John Capper, commanding 24th Division.

[10] Ibid., Percy Cyriac Burrell Skinner, b. 1871; 2/Lt., Northants.; Lt., 1893; Capt., 1901; Maj., 1912; Lt. Col., 2.6.15; O.C., 6th Bn. Northants, 4.10.15-22.4.15. Martin Alexander, b. Melrose, Roxburghshire, 1889; 2/Lt., 3rd Bn. Rifle Bde., 1909; Lt., 1911; T/Capt., 15.11.14; Capt., 20.12.14; Bde. MG Officer, 11.10.15. Reginald Playfair Hills, b. Kensington, London, 1877; educ. Malvern and King's Coll., Oxford; Barrister (Inner Temple), 1903; Board of Education, 1903-6; T/Lt., 1.2.15; Maj., 29.9.15 6th Bn. K.O.S.B.; DAAG, Gen. List, 27.2.16; Junior Counsel, Inland Revenue. Hugh Blackburn Hunter, b. Kelso, 1880; educ. Edinburgh Univ.; Manager; 2/Lt. R. Scots (Vols.), 1902; Lt., 1908; Capt., Sanitary Service, London Mtd. Bde. (TF), 1913; Lt., ASC, 4.11.14; Capt., 15.3.15; to BEF 25.8.15; T/Maj., 9.6.15.

[11] Ibid.

[12] Ibid., Testimony: Gray. Dvr. No.T2/14509 James Gray, 197th Coy., ASC; to BEF, 30.8.15.

[13] Ibid.

[14] Ibid., Testimony: Clayton. Dvr. No.T/36300 Richard P. Clayton, 197th Coy., ASC, to BEF 30.8.15.

[15] Ibid.

[16] Ibid., Testimony: Rush. Dvr. No. T4/036664 James Rush, 197th Coy., ASC; to BEF, 30.8.15.

[17] Ibid.

[18] Ibid., Testimony: Tarbuck. Pte. No.6150 Joseph Tarbuck, 13th Bn. Middlesex Regt.

[19] Ibid., Testimony: Stevenson. Pte. No.T4/040674 John Stevenson, 197th Coy., ASC.

[20] Ibid., Testimony: Bourton. Pte. No. SB/027912 Frank Bourton, 197th Coy., ASC; to BEF, 1.9.15. Re: 'Chuck it.' Likely to have been either a more robust expletive or 'Chuck it up' (i.e. Drop it or Stop).

[21] Op. cit., Testimony, Hanley.

[22] Testimony: Farrier Corporal No. T2/9413 Patrick Driscoll, 197th Coy., ASC; to BEF, 31.8.15.

[23] Ibid., Testimony: John Keith Grant Robertson, b. Petworth, Sussex, 1895; educ. Harrow and

Edinburgh Univ.; 1912-14; Pte. No.1765 RAMC; 2/Lt., ASC, 28.11.14.

[24] Ibid., Testimony: Cyril Herbert Thomas Ilott, b. Bromley, Kent, 1898; educ. Tonbridge Sch. And Caius Coll., Cambridge Univ.; MD, 1906; MB, BCh, 1908; London Hosp. and Gt. Ormond St. Hosp.; 2/Lt, RAMC, 8.4.15; Fort Pitt Mily. Hosp., Apl-May, 1915; to BEF June 1915; Surgeon, 26th Gen. Hosp.; MO, 74th Field Amb., 24th Divl. Train, Jan. 1916.

[25] Ibid.

[26] Ibid., Testimony: Lord. Frank Baigrie Lord, b.1876; 2/Lt., York & Lanc. Regt., 1896; ASC, 1898; Lt., 1899; Capt., 1901; Maj., 1912; to BEF, Dec. 1915; T/Lt. Col. & O.C., 24th Divl. Train, 18.12.15. From the written proceedings it is unclear whether Moore's complaint arose from the rough handling he experienced while having his legs bound together.

[27] Ibid., Testimony: Kenny, op. cit. Though not disclosed in court, after CSM Bagshaw complained about him hesitating to clean horse harness, on 31.12.15 Kenny was sentenced to 28 days' Field Punishment No.1 by Capt. Thompson.

[28] William Thomas Lee, b. Durham, 1880; builder's labourer; Dvr. No. T4/040832, 197th Coy., ASC, 8.1.15; to BEF, 1.9.15.

[29] All three punishments were awarded by Capt. Thompson. FGCM, op. cit., Form AFB 122: Dvr. Moore, T., ASC.

[30] Ibid., These offences seem to have arisen from a traffic accident witnessed by Cpl. No.49475 Alfred J. Luxton, RAMC and Lt. Campbell McNeil McCormack, RAMC.

[31] Ibid., e.g. During December 1915, both Dvr. Lee and Dvr. Kenny had separately been sentenced to spells of Field Punishment because CSM Bagshaw did not consider they had adequately cleaned the horses' harness.

[32] Ibid.

[33] Service Record: Thomas William Moore, b. Houghton-le-Skerne, Darlington, 1891; Farm Labourer; Spec. Res., 3rd Bn. Yorks. Regt., Jan-Feb 1911; Dvr. No.65067 131st Bty., RFA., 28.3.11; AWOL, 27.5.11-25.9.11; 2 mos. Imp. H.L. (Theft), 27.6.14; Disch. 27.7.14; Dvr. No.T4/040862, 197th Coy. ASC, 8.1.15.

[34] Ibid., WO 95/2203, 12.2.16.

[35] Ibid., Capper's nickname reflected his uncompromising support for military hierarchy.

[36] Ibid., The death sentence was approved by Lt. Gen. Edward Arthur Fanshawe (V Corps) on 20.2.16; General Herbert Plumer (2nd Army) on 21.2.6, and Field Marshal Haig on 23.2.16.

See also: Lord to HQ, 24th Div., 26.2.16, noting that Moore was buried at Devonshire Farm (a.k.a., Bossaert Farm, Reningelst), map reference: 28.G.22.b.8.8. After the war his grave was undisturbed by the Imperial War Graves Commission and his name was inscribed on the Menin Gate Memorial to the Missing.

[37] The authors are grateful to Sean Godfrey for this information and for generously sharing other details of his research about the Moore family.

Chapter 5

[1] Census, 1901 and 1911: Arthur Dale, b. 1871 Brailsford, Derbyshire.

[2] Circa 10% of 13th R. Scots were killed on 26-27.9.15 (CWGC).

[3] James Sneddon, b. 1887 Stirlingshire; coal miner; m. 1906 (x4 children); r. St. Mary's Wynd, Stirling; Pte. No.18547 13th Bn. Royal Scots, 19.1.15; to BEF 28.7.15.

[4] WO 71/451 FGCM: Testimony of Ptes. Wickham and Hutchinson. Pte. No.23220 Henry William Wickham, b. Birmingham 1896; res. & enl. Brighton, 7.6.15; to BEF 15.10.15; KIA 15.9.16. Pte. No.15127 Robert Hutchinson b. N/K; res. & enl. N/K; to BEF 9.7.15; demob. 22.3.19.

[5] FGCM: Testimony of Ptes. Wickham and Hutchinson.

[6] It is not clear from the written proceedings whether the No.45 Field Ambulance transport was a motor-powered or horse-drawn vehicle.

[7] WO 71/451 FGCM: Testimony of Cpl. No. P/188 William Howarth, Mounted Military Police and Cpl. No.3306 William Charles Rogers, 17th Lancers/MMP.

[8] FGCM: Testimony of Capt. John Berry Haycraft, b. Edinburgh 1888; M.B., Ch.B. Ed., (1909);T/2Lt., RAMC; to BEF 9.8.14; T/Lt., 10.8.14; Surgeon Specialist, No.1 CCS.; T/Capt., 10.8.15.

[9] Charles Maxwell Shurlock Henning, b. 1866. 2/Lt., Sco. Rifs., 1885; JP (Dorset) 1903; Maj., 1903; retd., 1913; T/Lt. Col., R. Scots, 7.8.15. James Edward Manning Farquhar, b. Devizes, 1870; Royal Fus., Pte. No.162; T/Major, 6th Cam. Hs.; to BEF, 9.7.15; KIA 15.9.16. James Thomas Rankin Mitchell, b. Airdrie 1888; Solicitor/Writer to the Signet, Edinburgh; T/2Lt., 11th Bn., A & SH, 19.9.14; T/Lt., 23.11.14; T/Capt., 6.3.15; to BEF 10.7.15; DOW (UK), 1.4.18. Neville Anderson, b. Earls Court 1881, educ. Rugby, Oriel Coll., Oxford Univ.; Barrister 1903; Midland Circuit; Spec. Commissioner of Income Tax; 2/Lt., 5th Bn., LRB, Feb. 1915; to BEF Jan. 1916; DAAG, att HQ, First Army, Jan.

1916; Capt., April 1916. Christopher Thomas Francis, b. Clapham 1888; Clerk (Co. Council), Pte. No.3468, Ox. & Bucks. LI; 2/Lt., R.Scots 13.11.14; Capt., 4.10.15. Charles Whitehead Yule, b. 1889, B.Litt., MA (St. Andrews Univ.); Asst. Curator (Historical Dept.), H.M. General Register House, 2/Lt, 13th Royal Scots, 14.11.14; Capt., 4.10.15; KIA, 11.5.16.

[10] FGCM, op. cit., Wickham.

[11] Ibid., Hutchinson. The WW1 British Army Medal Roll cites five soldiers named Rush who served overseas with the Royal Scots but it has not proved possible to specify the one to whom Hutchinson refers.

[12] Ibid., Howarth.

[13] Ibid., Rogers. The SMLE rifle Mk III featured a cut-off that separated the magazine from the firing chamber. With the cut off in operation each round would have to be inserted manually into the breach but it is not immediately clear why the cut-off should have figured in Rogers' evidence.

[14] Ibid., Haycraft.

[15] Ibid., Testimony of Cpl. No.22780 Robert Bain, 13th Bn. Royal Scots; to BEF 4.10.15.

[16] Ibid., Testimony of R.S.M./WO Cl. 1 No.4290 William Price, 13th Bn. Royal Scots; to BEF 9.7.15; Lt. & Qmr., 8.3.16.

[17] Ibid., Defence: Yule.

[18] Ibid.

[19] Ibid., Notes: Brig. Genl., OC, 45th Bde. To AA&QMG, 15th Div., 21.2.16; McCracken to 4th Corps, 22.2.16.

[20] Ibid., Note: Wilson to HQ, 1st Army, 25.2.16.

[21] Charles Carmichael Monro, b. 1860; educ. Sherborne Sch. & RMA Sandhurst; 2/Lt., 2nd Foot, 1879; Lt., R.W. Surrey, 1881; Capt.; Maj., 1898; Lt. Col. 1900; Col., 1907; Maj. Gen., 1910; GOC, 2 Div., 1914; GOC, 1st Corps, Dec. 1914-July 1915; GOC 3rd Army, July-Oct., 1915; C-in-C, Med. Exped. Force, Oct. 1915-Jan 1916; GOC 1st Army, 5.2.16.

[22] Ibid., Note: Monro to GHQ, 20.2.16.

[23] Ibid., The Haig marginalia consisted of? *Opinion* (45th Inf. Bde., op. cit.) and? *ditto* (McCracken, op. cit.).

[24] MML, ch.VII, sec.10.

[25] FGCM, op. cit.; WO 95/1946 War Diary: 13th Bn. Royal Scots, 13.3.16. Arthur Cyril Albert Jekyll, b. Eammaville, NSW, Australia, 1889; T/Lt, RAMC (T) 15.3.15; to BEF 1.6.15;

T/Capt., 15.3.16; KIA, 11.5.16 (obit. *British Medical Journal,* 27.5.16, p.768). Kenneth James Beatty, b. Australia, 1878, educ. Melbourne Univ.; Barrister; Lt. 5th Mtd. Rifs.; WIA 1901; Prosecutor/Judge, S.Africa, Gold Coast, Sierra Leone; T/Capt. (APM), 16.7.15.

[26] TNA, Statement of Service: James Sneddon 18547, 13th Bn., R. Scots.

Chapter 6

[1] On the casualties sustained by the Pioneers, see: Mitchinson, pp.290-298.

[2] TNA WO 95/335 War Diary: 173rd Tunnelling Company, R.E., 1915-1919. In addition to military mining, tunnelling companies engaged in trench digging and excavating underground military communications and medical facilities.

[3] Court of Inquiry (6.9.16), Witness Statement: Pte. No.14464, William Lynch, 6th Bn. Royal Scots Fus.; to BEF, 23.11.14.

[4] Ibid.

[5] Pte. No.1016 Harry Lionel Woodthorpe, b. Portsea, 1888; Registry Assistant, GPO; 15th Bn. London Regt.; to BEF, 18.3.15; A/Cpl., No.148565, 173rd Coy. Royal Engineers. William Damper, b. Hastings, 1873; Pte., 1st Bn. Sussex Regt., 1891; North West Frontier, India; South

Africa; Shoemaker, Cork; Labourer/Malster, Cork, 1911; Pte. No. G/7775, 2nd Bn. Sussex Regt., 14.8.15; Spr. No.155789, 173rd Tunnelling Coy., 23.2.16; Pte. No.155789, R.E.; Gas poisoning, 14-16.5.16.

[6] Robert Bell Turton, b. North Kilvington, Yorks., 1859; educ. Eton; Balliol Coll., Oxon.; Barrister, 1893; Yorks. Vols.; 4th Bn. Yorks. Militia; Maj., 1902; T/Maj. (SR), 3rd Bn. Yorks., 1908; 7th Bn. Yorks., 19.9.14; 12th Bn. Yorks., 12.4.15; to BEF, 1.6.16. Edward Betts Graham, b. Clapham, 1887; Pte., 14th Bn. London (Scottish), 1908-12; Insurance Broker's Clerk; Dvr. No.496, H.A.C., 25.8.14; T/2Lt., R.F.A., 13.4.15. Leslie Williams Burbidge, b. Bexhill-on-Sea, Sussex; Clerk; Pte. No.662, W. Kent Yeo., 1911; Pte. No. TS/2426, ASC, 12.8.14; Intell. Corps, att. HQ, Cav. Div.; T/2Lt., Sp. List, 14.8.14; to BEF, 14.8.14; 2/Lt., ASC, 19.10.14; 138th Coy., ASC, 15th Divl. Train; Lt., 19.11.15; A/Adjt., 40th Divl. Train, ASC, 15.3.16; Capt. & Adjt., 1.6.16. Edward Henry Chapman, b. London, 5.2.1874; educ. Eton; Magdalen Coll., Oxford Univ.; 4th Bn. Yorks Mil., Lt., 1891; Capt., 1895; Capt. (TF), 31.3.15; A.D.C. to G.O.C., 62nd Div.; to BEF, 9.3.16; CMO, 4 Army HQ, 9.6.16. Joseph Healy, b. Dublin, 1889; Barrister (Munster), 1912; Sub-Lt., RNVR (RND), 2.12.14; to Gallipoli, 23.10.15; trans. to Army, 6.6.16; T/Lt., RASC,

MT Sch. of Instr., St. Omer, 20.6.16; 411th Coy., ASC16th Amm. Sub-Park, 7th Corps.

[7] Bryan Caryl Taylor Freeland, b. 1889; Toft Monks, Norfolk, 1893; educ. Kelly College; Lt., OTC; T/Capt, 9th Bn. Devons, 30.8.14; T/Capt., R.E., 12.10.14. Testimony: Spr. No.82631 Richard Dobson, R.E.; to BEF, 9.3.15.

[8] Testimony: Pte. No.95854 Frederick G. Wells, 173rd Coy., Royal Engineers; to BEF, 30.10.15. Other than his rank, surname and military affiliation, no further details are recorded about Sapper Todd.

[9] Ibid.

[10] Testimony: Pte. No.1673, Hugh Rice, Scottish Rifles; to BEF, 21.3.15; Pte. No.79685, 173rd Coy., Royal Engineers.

[11] Ibid.

[12] Ibid., Testimony: Arthur Campion Pritchard, b. New Cross, 1887; Secretary; 26th Bn. Middx (Cyclist) VRC; Pte. No.157, 25th Bn. London Regt., 1908-9; T/Lt., 11th Bn. Northumberland Fus., 20.10.14; to BEF, 25.8.15; T/Capt., 30.8.16; att. 173rd Coy. Royal Engineers.

[13] Ibid.

[14] Ibid.

[15] Ibid.

[16] Ibid., Ch.VI, sec 15, p.59.

[17] MML (1914), Rules of Procedure, 85 (A), p.621.

[18] FGCM, op. cit., Testimony: Pritchard.

[19] Ibid., sec.63, pp.71-2: The general rule is that the opinion or belief of a witness is not evidence. A witness must depose to the particular facts that he has seen, heard or otherwise observed, and it is for the court to draw the necessary inference from these facts.... The examination of the witness should be confined ... to such other facts relevant to the charge as may be within the knowledge of the witness; sec.64, p.72. The chief exception to this rule relates to the evidence of experts. The opinion of an expert, that is to say, a person specially skilled in any science or art, is admissible as evidence on any point within the range of his specialist knowledge; ibid., sec.65: Thus ... a doctor may be asked as an expert.... And, where lunacy is set up as a defence, an expert may be asked whether, in his opinion, the symptoms proved to be exhibited by the alleged lunatic commonly show unsoundness of mind, and whether such unsoundness of mind usually renders persons incapable of knowing the nature of their acts, or of knowing that what they do is either wrong or contrary to law.

[20] MML (1914), sec 85 (A), p.621.

[21] FGCM, Testimony of Dvr. No.1025 George Alexander, 2 Bty., Royal Horse Artillery.

[22] Ibid.

[23] Ibid., Testimony of Sgt. No.6624 James Currie, Royal Scots Fus.; to BEF, 21.1.15; Sgt., No.86421, 173rd Coy., Royal Engineers.

[24] Ibid.

[25] Pte. William W. Damper was buried on 4.9.16 at Barlin Communal Cemetery Extension., Plot 1.D 5.

[26] FGCM, op. cit., Testimony of Capt. Owen William Richards, b. Isleworth, 1873; educ. Eton; New Coll., Oxford Univ.; Lt., RAMC, 30.9.14; T/Capt., 21.5.16; att. No.6 C.C.S.

[27] Ibid., Testimony of Pte. No.14466 James Glen, Royal Scots; to BEF, 2.9.15.

[28] Ibid., Statement: Pte. No.12692 Duncan Scully, 6th Bn. Royal Scots Fusiliers. Removing bolts from the rifles rendered them useless as firearms but it is unclear in whose interests the disarmament was conducted.

[29] Ibid., Testimony of Pte. No.2889 Francis Murray, 9th Bn. Gordon Highlanders.

[30] Ibid., Defence Statement: Healy.

[31] Ibid., Statement dictated by Cpl. H.L. Woodthorpe to Capt. A.C. Pritchard, 3.9.16.

Unsigned but Woodthorpe's mark witnessed by Pritchard. No other witness refers to Murray's shirt being torn or aiming from a prone position and the only person lying prone at the time was Pte. Todd.

[32] Ibid., Army Form AFB 122, Pte. No. S/2889 Francis Murray, H Company, 9th Bn. Gordon Highlanders.

[33] Ibid., Schedule.

[34] Harold Goodeve Ruggles-Brise, b. Finchingfield, Essex, 1864; Lt., Gren. Gds., 1885; Adjt., 1893-6; Capt., 1897; Brev. Maj., 1900; Maj., 1902; Lt. Col., 1907; Col., 1911; T/Brig.-Gen., 15.9.14; T/Maj.-Gen., 25.9.15.

[35] Ibid.: Ruggles-Brise, HQ, 40th Div. to HQ, 1 Corps, 25.9.16.

[36] MML. (1914), Ch.III, sec.30, p.22; see also King's Regulations, 510.

[37] Havelock Hudson, b. 1862; Lt., Northants., 1881; Indian Army, 1885; Capt., 1892; Maj., 1901; Brev. Maj., 1906; Lt. Col., 1907; Col., 1911; T/Brig. Gen., 1912; Brig.-Gen., Indian Corps, 30.9.14-30.7.15; OC, Maj. Gen., 18.2.15. On 1.7.16 under Hudson's command, 8th Division lost 218 of its 300 officers and 5,274 of its 8,000 rank and file. Perhaps understandably, Hudson omitted reference to 8th Div. in his *Who's Who* entry.

[38] Ibid., Hudson, HQ, 1st Corps to First Army A', 26.9.16.

[39] Op. cit., MML (1914), Ch.VII, para. 10, p.88. The MML holds that voluntary intoxication ought to be taken into consideration by the court. If a man was so drunk that he was incapable of forming the intent to kill, it may serve to reduce the charge to one of manslaughter. The military courts were bound to follow the rulings of the Courts of England in civil matters and the intoxication defence was well established in the case of *R.v. Meade* [1909] 1KB, 895. *Meade* held that if a man was so drunk as to be incapable of understanding the nature of his actions, he could not be convicted of the intentional act of murder. The case was overturned by the House of Lords in 1920 but when Murray was convicted, it was still good law.

[40] Richard Cyril Byrne Haking, b. Halifax, 1862; Lt., Hants., 1881; Adjt., 1886; Capt., 1889; Maj. 1899; Lt. Col., 1903; Brev. Col., 1905; Brig. Gen., 1908-27.12.14; Maj. Gen., 28.12.14; C.E.W. Bean – *The Official History of Australia in the War of 1914-1918,* Vol.3, *The AIF in France: 1916,* p.444.

[41] FGCM, op.cit., Haking to A.G., GHQ (thro' DJAG), 27.9.16.

[42] Alexander Gordon Maxwell, b. Meerut, India, 1867; 6th King Edward's Own Cavy. Indian Army, Capt., 1900; Maj., 1907; retd. 3.8.09; APM, 40th Div., 3.5.16.

[43] The 1911 Scottish census and CWGC Register: Nouex-les-Mines Comm. Cemetery states Francis was the son of William Murray, 2, Welsh Row, Calderbank, South Airdrie, Scotland.

Chapter 7

[1] WO 71/540: FGCM, Testimony: Pte. No.12384 Alexander Reid, 16th Bn. Highland Light Infantry (HLI). 10th Bn., HLI, 46th Bde., 15th (Scottish) Division.

[2] WO 95/2403, War Diary: 16th (Service) Bn. HLI (2nd Glasgow), 97th Bde., 32nd Div.: Casualties, 1-3 July 1916, 554 All Ranks; 18-19 November 1916, 403 All Ranks. See also, Chalmers, pp.31-68.

[3] Winter 1916-1917 was one of the coldest in Western Europe during C20th; during the five weeks prior to 6.1.17, 10,450 (all ranks) were admitted to BEF medical units suffering from Trench Foot or Frostbite, Mitchell & Smith, p.89. Typically, billeting officers made use of farm buildings, large sheds and vacant residential properties.

[4] Op. cit., Testimony: Reid. Inhabitants of Rubempre: 1911-673; 1921-568 (www.annuaire mairie.fr/statistique-rubempre.html).

[5] Ibid., Testimony: Reid. Pte. No.3981 James Henry Kean, b. Lochee, Angus, 1895; r. Glasgow; enl. 16th Bn. HLI; to BEF 24.11.15. Pte. (L/Cpl.) No.13527 William Cumberland, b. & r. Glasgow; Brewer's Clerk; enl. 16th Bn. HLI; to BEF 23.11.15; KIA 23.11.17.

[6] Ibid., Testimony: Reid. Testimony: J. Kelley, i.e. Pte. No.8099 John Kelly, b. Dunblane, 1895; Labourer; enl. HLI, 14.8.14; to BEF 1.1.15-5.3.15 (1st Bn.); 4th Bn. HLI, 27.8.15; Civil Court: Breach of peace & assault (29 days Imp.), 25.10.15; DCM: Desertion (1 year, comm. to 6 mos. Detn.); to BEF, 24.6.16. Testimony: H. McClean, i.e. Pte. No.1586 Hector McClean, enl. 12th Bn., HLI; to BEF 28.7.15. Although Kelly was repeatedly jailed for absence or desertion in the UK, it is unclear why he and McLean were detained in the guardroom on 5.1.17.

[7] Ibid., Reid; Testimony: G. Thompson, i.e. L/Cpl. No.43131 George Thompson, 16th Bn. HLI. L/Cpl. No.13913 Peter Spence, 15th Bn. HLI; to BEF, 23.11.15.

[8] Ibid., Testimony: Thompson.

[9] Ibid., Schedule. Edward Harrison Rigg, b. Scarborough, 1880, 2/Lt, 2nd KOYLI, 1889; Lt., 1901; Capt., 1906; T/Maj. 29.10.14; T/Lt. Col. 20.11.15-7.1.17; A/Lt. Col., Innis. Fus. John Ferguson Muir, b. Glasgow, 1889; Solicitor; T/2Lt., 1/5th HLI (TF); T/Lt., 22.12.14; T/Capt., 13th Bn. HLI, 5.5.15; to Balkans 30.5.15; 17th Bn. HLI. John Stanley Griffith-Jones, b. 1877, educ. Univ. Coll. Sch. & Trinity Coll., Cambridge; barrister; T/2Lt., 10th Bn. SWB, 9.4.15; T/Lt., 5.12.15; T/Capt., Gen. List, 30.10.16.

[10] Andrew Macfarlane, 2/Lt., 16th Bn. HLI, 14.4.15; T/Lt., 2.9.16; Adjt., 20.10.16. Charles Bell Buddle, b. Auckland NZ, 1884; LLB, Auckland Univ., 1909; barrister 1910; Lt., ASC; to BEF 1915; T/Capt., 1.11.15; 32nd Div. Train, ASC.

[11] Vincent Edgar Badcock, b. Auckland (UK), 1884; MB, 1906; MD, 1909 (Durham); T/Lt, RAMC, 25.6.15; to BEF 11.11.15; Capt., 25.6.16.

[12] Testimony: Badcock, op. cit.

[13] Testimony: Thompson, op. cit.

[14] Ibid.

[15] Testimony: Spence, op. cit.

[16] Testimony: Pte. No.43128 Thomas Robertson, 16th Bn. HLI.

[17] Testimony: CSM No.43617 James Allison, 16th Bn. HLI; formerly No.1012, Highland Cyclist Bn. and 10th Bn. HLI.

[18] Testimony: Label, i.e. Pte. No.552 Peter Lavelle, 16th Bn. HLI; formerly 11th Bn. HLI; to BEF, 13.5.15; 15th Bn. HLI, KIA, 26.5.18. James Marr, b. Alnwick, 1895; educ. Duke's School; Black Watch, 7.8.15; Pte. No.33395, 16th Bn. HLI; to BEF Oct. 1916; DOW, 3.12.17.

[19] Ibid., Reid maintained they were infantrymen serving in France with the Royal Scots, Seaforth Highlanders and Northumberland Fusiliers.

[20] Service Reserve Department rum was 95.5 proof spirit and the official daily allowance was 1/12 of a gill, so Reid's intake was circa half a dozen modern-day single measures of spirits.

[21] Ibid., Reid. Because the bottled stout had been purchased at an *estaminet,* it is likely to have been *Cuvee de Noel* (Christmas beer), a strong, dark ale akin to an English winter warmer.

[22] Testimony: Kelly, op. cit.

[23] Testimony: Pte. No.8057 William McCheyne, 16th Bn. HLI; to BEF, 5.1.15.

[24] Testimony: Pte. No.7037 John Simpson, 16th Bn. HLI; formerly 1st Bn. HLI; to BEF 5.1.15.

[25] Testimony: E. Gallagher, i.e. Pte. No.3324 Alexander Gallagher, 16th Bn. HLI.

[26] Testimony: W. Grant, i.e. Pte. No.33125 William Grant, 16th Bn. HLI.

[27] R.v. Steadman, Foster, 292., Archbold.

[28] Rex v. Lynch, [1883] 5 C. & P., Court of Criminal Appeal, ibid., *Archbold.*

[29] MML (1914), p.22, sec.31.

[30] FGCM, op. cit., Prisoner's Friend: Summary.

[31] Ibid., Character and Particulars of Service.

[32] Ibid., Plea in Mitigation.

[33] Ibid., Remarks: Jardine, 18.1.17; Barnes to HQ, 5th Corps, 19.1.17.

[34] Ibid., Fanshawe to HQ, 5th Army, 22.1.17.

[35] Ibid., Gough to AG, GHQ, 25.1.17.

[36] Charles Dickson, b. Dromore, Co. Down, Ireland, 1866; educ. Royal Belfast Acad. Inst. and Queen's Coll., Belfast; MB, BCh, BAO, RUI, 1908; DPH, 1910; MD, Belfast, 1911; Lt., RAMC, 9.8.15; T/Capt., 9.8.16.

[37] CWGC Bertrancourt Military Cemetery: Pte. No.12384 Alexander Reid, 16th HLI. Plot 2. Row A Grave 7. Research conducted by Mark Thomas, Dominiek Dendooven and CWGC staff suggest the inscription was chosen by his sister, Mrs A[nnie] Stirling, Edinburgh.

Chapter 8

[1] Thomas McCain, b. Gloucester, 1877; Engine Cleaner; Spr., Royal Engineers, 1894; Plymouth, 1896; Falmouth, 1897; Bermuda 1900; Greenock, 1904; Malta, 1908; Sgt., 1911; Gosport, 1912.

[2] Details about the activities and generally unsuccessful record of the 50th Field Searchlight Coy. may be gathered from Addison, pp.314-6.

[3] Beresford Finniston, b. Shankill, Belfast, circa 1880; Plasterer; Cpl., R.E., South Africa, 1911; CQMS No.6616, 50th Searchlight Coy.; d. Edinburgh 1958.

[4] WO 71/603, FGCM, Testimony: Horace G. (a.k.a. Fred) Anson b. Pontefract, 1897; Messenger Clerk, Labour Exchange, Castleford; Spr., No.23611, R.E., 50th Field Searchlight Coy.

[5] Ibid.

[6] CWGC Register: La Chapelette British and Indian Cemetery, Peronne; McCain T., Company Sergeant Major No.28347, RE. Grave 1.G.5.

[7] FGCM: Schedule, op. cit. does not identify the exact location but at the time 123rd Brigade HQ was situated at St. Idesbalde.

[8] Ibid., Sydney Herbert Beattie, b. Dublin, 1888; 2/Lt., Northants., 1911; Lt. 1912; to BEF,

6.10.14; Capt., 14.3.15; T/Maj., 10th Bn. R.W. Kents, 3.5.16; Lt. Col. 1.7.17. Noel Eric Hayward Sim, b. Derby, 1890; 2/Lt, Y. & L. Regt. 1910; Lt., 1912; to BEF, 7.9.14; T/Capt., 10.6.15; Capt., 25.7.15; A/Maj., 20th Bn. D.L.I., 15.8.17; Charles Hext Cotesworth, b. Dover, 1879; 2/Lt., 21st Lancers, 1902; Lt., 1909; ADC to CO, 2nd Rawalpindi Div., 9.7.14; Capt., 21st Lancers, 4.5.14; att. MG Corps, 3.4.16; to BEF 1.12.16; att., 23rd Bn. Middx.

[9] Ibid., Oscar Follett Dowson, b. Stockport, 1879; educ. Rugby, New Coll. Oxford Univ.; Barrister (Inner Temple), 1905; 2/Lt., A.S.C., 29.9.14; T/Capt. & CMO, 30.10.16. Ernest Edward Green, b. Cardiff, Solicitor; Capt., 7th Bn. Welsh Regt., 4.8.14; Capt., 1.1.15; Staff Capt., 7.7.15; T/Maj., 16.9.15; Maj., 1.6.16; to BEF, 24.2.17. Gonne St. Clair Pilcher, b. Woolwich, 1890; educ. Wellington Coll. & Trinity Coll., Cambridge Univ.; T/Lt., Intell. Corps, att. R.E., 6.8.14; Barrister (Inner Temple), 1915.

[10] Ibid., Testimony: Anson, op. cit.

[11] Ibid.

[12] Ibid.

[13] Ibid., Testimony: L/Cpl. 13551 Lewis B. Boyce, R.E., 50th Field Searchlight Coy.

[14] Ibid.

[15] Ibid., The exact meaning of 'I will go up against the wall for one bloody man' is rather unclear but it is most likely an expression of personal exasperation, a reference to being executed (against a wall) because of one particular man's (in)action or attitude.

[16] Ibid., Testimony: Spr. No.26415 Daniel Lawlor, R.E., 50th Field Searchlight Coy.

[17] Ibid.

[18] FGCM: Spr. Arthur Oyns, Form AFB 122.

[19] Field Punishment No.2 involved soldiers undergoing sentence losing privileges; being required to carry out heavy labour, extra fatigues and generally being harassed. Field Punishment No.1 also involved heavy labour; extra fatigues; loss of pay and privileges and being tethered to a fixed post or wheel for two hours a day for up to three out of every four consecutive days for up to 3 months.

[20] FGCM, op. cit., Testimony: Sidney Ernest Willoughby Hathaway, b. Aston, 1883; House Painter; Spr. No.496753, R.E.

[21] Ibid., Testimony: Sgt. No.17394 William Pritchard, 7th Bde. RHA; to BEF, 15.8.14.

[22] Ibid., Testimony: Thomas George Windebank, b. Southampton, 1889; Cleaner (Dyer); Bdr., No.168323, RGA.

[23] Ibid., Testimony: L/Cpl. No.23722 W. Taylor, 50th Field Searchlight Coy.; Pte. No.43078 A.P. Hand, RAMC.

[24] Ibid.

[25] Though Oyns fired his rifle twice, there remains a possibility that only one shot wounded both sergeants.

[26] FGCM, op. cit., Testimony: Spr. No.94236 Arthur Philip Oyns, b. Whitehaven, 1884; Electrician; enl. 35th Sig. Coy., R.E., 17.4.15; 50th Field Searchlight Coy., R.E., 11.1.16; to BEF, 7.4.16.

[27] Ibid.

[28] Ibid., Testimony: Douglas Ronald St. Jarlath ffrench-Mullen, b.1892; 2/Lt., R.E., 1911; Lt., 1914; Capt., 26.6.17.

[29] FGCM, op. cit., Testimony: ffrench-Mullen. Oyn's personal record indicates he was classified as a Skilled Electrician (Light & Telegraph work) on 10.7.16.

[30] Robert William Benjamin Simms, b. Portsea, 1865; Tailor, enl. RM Artillery, 1881; Sgt., 1889; Sgt, No.6569, 6th Bn. Northumberland Fus., 1906; T/Lt., 14th Bn. Hants., 30.11.14; T/Capt., 11.3.15; T/Capt., Gen. List. &APM, 21.4.17.

[31] Capt. J.C. Davidson, RAMC certified that both men perished at 6.10am.

[32] Op. cit., Personal Record: Oyns. In 1916, Julia Isabel Oyns (1846-1918), Arthur's twice-widowed mother resided at 11, North Street, Portsea, Hants.

[33] Ibid., Medical History: (sd.) Lt. Gordon Johnson, RAMC, 17.4.16.

[34] R.E. Record Office, Chatham to Mabel McCain, Ferndale, Sydney Road, Gosport, 3.7.18. op. cit., Personal Record: McCain.

Chapter 9

[1] *Maison tolérée* or *Maison de tolerance:* Brothel; *Maison d'abbatage:* (colloq.) Slaughter house, a brothel specializing in a quick turnover (Corbin, 1990). See also: Stanley, pp.84-5.

[2] Lamps: 'Red' for soldiers; 'Blue' for officers; Harrison, pp.143-146.

[3] WO 71/636, FGCM: Cpl. (L/Sgt.) No.3019 Arthur Wickings, 9th Bn. Rifle Brigade, Statements: Gremond; Lemoine; Defraey; Supplementary Summary: Bergilez.

[4] FGCM: Report: Chef du Service Anthropometrique, Commissariat de la Surete, Ville du Havre to Juge d'Instruction du Havre,

20.12.17, p.1; Statement: Mme. Virginie Gremond.

[5] Ibid., Statement: Lemoine.

[6] The use of 'excited' by Gremond in this context could refer to the man appearing to be sexually aroused. However, in her Witness Statement (op. cit.) Gremond stated, 'He appeared to be somewhat nervous, he had been drinking but was not drunk.'

[7] Ibid., Witness Statement and Testimony: Gremond.

[8] Ibid., Statement: Defraey.

[9] Op. cit., Statement: Defraey; Witness Statements: Pte. No.14286, J.A. Adams, Manchester Regt.; to BEF 8.11.15; L/Cpl. No. P/4190, MFP. Sgt. No.871 Ralph Wilson Waugh, ANZAC Provost Corps; Harry William Woodgate, b. Salisbury, 1881; Clerk, Govt. Dockyard; L/Cpl. No.9044, MFP; to BEF, 24.6.17; att. APM, Le Havre, 3.8.17-10.1.18.

[10] Bergilez did not engage more actively because he was an invalid recovering from a nervous collapse. Supplementary Summary: Corporal No.53010 Arthur Bergilez, Belgian Army.

[11] Statements: Adams, Waugh, Woodgate, op. cit.

[12] Testimony: Ford. Charles William Ford, b. Woolwich, 1890, Pte. L/8884, 1st Bn. R.W.

Kent; L/Cpl. No.6278, MFP. Testimony: Gremond.

[13] Statement: Dr M.P. Klein.

[14] Statement: Victor Frambourg, Commissionaire de Police. Faubourg made no reference to a very heavy marble table having been completely overturned in the centre of the room because Gremond had righted it. See, Statements: Bergilez, Waugh, op. cit.

[15] Statement: Thomas William Fitzpatrick, b. Enniscorthy, Wexford, 1876, Pte. No.5637, 18th Bn. R. Irish Regt. 1895; RQMS, 2nd Bn.; to BEF, 14.8.14; 2/Lt & Lt./Adjt., 1.10.14; T/Capt. & APM, 22.4.16; Capt. (Brev. Maj.), 28.12.17.

[16] Berliere, pp.225-230.

[17] Statements: Frambourg (op. cit.); Maurice Ternon, Chief of the Identification Department, Le Havre Police.

[18] Statement: Dr Balard D'Herlinville (Police Pathologist), Post-Mortem Report on Mme Henriette Tremerel (née Mont), 22.12.17.

[19] Statement: Captain Leonard Gibson, Adjutant, Employment Base Depot, No.17 Camp, Harfleur.

[20] C/Sgt. No.7080 Thomas Bernard Collins, b. Exeter, 1882; Sgt., 1st Bn. Devons; to BEF, 22.8.14, att. Employment Base Depot, No.17 Camp, Harfleur.

[21] Testimony of Capt. Ralph Rimmer, MB, ChB, RAMC; Bacteriologist, No.2 Gen. Hosp., Le Havre.

[22] Ibid., Testimony: Gremond., op. cit. The identity parade took place at the office of the APM, Le Havre but she was directed to pick out the wanted man by the Juge D'Instruction (Investigating Magistrate).

[23] Ibid., Testimony: Geroult.

[24] Statements: Rifleman No. Z/1954 Harry Binks, 2nd Bn. Rifle Brigade; A/Cpl. No.412186. Pte. No.1489 Arthur Charles Hawes, 2nd Bn. Rifle Brigade; to BEF, 7.11.14; No.412093, Labour Corps. Pte. No.5/408 Henry Johnson, 3th Bn. Rifle Brigade; to BEF, 13.11.14; No.412187, Labour Corps. All three were attached to 893rd Garr. Guard Coy. (formerly 10th Bn. Rifle Brigade), Cinder City Camp, Le Havre.

[25] Ibid., Testimony.

[26] William Henry Jefferis, b. 1889 Hermitage, Sussex. Police Clerk (Constable), Salisbury, Wilts.; Staff Qmr. Sgt., No. S3/25430, ASC; to BEF; T2/Lt., ASC, 25.10.16.

[27] Statement: Defence – Wickings.

[28] Ibid., Schedule: Godfrey Massy, b. 1863; 2/Lt., Norfolks, 22.10.81; Lt/Col., 12.1.05; Brev. Col., 12.1.05; retd. 12.1.09; Commandant, DAAG,

5.8.14; to BEF, 20.8.14; Commandant, No.4 IBD, Le Havre. Lord Louth, Randal Pilgrim Ralph Plunkett, DL, JP, b. 1868; Lt., 3rd Bn. Wilts. Militia; Capt., London Yeo., 10.9.14; Maj., 4.12.14; No.831 Area Employment Co. John Herbert Grindley, b. Liverpool, 1874. Art Dealer; Lt., 1/5th Bn. Liverpool, 27.12.00; Capt., 2.4.08; to BEF; T/Maj., 20.11.15; T/Lt. Col., 29.1.16; Adjt., 4th Garr. Bn. R.W. Fus., 9.5.16. William Morse Crowdy, b. Newton Abbott, 1866, educ. Brasenose Coll., Oxford; Barrister (Lincoln's Inn); 3rd Bn. Devons; Capt., 30.3.15.

[29] Ibid., Schedule: Hugh Gatehouse, b. Chichester, 1872; educ. Charterhouse and Clare Coll., Oxford Univ.; Barrister (Lincoln's Inn), 1897; T/2Lt., RE, 6.2.15; T/2Lt., ASC, 18.10.16; to BEF, 6.1.17; CMO and T/Capt., Gen. List, 24.10.17.

[30] Testimony: T/Sgt. G. Ellis, MFP; to BEF, 11.10.14. See MML, Ch.VI, sec.58.

[31] Ibid., Testimony: Gueroult.

[32] Arthur Wickings, Attestation Papers: 18.8.08, Medical Examination of Pte. No.3019 Arthur Wickings, Marks: 'Large scar on right side of neck; scar of abscess, right side of neck.'

[33] Testimony: Binks.

[34] Testimony: Hawes.

[35] Testimony: Johnson.

[36] Testimony: Gremond.

[37] On enlistment, Wickings weighed 51 kilogrammes and by late 1917 he may have put on weight but his height was only 1.6 metres.

[38] Gremond's statement was probably admissible as part of the *res gestæ.* The doctrine of *res gestæ* is founded upon the belief that some statements are made spontaneously during the course of an event. Such accounts leave small room for misunderstanding when heard by someone else therefore the law holds that such evidence carries great weight. MML, Ch.VI, sec.58 & 59.

[39] Testimony: Gremond, op. cit.

[40] Ibid.

[41] Arthur Wickings, Attestation Papers, op. cit., records Wickings had been shot in the head on 7.5.15 and was wounded in the back by shrapnel on 15.4.16. The age cited in his attestation papers is also corroborated by the 1891 census data.

[42] Waugh arrived in France on 25.6.17 and there is no evidence that he spoke French. Ralph Wilson Waugh, Attestation Papers, Australian National Archives.

[43] Testimony: Gremond, op. cit.

[44] Ibid.

[45] The high proportion of British born pre-war emigrant settlers who enlisted in the ANZAC forces and were encamped in the vicinity of Le Havre further complicates the issue of accents.

[46] Testimony: Gremond, op. cit.

[47] Ibid.

[48] Testimony: Lemoine.

[49] Testimony: Mills. Rather curiously, the WW1 British Army Medal Roll does not include a reference to Sgt. No.476111 F. Mills, Rifle Bde, the witness entered in the written proceedings. However, it does include Sapper No.476111 Harry Marshall, Royal Engineers. There were only two soldiers serving with the Rifle Bde., whose names match those of the witness: Sgt. No.211985 H.F. Mills and Pte. No.57287 F. Mills. Of Mills, Jefferis stated: 'Every endeavour is being made to trace this man ... but it is understood that he has been evacuated. If he cannot be traced Det. Sgt. Roberts who was present at the Identification parade when this man was selected will give the court the necessary particular.' FGCM: Opening Address by Prosecutor, p.2.

[50] Testimony: Lemoine, op. cit.

[51] Testimony: Defraey.

[52] Ibid.

[53] Testimony: Bergilez.

[54] Testimony: Adams (op. cit.), stated that he and L/Cpl. Woodgate had been walking from the Hotel de Ville along the Rue de Paris and were in the Place Gambetta when Waugh first met them.

[55] The winter equinox was 22 December 1917.

[56] Testimonies: Waugh; Ford.

[57] Statement, op. cit., Frambourg; Statement: Gremond (op. cit.). 'I picked up the table again.' With reference to the counterpane and sheet hanging out of the window, she stated, 'I unfastened these articles.' However, the latter sentence was struck out and initialled by Jefferis.

[58] Testimony: Waugh

[59] Testimony: Murray. Sgt. No.16027 Christopher Murray, R. Irish Fus., att. Chinese Labour Depot, Noyelles.

[60] Testimony: Smyth. Sgt. No.159 Robert Smyth, 11th Bn. R. Irish Rifs., att. 142nd POW Coy., Le Havre.

[61] Testimony: King. Sgt. No.8/15077 Mark King, 8th Bn. R. Irish Rifs.; to BEF, 2.10.15; att. No.2 Employment Base Depot, Harfleur.

[62] Ibid.

[63] Ibid., At 10.00pm a bugle call sounded Lights Out.

[64] Ibid.

[65] Testimony: Mallon. Sgt. No.2396 William Mallon, 2nd R. Innis. Fus.; to Balkans 24.5.15; WIA; att. 893rd Garr. Guard Coy., Cinder City Camp, Le Havre.

[66] Ibid.

[67] Op. cit., Statement: Smyth. The written proceedings and associated material in the trial dossier do not contain enough information about Sgt. Lynas to permit his identification, service affiliation or service details.

[68] Testimony: Barber. L/Cpl. No.1237 James H. Barber, 2nd Bn. King's Royal Rifle Corps; to BEF, 27.1.15. In the written proceedings he is incorrectly cited as No.1236.

[69] Ibid.

[70] Testimony: Gibson. Leonard Gibson, b. St. Albans, 1866; Capt., 9th Bn. R. Innis. Fus., 14.9.14; to BEF, 5.10.15; Camp Adjt., 3.3.16.

[71] Ibid.

[72] Testimony: Fitzpatrick.

[73] Ibid.

[74] Statements: Adams, Waugh and Fitzpatrick all said that the night had been 'dark' or 'very dark'.

[75] *Garamouched,* i.e. fellatio.

[76] Testimony: Defence: Gatehouse, Precis. Wickings' complaint was subsequently investigated and rejected. He was only kept in solitary confinement at night and issued with three blankets; his clothes were washed and he was only handcuffed 'when it was considered necessary for his own safety' and he was allocated a cigarette ration. FGCM, op. cit., Memo., APM, Havre Base, 25.2.18.

[77] Putkowski (1998), p.22; Putkowski (2002); Baxter, ch.5.

[78] MML (1914) Rules of Procedure, p.72, 4(E), f.n. 8.

[79] Testimony: Defence: Gatehouse, Precis, op. cit.

[80] Testimony: Defence, Wickings. Attestation Papers: Wickings. He was awarded a 3rd Class Army Cert. Educ. on 13.12.14.

[81] Wickings joined the Army in 1908 and had already served with the Rifle Brigade in India, Sudan and Ireland before embarking for France.

[82] Testimony: Defence, Wickings, op. cit.

[83] Testimony: Ford, op. cit.

[84] Ibid., (trans.): 'He was big like you, with a wound in the neck and also here [on the side of his nose], with a small moustache, [He had] three stripes [chevrons), he [sic] is a Sergeant.'

[85] Prosecution: Argument.

[86] Defence: Argument.

[87] John Sanctuary Nicholson, b. 1863; 2/Lt., 1884; Col., 1905; Commandant, Calais Base, 24.4.15; Commandant, Le Havre Base, 2.12.16. Joseph John Asser, b. 1867; ADC to GOC, Egypt, 1892; AAG, 1900; AG 1907-1914; Commandant, No.3 Base; Commandant, Boulogne Base, 13.10.14; Commandant, Le Havre Base, 18.7.15; Inspector General of Communications, Lines of Communication, 2.12.16.

[88] Arthur Wickings, Attestation Papers, op. cit. In 1908 his physical description refers to him having light brown hair, a fresh complexion and blue eyes.

[89] FGCM: Memo: Capt. C.W. Crowdy, CMO to DAAG, HQ, L. of C. Area, 17.2.18.

[90] Op. cit.: Report of Medical Board, Le Havre, 25.2.18.

[91] Putkowski (1998), pp.24-31.

[92] Baron Charles Francois Edouard Didelot, b. Brest, 1861; joined French Navy, 1878; Captain, 1900; Squadron Commander, 1908; Commandant, Cherbourg, 1914; Vice Admiral, 15.3.16; Marine Base Commandant and Mil. Govnr., Le Havre, 8.2.17.

[93] FGCM, op. cit., Didelot to M. le General de Division, Commanding the French Mil. Miss. att. to the British Army, 21.2.18.

[94] Ibid., Schedule.

Chapter 10

[1] WO 71/641 FGCM: Pte. J. Skone a.k.a. James Skone, b. Pembroke, 10.6.79; Pte. No.15071, South Wales Borderers, 15.10.14; to BEF 30.11.14; No.36224, 2nd Bn. Welsh Regt. The FGCM cites his forename as John but his family; Admiralty; WWI Medal Roll and the CWGC refer to his forename as James.

[2] Edwin Williams, b. Llantrisant; m. Hannah Mays, 1906; enl. Pontypridd, L/Sjt. No.25585, 2nd Bn. Welch Regt. He was buried in Beuvry Communal Cemetery, Grave III B3.

[3] Ibid., Schedule: Grenville Arthur Battock, b. Cookham, Berks., 1882; 4th Bn. R. Berks.; educ. Winchester; Trinity Coll., Oxford Univ., 1901;

Solicitor, 1910; Capt., 1910; to BEF, 28.3.15: Maj.; att. 1st Bn. Loyal N. Lancs., 19.4.16. Murdo McKenzie, Capt., 4th att. 1st Bn., Cam. Highlanders; George Henry Goldie, b. India, 1888; 2/Lt, 2nd Bn. Loyal N. Lancs, 1906; Lt., 1910; Lt., 1st Bn. Loyal N. Lancs.; Hugh Loveday Beazley, b. Birkenhead, 1880, educ. Cheltenham Coll.; Oriel Coll., Oxford Univ.; Barrister (Inner Temple), 1905; T/2Lt., King's L'pool; to BEF 1917; T/Capt, Gen. List & C.M.O., 8.1.18; T/Capt., Staff, 25.4.18; Claude Prichard Lewis, b. Brecon, 1882; Cashier, Metropolitan Bank, Cardiff; 2/Lt., 12th Bn. Welsh, 17.12.14; to BEF, 20.10.15; Lt., 2nd Bn., Welsh, 19.10.16. Louis Gurney Hoare, b. Jesmond, 1879; educ. Harrow, King's Coll., Cambridge Univ.; Barrister (Inner Temple), 1905; 2/Lt. (SR), 3rd Bn. D.L.I., 15.10.14; Lt., 12.10.15; T/Capt, 18.5.16; CMO, att. HQ, 1st Army, 25.4.18.

[4] Cpl. No.34428 Thomas Lynch, 2nd Bn. Welsh Regt.; to BEF, 20.10.15.

[5] L/Cpl. No, 1518 W. Smith, 2nd Bn. Welsh Regt.

[6] Pte. No.202463 Herbert Scrase, b. Cardiff, 1891; Butcher; 2nd Bn. Welsh Regt.

[7] Reginald Arthur Morrell, b, Bradfield, Berks, 1883; LRCP, MRCS 1908; T/Lt., RAMC, 1.2.15; to BEF, May 1915; Capt., RAMC, 1.2.16.

[8] MML. Chapter VII, Section 9.

[9] NYD(N): Not Yet Diagnosed, Nerves was one of a number of medical references used for shell shock.

[10] Ibid., Rules of Procedure, 13, sec.65 [A]; ibid., f.n. 3: 'The court, however, should not as a rule permit an adjournment for the purpose of obtaining further evidence on the part of the prosecution, and should only adjourn for the production of evidence for the accused, where they consider that he has not previously had sufficient opportunity for procuring his witnesses, or where it would be unjust to the accused not so to adjourn. Great care must be taken both by the prosecutor and by the accused, to have ready at the trial all the witnesses and documents they desire respectively to produce.'

[11] FGCM: Schedule, op.cit.

[12] Ibid., Herbert Horatio Shirley Morant, b. New Forest, Hants., 1870; 2.Lt., D.L.I.; Lt., 1892; Capt., 1899; Maj., 1910; Lt. Col., 10th Bn. D.L.I., 19.8.14; T/Brig. Gen., O.C. 3rd Inf. Bde., 29.1.18; Morant to O.C., 1st Div., 29.4.18. Edward Peter Strickland, b. 1869; 2/Lt., Norfolk Regt., 1888; Lt., 1891; Capt., 1899; Brev. Maj., 1899; Maj., 1908; Lt. Col., Manch. Regt., 1914; T/Brig. Gen., 4.1.15; T/Maj. Gen., 12.6.16; Maj. Gen., 1.1.18; Strickland to Corps 'A', 30.4.18. Arthur Edward

Aveling Holland, b. 1862; Lt., R.Arty., 1880; Capt., 1888; Maj., 1898; Lt. Col., 1905; Brev. Col., 1907; T/Brig. Gen., 1913; Maj. Gen., 1.1.16.; Holland, O.C., Lt. Gen.; Holland to D.A.A.G., 1st Army, 2.5.18. Henry Sinclair Horne, b. 1861; Lt., R.Arty., 1880; Capt., 1888; Maj., 1889; Brev. Lt. Col., 1900; Col., 1906; T/Brig. Gen., 1912; Maj. Gen., 26.10.14; T/Lt. Gen., 12.1.16; Lt. Gen., 1.1.17; T/Gen., 30.9.16. Horne to Adjutant General, 3.5.18.

[13] Joseph Harold Stops Westley, b. 1882; 2/Lt., Yorks., Regt., 1902; Lt., 1904; Capt. & Adjt., 1911; Brigade Maj., 23.7.15; D.A.A. & Q.M.G., 23.7.15; D.A.A.G., 5.2.16; Maj., 18.1.17. FGCM, op. cit., Westley, D.A.A.G., 1st Div., to HQ, 3rd Div., H.Q., 8.5.18.

[14] Ibid., Schedule. John Skone's father, James, latterly a boot and shoe repairer, died in 1916 and his widowed mother, Mary Skone, is recorded as living at 13 Thomas Street, Orange Gardens, Pembroke.

Chapter 11

[1] Family details from 1911 Census. Notwithstanding his father's declaration of widower status, the Commonwealth War Graves Commission notes that circa 1920, Mrs Annie Bell was still alive and residing at 84, Big Jug Yard, Claypath, Durham. On the Block Strike, see: 'The Strike',

Aberdare Leader, 12.11.10; http://webapps.rhondda-cynon-taff.gov.uk/heritagetrail/cynon/aberaman/aberaman.htm. See also: Evans & Maddox (2010).

[2] TNA, WO 71/640 FGCM: Spr. R.Bell, form AFB 122. George Stuart Knox, b. 1871; educ. Cheltenham College and RMA, Woolwich; 2/Lt., 1891; Lt., RE, 1894; Capt., 1902; Dir. Surveys, Brit. E. Africa 1906-12; Maj. 1911; Surveyor General, FMS, 1913-4; Lt Col, 19.5.16.

[3] On foraging, see: MacDonald (1998), pp.196-7, 330-1.

[4] Wynell Hastings Lloyd, b. 1894; educ. Malvern Coll., 1909-12; Apprenticed to an Architect; Pte. No. PS/622, R. Fus.; to BEF, 25.12.15; 2/Lt., RE, 9.1.16.

[5] FGCM, Schedule. Major Richard David Williams, b. 1879, educ. Aberystwyth U.C.; Capt., 12th Bn. Welsh Regt. 18.3.15; 13th Bn. Welsh Regt.; to BEF, 2.12.15; Maj., 14.9.17. Major Frederick Rainsford Hannay McLellan, b. Scotland, 1890; educ. Christ's Hosp. Sch.; Capt. OTC, 9.9.09; Maj., 16th Bn., RWF, 1.3.15; to BEF, 3.12.15. Evan Howells Evans, b. Aberdare, 1882; Solicitor; A/Sgt. No.4471, Pembroke Yeo.; A/Capt., 2nd Bn. RWF, 27.3.17. Douglas Cecil Rees Stuart, b. Kingston, 1885; educ. Cheltenham Coll. and Trinity Hall, Cambridge Univ.; Solicitor, 1909; 2/Lt., 1st Bn. Border Regt,, 22.7.15; WIA, July

1916; Lt., 1.7.17; T/Capt., 18.7.17. Lieutenant Claude Meeson, b. Rawreth, Essex, 1891; Solicitor, Battlebridge, Essex, 1913; Pte., 19th Bn. R. Fus., 16.9.14; 2/Lt., 38th MGC, 26.9.16; Lt., 26.3.18. Major John Chancellor Irving Wood, b. India, 1882; 2/Lt., R.E., 1901; Lt., 1904; Capt., 1911; Maj., 2.11.16.

[6] FGCM, Testimony: Pears. Spr. No.285582 Edward Richard Pears, b. Shoreditch, 1893; Pnr. No.285582; Pte. No.83833, RAMC; Spr. No.285582, 123rd Field Coy. RE.

[7] Ibid.

[8] Testimony: Ordish. 2nd Cpl. No.146629 Rowland Ordish, 123rd Field Coy. RE.

[9] Ibid.

[10] Testimony: Prior. Cpl. No.62629 Reuben Prior, 123rd Field Coy., RE.

[11] Ibid.

[12] Ibid.

[13] Testimony: Foster. CSM [No.4218 or 4215?] Foster [poss. No.4218 Sgt. John Flaherty?], 123rd Field Coy., RE. Reference to the cut-off suggests that Bell and his comrades had been issued with pre-1916 pattern rifles.

[14] Ibid.

[15] Testimony: Ferris. Sgt. No.82567 William R. Ferris, 123rd Field Coy., RE.

[16] Ibid.

[17] Testimony: Gold. Joseph Brand Gold, b. Rochester, Pa., USA, 1890; MD, US Army, Capt., att. Orthopaedic Unit, RAMC; to BEF, 12.8.17. *Gazette Times* (Pittsburgh), 15.5.19.

[18] Testimony: (sic) Shortt, i.e. Sapper No.140368 Walter E. Short, 123rd Field Coy., RE.

[19] Ibid., Defence.

[20] MML (1914), Ch.VII, sec.52, p.99.

[21] *Hansard,* House of Commons, Written Answers, 14.3.18, col.573.

[22] Maj. Gen. Charles Blackader, b. 1869; 2/Lt., Leics. Regt., 1888; Lt., 1890; Capt., 1895; Maj., 1904; Lt. Col., 1912; Col., 18.2.15; T/Brig. Gen., 27.5.15; T/Maj. Gen., 3.1.16; Maj. Gen., 1.1.18. Blackader was one the officers responsible for sentencing to death the Irish rebel leaders of Easter Rising in 1916. In Robert Bell's case, the other confirming officers were Lieutenant General Shute, OC 5th Corps and General Julian Byng, commanding 3rd Army and Field Marshal Haig.

[23] Claude Lewis Devenish Tully, b. Croydon, 1889; Asst. Sec., Boy Scouts Orgn.; T/Lt., 10th Bn. A. & S.H., 28.12.14; to BEF, 9.5.15; Capt.,

10.6.15; Capt., Gen. List & APM, 1.9.16. Blackader fell ill, so notification of the time and location of Bell's was forwarded by Brig. Gen. Henry Edward Ap Rhys Pryce, Indian Army, T/OC, 38th Division, 20-23.5.18.

Chapter 12

[1] Babington, op. cit. pp.184-6. For a breezy dismissal of Babington's mystification, see Corns & Hughes-Wilson, p.378. The transcript of Paterson's trial by GCM (TNA, WO 71/1028) was finally declassified in 1994.

[2] Nannestad, pp.3-6; Topical Budget, Clapton's Khaki Team; WO 339/111890, Attestation Papers & Service Record: John Henry Paterson, b. 22.5.90; Storekeeper; Pte. No. F/1239, 17th Bn. Middx. Regt.; enl. Kingsway, 6.4.15; to BEF, 17.11.15. *Police Gazette,* 23.6.18, p.3.; Riddoch & Kemp, pp.37-56, illus., pp.54 et seq.

[3] WO 339/111890, ibid., A' Company Conduct Sheet: 17th Bn. Middx. Regt.: Pte. No. F/1239 J. Paterson. See also Riddoch & Kemp, ibid., p.62.

[4] Annequin was a small coal mining village situated circa 8 kilometres East of Bethune. WO 95/1361, War Diary, 17th Bn., Middx. Regt., 2.2.16; WO 339/111890 Personal Record: 2/Lt. J.H. Paterson, Casualty Form – Active Service, refers to

Paterson being unfit due to 'ITC' [Interconnective Inflamed Tissue], 'Left Foot' and being treated at 100th Field Ambulance and No.6 Casualty Clearing Station, 8.2.16-23-2.16. He rejoined the battalion on 26.2.16.

[5] Riddoch & Kemp, op. cit., pp.117-128.

[6] WO 339/11890, op. cit., Paterson was discharged from No.13 General Hospital on 12.8.16. He contracted scabies during convalescence at No.41 IBD for which he was treated at No.20 Gen. Hosp. and discharged, 29.8.16. He rejoined the battalion on 1.9.16.

[7] Ibid., Paterson's Military History Sheet erroneously records him suffering a 'G[un] S[hot] W[ound] L[eft] Hand', 13.11.16 and 20.12.16. The attack was hampered by fog, a muddy terrain and uncut barbed wire. Over 300 (all ranks) were killed wounded or missing before the battalion was withdrawn. Wyrall, p.311; Riddoch & Kemp, op. cit., pp.162-178.

[8] Ibid.: Casualty Form. The 'Bullring' was a generic term applied to a battlefield combat skills training area. The Étaples Bullring regime was reckoned by many soldiers to be especially demanding. See: Putkowski (1986); Gill & Putkowski (1997).

[9] Ibid., Statement of Services: 2nd Lieutenant J.H. Paterson, 3rd att. 1st Bn. Essex Regt. The

military debacle at Bourlon Wood marked the end of the battle of Cambrai, in which 29th Division suffered 4,500 casualties and its commander barely escaped capture by the enemy. See: Moore, pp.143-164; Cave & Horsefall, (2001).

[10] For a contrary opinion see: Hughes-Wilson & Corns, p.378. On Paterson's movements, see: WO 71/1028, op. cit.: Officer's Advance Book.

[11] Maida Camp was one of a series of hutted encampments located immediately North-East of Kruisstraathoek.

[12] Ibid., GCM, Statement: Sidney Charles Appleton, b. Colchester, 1888; Pte. No.8272, 1st Bn. Essex Regt., 1910(?); India; Sgt. No.8272, 2nd Bn. Essex Regt.; to BEF, 24.8.14; WO Cl. 2, 1st Bn., Essex Regt. Shrapnel Corner was an exposed, dangerous road junction situated about one and a half kilometres S. of Ypres.

[13] Ibid., GCM: Officer's Advance Book, op. cit.; Statements: M. Capelle, Cashier, Banque de France, Calais and A.E. Giles, Representative, Cox & Co., London.

[14] *Police Gazette,* 23.6.18, p.3. William Stockton, b. Peckforton, Cheshire, 1882; Railway Policeman; L/Cpl. No. P/1199, MFP; to BEF, 3.6.15; att. GHQ, St. Omer. Harold Arthur

Collison, b. Staplehurst, Kent, 1877; Gnr. No.14573, RA, 1896; Policeman, Middlesborough, 1903; Police Sgt., 1912; Gnr. No.126485, RHA/RFA, 3.12.15; Pte. No. P/3479, MFP; to BEF, 30.7.16; att. APM, Boulogne, 1.8.16; Det. Sgt. No. P/3479, MFP; att. GHQ, St. Omer.

[15] WO 71/1208, op. cit., GCM, Testimony: Stockton.

[16] Ibid.

[17] Ibid., Testimony: Duquenoy.

[18] Personal File: H.A. Collison, Court of Enquiry, 9.7.18; WO 339/111890, op. cit., Circular Memorandum to all APMs: 2nd Lieutenant J.H. Paterson, GHQ, Great Britain, 15.7.18. WO 71/1208, op. cit., Translation No.1055, Extract from Proces-Verbal, Eugene Mollex, Commissaire Special, Chef du Service de Surete, att. 1(b) 2nd British Army., n.d.

[19] Francis Douglas Lumley, b. Fareham, Hants., 1857; 2/Lt., 1875; Brev. Col., 1904; Col., 1907; O.C. District, 1911; to BEF 7.12.15; Brig. Genl., 12.4.17; Hugh Rosceter Rice, b. Boston, Lincs., 1867; 2/Lt., Essex Regt., 1888; Lt., 1891; Capt., 1898; Maj., 1908; to Gallipoli, 1915; Lt. Col., 6.6.15; O.C. 1st Garr. Bn., N. Staffs., 11.5.16; Lt. Col., 4th Labour Group. William Bertram Squire Hickson, b. Islington,

London, 1873; Lt., Northants, 1898; Capt., 1901; Maj., 6th Bn. Northants., 16.3.15; to BEF, 24.7.15. Thomas Rothwell Paget-Tomlinson, b. Gt. Crosby, Lancs., 1875; educ. Aldenham Sch. & Trinity Coll., Cam. Univ.; JP (Westmorland), 1899; 2/Lt., RGA (W. Scotland), 1900; Lt., 1911; Maj., W'land & C'land Yeo., 21.12.14; to BEF, 25.5.17. Nicholas Augustine Leadbitter (-Smith), b. Brandon, Co. Durham, 1880; 2/Lt, 4th Bn. DLI; Lt., 1903; Capt., 3rd Bn. DLI, 1906; res. comm., 1908; Capt., 3rd Bn. DLI, 8.8.14; to BEF, May 1915; Staff Officer, 27.5.15; Chinese Lab. Corps, 4.5.17; T/Maj., Lab. Corps, 26.2.18. Walter Blake Odgers, b. 1880; educ. Sedburgh & Balliol Coll., Oxford Univ.; Barrister (Middle Temple), 1906; Pte. No.6/7803, Inns of Court OTC; 2/Lt, RASC, 29.3.16; to BEF, 10.10.16; Lt., 1st Aux. Horse, Rouen, 23.6.17; Capt. & CMO, Gen. List., 7.12.17. Ernest Edward Green, Solicitor, 1906; Capt., 1.1.12; Capt., 7th Bn. Welsh Regt., 4.8.14; Staff Capt., 7.7.15; T/Maj., 16.9.15; Maj., 1.6.16. Ernest Percival Walsh, b. Bicester, Oxon., 1876; educ. Rossall Sch.; Solicitor's Clerk, 1901; Barrister (Inner Temple); 2/Lt., Gen. List, 20.10.16; CMO.

[20] WO 71/1208, GCM, op. cit., Schedule.

[21] Ibid., Testimony: Appleton.

[22] Ibid., Testimony: Stockton.

[23] Ibid.

[24] Ibid.

[25] Ibid.

[26] Ibid.

[27] Ibid., Testimony: Augustine Duquenoy.

[28] Ibid.

[29] Ibid.

[30] Personal File: H.A. Collison, Court of Enquiry, op. cit.: Statement of Augustine Duquenoy.

[31] Testimony: Augustine Duquenoy, op. cit.

[32] Statement: Augustine Duquenoy.

[33] Ibid.

[34] Ibid.

[35] Ibid., Testimony: Neomi Duquenoy.

[36] Ibid., Testimony: Lt. J.G. Allen. John Gibson Allan, b. 1888, Scotland; educ., Edinburgh Univ., BSc., 1910; MB, ChB., 1917; Lt., RAMC (SR), 16.8; to BEF, 14.10.17; Capt., 16.8.18.

[37] Ibid., Testimony: Pryce. Arthur Meurig Pryce, b. Carmarthen, 1878; educ. Clifton Coll., Aberystwyth Univ.; MB, ChB (Edin.), 1903; MD; Lt., RAMC, 4.3.15; to BEF, 1.12.15; Capt., 4.3.16.

[38] Ibid., Testimony: Pte. No.53904 E. Roper, 2nd. Bedford Regt., i.e. Pte. Edward Roper, 2nd Bn. S. Lancs. Regt.; to BEF, 5.12.14; No.68700, Liverpool Regt.; No.43594, Bedfordshire Regt.

[39] Ibid., Testimony: Mollex.

[40] Ibid., Testimony: Campbell. John Campbell, Pte. No.3/2561, Royal Highlanders; to BEF, 4.8.15; Pte. No. S/41046, 11th Bn. A&SH.

[41] Ibid., Testimony: Landan, i.e. Pte. No.202616 Jack Karl Landau, 5th Bn. North Staffs. Regt.

[42] Ibid., Testimony: Stockton.

[43] Ibid., Testimony: Paterson.

[44] Ibid., Prosecution: Closing Address.

[45] Ibid., Judge Advocate: Summation.

[46] Ibid., Testimony: Sword. Percy Sword, b. Trowse, Norfolk, 1890; Mill Sawyer; Pte. No.23996, Norfolks; Cpl. No.32974, 1st Bn. Essex Regt.; KIA, 8.10.18.

[47] Ibid., Eusabius A. Andrewes, b. 1875; 2/Lt, 5th Bn. Northumberland Fus.; Lt., 22.11.05; Capt., Northants Yeo., 1.4.14; Adjt., 26.8.14; Staff Capt. (DAPM), 28.3.17; T/Maj. 23.7.18. 2/Lt. J.H. Paterson: Certificate of Death: 2nd Lieut. J.H. Paterson.

[48] Collison's war service record (op. cit.) notes he worked peripatetically, attached to various

Army HQs; the London Gazette, 10.6.18 notes he was awarded a DCM for investigating looting of corpses. 1911 Census: Louisa Esther Collison (nee Perkins) and two children lived in Middlesborough.

[49] Ibid., Translation No.1055, Extract from Proces-Verbal, op. cit.: '7 postcards 2 of which bearing the mention "to my dear Jim" and signed "Augustine". This Christian name applies to the woman the photo of which is one of the postcards and not to the one called Allienne.'

[50] Ibid., Statement: Augustine Duquenoy; Personal File: H.A. Collison, op. cit., Statement of Augustine Duquenoy.

[51] Corns & Hughes-Wilson, op. cit., pp.377-8.

[52] West Ham Registry Office, Wedding Cert.: Alice Willett, b. Forest Gate, 1879, eldest dau. of May Ann and Arthur Willett, Builder, Leytonstone m. James Henry Paterson, s. of Joseph Paterson (dec'd.), Builder, 12.11.17. A photograph of the newlyweds was subsequently cropped and featured alongside the groom's personal details in the *Police Gazette.*

[53] WO 339/111890, op. cit., Telegram: WO to Mrs Alice Paterson, 13 Matcham Road, West Ham, 18.4.18; Letters: Alice Paterson to WO, MS3. Cas/518 (A), 5.8.18; WO, MS3. Cas/518 (A) (to Alice Paterson), 8.8.18; WO, MS3.

Cas/518 (A) (to Alice Paterson), 3.10.18; WO, MS3. Cas. to Alice Paterson, 4.10.18; Alice Paterson to WO, 20.10.18.

[54] Ibid., Letters: H.E.A. Phillips to WO, MS3. Cas., 23.10.18; WO, MS3. Cas. to H.E.A. Phillips, 23.10.18.

[55] Ibid., in Draft Letter: WO to Mrs Alice Paterson, 25.11.18 reference to Paterson's 'murder of a soldier and forgery' was crossed out. For her husband's service in the ranks, in March 1920 the WO awarded Mrs Paterson a £20 gratuity.

[56] Ibid., WO Memo. re: Cox & Co., Claim for £52. 4/8d, initialled F.M.R, 18.2.20; Letter: Anderson & Sons, Edinburgh to WO, 27.5.19.

[57] Ibid., No.211008/61 – WO Effects Form 107, (sd.) Alice Paterson, 24.9.18.

[58] 1911 Census: Home address: 81 Ham Park Road, West Ham.

[59] Op. cit., Attestation Papers: John Henry Paterson.

[60] WO Memo. re: Cox & Co., op. cit.. See also Payments on Account, 17.12.17-5.6.18.

Conclusion

[1] MML (1914), Ch.II, sec.2, p.6.

[2] See Wilson's comments about Ptes. Dale and Barnes' observations about Pte. Reid.

[3] See Appendix 3.

Appendix 1

[1] If a special plea about the general jurisdiction of the court was offered by the Accused, and found by the court to be proved, the court referred the matter to the Convening Officer for consultation.

[2] Army Act, Part I, section 51 (1). Any Accused may object, for reasonable cause to any member of the court.

[3] e.g. WO 71/673 FGCM Pte. Ernest Jackson, Memo: J[ohn].B[artholomew].W[roughton]. to A[djutant]. G[eneral], 26.10.18.

APPENDIX 1

Courts Martial Procedure

Wartime field general courts martial generally required a minimum of three officers to be empanelled and, after 1914, in many capital cases a court martial officer was on hand to provide legal advice.

General courts martial convened overseas required five or more commissioned officers and the attendance of a judge advocate, an expert in military law, who presented a summary of legal issues before the President and Members retired to consider their verdict. Trial by field general court martial tended to be comparatively brief and as Appendix 3 indicates, general courts martial were mostly convened to try officer-defendants.

Aside from the role of the Judge Advocate General and interventions by a Prisoner's Friend, there was otherwise procedurally little difference between field general courts martial and general courts martial.

Proceedings before the trial

The Members of the Court read the charge sheet and particulars, comparing them with the corresponding section of the Army Act, ensuring that the charges have been correctly framed and worded. The court was also required to familiarize itself with the relevant sections of the *Manual of Military Law,* analyse the charges and note particular points that had to be proved by the evidence in order to convict.[1]

The Members had to satisfy themselves that the court was duly constituted. A defendant, the prosecuting officer and any witnesses and interpreters were admitted and the Convening Order was read out. A defendant was informed of his 'right of challenge' and asked if he wished to avail himself of the right.[2] If there was no objection by a defendant, the Members of the Court were sworn. Then everyone except a defendant, his escort, the prosecuting officer and the Prisoner's Friend were ushered out of court and a defendant was formally arraigned and required to plead.

Procedure on a plea of guilty

If a defendant entered a guilty plea to a non-capital offence, the court made a formal finding of guilty and the Summary of Evidence was admitted. If there was no Summary, sufficient evidence was taken under oath to enable the Convening Officer to judge the gravity of the offence. A defendant could then make a statement and call witnesses to testify about his character. Thereafter, the court would close and the Members would consider their findings. After their deliberations the court re-opened and announced its verdict.

Evidence of character, particulars of service, and details of disciplinary offences recorded on a Field Conduct Sheet were admitted. The defendant was then asked if he wished to say anything in mitigation and his statement was entered in the written proceedings. The sentence of the court was then announced.

Procedure on a plea of not guilty

After February 1915, if a defendant faced a capital charge, a formal plea of not guilty was entered in the record. The prosecution presented its case and summoned witnesses to testify and after direct examination, the defence could conduct a cross-examination. All questions addressed to the witness by the court had to be posed by the President; no other Member was permitted to directly question a witness.

A Defendant then had four options:

(a) He could give evidence on oath and be cross-examined by the prosecution and questioned by the court.

(b) He could make a statement to the court not on oath. This was not subject to cross-examination and in the court's deliberations an unsworn statement would carry less weight than a sworn statement.

(c) He could submit a written statement.

(d) He could exercise his right to silence and say nothing.

The accused could then call any witnesses, including character witnesses, whose testimony had to be confined only to the general reputation of the accused.

Evidence of character, particulars of service, and the defendant's Field Conduct Sheet were admitted. A defendant was invited to make a statement in mitigation, which was entered in the written proceedings. The sentence of the court was then announced. If the finding was found not guilty, the President announced the verdict and a defendant was released. The proceedings would then be signed by the Judge Advocate, if one was present. When a defendant was found guilty of a capital offence, the President and Members had to be unanimous in deciding to award a death sentence. In all cases in which a defendant was found guilty, the written proceedings and outcome of the trial was referred to the confirming authority and the prisoner was detained in custody until his sentence was confirmed.

Proceedings after sentence

After confirmation, a dossier containing the pro forma schedule, written proceedings and sentence was passed up the chain of command. At each stage, a confirming officer was invited to reflect on the sentence but not the verdict. Confirming officers were required to consider the gravity of the offence; the convicted man's performance as a soldier; the morale and discipline of the formation to which he belonged; the sentence passed by the court and any recommendation to mercy. Thereafter, the trial dossier was reviewed by the Judge Advocate or Deputy Judge Advocate General, who verified that the proceedings were legally sound, and in some cases comments by the Director of Personal Services were also attached to the dossier.[3] Finally, if the Commander-in-Chief decided the execution should go ahead, his confirmation was communicated to the Assistant Provost Marshal and other relevant authorities, and the condemned man was informed about the outcome, usually during the late afternoon or early evening before he was executed. In some cases a victim's unit was immediately informed about the killing but more generally the news was circulated throughout the Army via a posthumous entry in Army Routine Orders and announcements to troops on parade.

APPENDIX 2

Sites of Mourning

Location	*Unit or Formation*	*Died*	*Grave*
Bethune Town Cem			
HAYES, Hughie Job	2nd Bn Welsh Regt	21.1.15	3/B/62
MORGAN, Richard Pte	2nd Bn Welsh Regt	15.2.15	4/A/17
PRICE, William L/Cpl	2nd Bn Welsh Regt	15.2.15	4/A/18
Bailleul Communal Cem Extension			
LEWIS, Robert	20th Fortress Coy, RE	5.5.15	11/A/172
Chapelle d'Armentieres Old Military Cem			
CHISHOLM, Alexander A/Cpl	20th Fortress Coy, RE	17.5.15	B/27
Eecke Churchyard			
EDWARDS, Alfred Pte	10th Bn Royal Welsh Fus	3.11.15	A/3
Le Grand Hazard Military Cem, Morbecque			
KNIGHT, Charles William Pte	10th Bn Royal Welsh Fus	15.11.15	3/B/9
Poperinghe New Military Cem			
PICK, James A/Staff Sgt Farrier	4th Coy, ASC, 24th Div Train**	11.2.16	1/F/12
Menin Gate Memorial			
MOORE, Thomas Pte	4th Coy, ASC, 24th Div Train	26.2.16	
Chocques Mil Cem			
SNEDDON, James L/Cpl	13th Bn Royal Scots	7.2.16	1/H/93
Mazingarbe Communal Cem			
DALE, Arthur Pte	13th Bn Royal Scots	3.3.16	103
Barlin Communal Cem Extension			
DAMPER, William	173rd Tunnelling Coy, RE	2.9.16	1/D/5
Noeux-les-Mines Communal Cem			
MURRAY, Francis Pte	9th Bn Gordon Highlanders att RE	1.10.16	1/P/2
Rubempre Communal Cem			
KEAN, James Henry Pte	16th Bn Highland Light Inf	5.1.17	3

Location	*Unit or Formation*	*Died*	*Grave*
Bertrancourt Military Cem			
REID, Alexander Pte	16th Bn Highland Light Inf	31.1.17	2/A/17
La Chapelette British & Indian Cem, Peronne			
McCAIN, Thomas CSM	50th Field Searchlight Coy, RE	14.7.17	1/G/5
Coxyde Military Cem			
OYNS, Arthur Philip Spr	50th Field Searchlight Coy, RE	20.10.17	IV/G/24
Le Havre			
TREMEREL, Henriette Mme	Civilian	19.12.17	N/K
Ste Marie Cem, Le Havre			
WICKINGS, Arthur L/Sgt	9th Rifle Bde	7.3.18	Div.62.1.K.3
Beuvry Communal Cem Extension			
WILLIAMS, Edwin L/Sjt	2nd Bn Welsh Regt	13.4.18	III.B.3
Hersin Communal Cem Extension			
SKONE, James [John] Pte	2nd Bn Welsh Regt	10.5.18	3/B/1
Warloy-Baillon Communal Cem Extension			
LLOYD, Wynell Hastings 2/Lt	123red Field Coy, RE	17.4.18	II.E4
Toutencourt Communal Cem			
BELL, Robert Spr	123rd Field Coy, RE	22.5.18	2/A/9
Les Baraques Military Cem, Sangatte			
COLLISON, Harold Arthur A/Sjt DCM, MSM	Military Foot Police, GHQ Staff	3.7.18*	IV/C/13
Terlincthun British Military Cem			
PATERSON, John [James] Henry 2/Lt	3rd att 1st Bn Essex Regt	24.9.18	IV/B/48

*CWGC cites 4.7.18
**aka 197th Coy; CWGC states 192nd Coy

APPENDIX 3

Statistics

British Army Officer & Other Ranks Court-Martialled for Captial Offences other than Murder 1914-1918**

Offence & charge	*4.11.14-30.9.14*	*1.10.14-30.9.15*	*1.10.15-30.9.16*	*1.10.16-30.9.17*	*1.10.17-30.9.18*	*1.10.18-11.11.18**	*Total*
General Courts Martial							
Officers:							
Mutiny							nil
Cowardice		2	4	1	2		9
Desertion			7	3	3	5#	18
Striking			2	1			3
Quitting/Sleeping Post	1	1	5	2	9	1#	18
						Total	**48**
Other Ranks:							
Mutiny		7	20	13	2	084#	126
Cowardice							2
Desertion			2				
Striking		4	6	1	2	2#	15
Quitting/Sleeping Post		1					1
						Total	**144**
Field General Courts Martial							
Officers:							
Mutiny							nil
Cowardice							nil
Desertion					1	2#	3
Striking				1			1
Quitting/Sleeping Post							nil
						Total	**4**
Field General Courts Martial							
Other Ranks:							
Mutiny		6	19	98	383	168*	506
Cowardice		126	136	161	90	14*	513
Desertion	1	380	881	1555	2596	409*	5413
Striking	5	568	1505	1326	1723	257*	5127
Quitting/Sleeping Post	2	1453	2040	1221	862	129*	5578
						Total	**17137**
District Courts Martial (not empowered to award death sentences)							
Other Ranks:							
Mutiny			1				1
Cowardice							
Desertion	13	28	16	20	55	7*	132
Striking	7	141	96	156	188	28*	588
Quitting/Sleeping Post	9	108	59	37	32	5*	245
						Total	**nil**
				Total:	*52 Officers*	*17178 Other Ranks*	

**Derived from TNA Files: W0213/25-28 official Statistics: All overseas theatres of operations. Between August 1914 and November 1918 no British Army officers or soldiers were condemned to death or executed after being tried by courts martial convened in the United Kingdom. After 11 November 1918, official policy decreed that death sentences passed by courts martial on British military personnel was only liable to be confirmed in cases involving murder or mutinies that involved loss of life.

*estimated (based on the 1918 monthly average) #figs.1.10.18-30.09.19

Offence & charge	*4.11.14-30.9.14*	*1.10.14-30.9.15*	*1.10.15-30.9.16*	*1.10.16-30.9.17*	*1.10.17-30.9.18*	*1.10.18-11.11.18**	*Total*
Punishments Awarded							
Totals: 4.8.14-11.11.18	Death Penal Servitude:						
		3 years	6 years	9 years	12 years	15 years	Life
Officers: GCM	2	1*	2		1*		
Other Ranks: GCM	6	3*	8*		2*	2*	1*
Officers: FGCM		1					
Other Ranks FGCM	357*	1216*	2450*	358*	1519*	390*	104*
	Imprisonment with Hard Labour, Detention or Imprisonment:						
	6 months IHL	12 months IHL	18 months IHL	24 months Imp	6 mos Detn./Imp		
Officers: GCM	3*	4*	3*	1	1		
Other Ranks: GCM	6*	10*	7*		2*		
Officers: FGCM				1			
Other Ranks FGCM	302*	6298*	1237*	4670*	7412*		
	Imprisonment or Detention:						
	12 months Imp	18 months Imp	24 months Imp	3 months Detn	6+ months Detn.		
Officers: GCM					2*		
Other Ranks: GCM			28*	9*	4*		
Officers: FGCM							
Other Ranks FGCM	128*	27*	79*	509*	60*		

Bibliography

UNPUBLISHED SOURCES

The National Archives, Kew

WO 71/437 Knight: FGCM
WO 71/446 Moore: FGCM
WO 71/415 Chisholm: FGCM
WO 71/451 Dale: FGCM
WO 71/504 Murray: FGCM
WO 71/540 Reid: FGCM
WO 71/603 Oyns: FGCM
WO 71/636 Wickings: FGCM
WO 71/640 Bell: FGCM
WO 71/641 Skone: FGCM
WO 71/1028 Paterson: GCM
WO 329/Service Medal and Award Roll 1914-1918
WO 339/111890 Paterson: Attestation & Service
and Official War Diaries (series WO 95)

Australian War Memorial & Australian National Archives

ANZAC Attestation papers and records of service

Film

Topical Budget: *Clapton's Khaki Team* (Youtube.com)

PUBLISHED SOURCES

Newspapers

Aberdare Leader
British Medical Journal
Forward
Gazette Times (Pittsburgh)
Guardian
Le Petit Havre
Police Gazette

Official Publications & Works of Reference

Addison, G.H. (ed.), *Work of the Royal Engineers in the European War, 1914-1918, vol.8,* (miscellaneous) (Chatham, Inst. of Royal Engineers, 1926)

Army Lists and *Indian Army Lists* (various)

Becke, A.F. (ed.), *History of the Great War based on Official Documents by Direction of the Historical Section of the Committee of Imperial Defence – Order of Battle,* Pts. 1-4 (London, HMSO, 1935-1945)

Commonwealth War Graves Commission, *War Graves Registers* (various)

King's Regulations, 1914, (London, HMSO, 1914)

Manual of Military Law, 1914 edn, (London, HMSO, 1914)

Mitchell, T.J. & Smith, G.M., (1931) *Medical History of the War: Casualties & Medical Statistics* (London, HMSO, 1931)

Parliamentary Papers (Hansard)

Report of the Committee Constituted by the Army Council to Enquire into the Law and Rules of Procedure Regulating Military Courts Martial (London, HMSO, 919)

Report of the War Office Committee of Enquiry into Shell Shock (London, HMSO, 1922)

Soldiers Died in the Great War, (London, HMSO, re-printed J.B. Hayward, 1988)

Who's Who and *Who Was Who* (various)

Young, M., *Army Service Corps 1902-1918* (London, Leo Cooper, 2000)

Articles & Essays

Berkovic, S. & Crompton, D.E., The borderland of epilepsy: A clinical and molecular view, 100 years on, *Epilepsia,* 51, S.1, Feb. 2010

Gill, D. & Dallas, G., Mutiny at Etaples Base in 1917, *Past & Present,* Nov.1975

Harrison, M., The British Army and Venereal Disease during the First World War, *Medical History,* 39, 1995

Nannestad, I., 'The charge at Football is good, that with the bayonet finer': The formation of the Footballers' Battalion, 1914, *Soccer History,* 1, Spring 2002

Putkowski, J.J., Toplis, Etaples and the "Monocled Mutineer", *Stand To!,* 18, Winter 1986

Books

Babington, A., *For the Sake of Example: Capital Courts Martial 1914-18, The Truth* (London, Leo Cooper, 1983)

Baxter, A., *We Will Not Cease: The Autobiography of a Conscientious Objector* (London, Gollancz, 1939)

Berliere, J-M., *Le Préfet Lépine: aux origines de la police moderne* (Paris, Denoël, 1993)

Blackburne, H.W., *This also happened on the Western Front* (London, Hodder & Stoughton, 1932))

Bourke, J., *An Intimate History of Killing* (London, Granta Books, 1999)

Burton, F.N. & Comyns, A.P., *The War Diary (1914-1918) of 10th (Service) Battalion, Royal Welsh Fusiliers* (Plymouth, Brendon & Sons, 1926)

Cave, N. & Horsefall, J., *Bourlon Wood* (Barnsley, Pen & Sword Books, 2001)

Chalmers, T. (ed), *A Saga of Scotland – History of the 16th Battalion, the Highland Light Infantry* (Glasgow, McCallum, 1931)

Corbin, A., *Women for Hire: Prostitution and Sexuality in France after 1850* (Rhode Island, Univ. Harvard Press, 1990)

Corns C. & Hughes-Wilson, J., *Blindfold and Alone: British Military Executions in the Great War* (London, Cassell, 2001)

Crase, W.F. & Roome, H.D., *Archbold* [J.F.]: *Summary of the Law Relative to Pleading and Evidence in Criminal Cases* (24th edn, London, 1910)

Evans, G. & Maddox, D., *The Tonypandy Riots 1910-1911* (Plymouth, Univ. Plymouth Press, 2010)

Dunn, J.C., *The War the Infantry Knew* (London, Cardinal, 1989 edn)

Gill, D., & Dallas, G., *The Unknown Army* (London, Verso, 1985)

Gill, D. & Putkowski, J.J., *Le Camp Britannique d'Etaples* (Etaples, Musee Quentovic, 1997)

Gowers, W., *The Borderland of Epilepsy* (London, Churchill, 1907)

Graves, R., *Good-Bye to All That* (London, Jonathan Cape, 1929)

Hanna, E., *The Great War on the Small Screen* (Edinburgh, Edinburgh University Press, 2009)

Howard, M. (ed), A *Part of History* (London, Continuum, 2008)

Leonard, J. & Leonard-Johnson, P. (eds), *The Fighting Padre* (Barnsley, Pen & Sword Books, 2010)

MacDonald, L., *To the Last Man: Spring 1918* (London, Viking, 1998)

Marden, T.O., *History of the Welch Regiment,* vol.2, 1914-1918 (Cardiff, *Western Mail & Echo,* 1932)

Millen, J., *The Story of Bell Buddle Gully Weir* (Auckland NZ, Bell Gully, 1990)

Mitchinson, K.W., *Pioneer Battalions in the Great War* (Barnsley, Leo Cooper/Pen & Sword Books, 1997)

Moore, W., *The Thin Yellow Line* (London, Leo Cooper, 1974)

Moore, W., *A Wood Called Bourlon: the Cover-up After Cambrai, 1917* (London, Leo Cooper, 1988)

Oram, G.C., *Military Executions During World War 1* (London, Palgrave Macmillan, 2003)

Osler W., *The Principles and Practice of Medicine* (8th edn, London, Appleton, 1916)

Putkowski, J.J. & Sykes, J., *Shot at Dawn* (London, Leo Cooper/Pen & Sword, 1989)

Putkowski, J.J., *British Army Mutineers* (London, Francis Boutle, 1989)

Putkowski, J.J., *Les Fusilles de King Crater* (vol.2): *L'incident de King Crater et les cours martiales de la Somme* (Louviers, Editions Ysec, 2002)

Riddoch, A., & Kemp, J., *When the Whistle Blows: the Story of the Footballers' Battalion in the Great War* (Yeovil, Haynes Publishing, 2008)

Sambrook, J., *With the Rank and Pay of a Sapper* (Nuneaton, Paddy Griffiths Associates, 1998)

Stanley, P., *Bad Characters* (Millers Point, Murdoch Books, 2010)

Walker, S., *Forgotten Soldiers* (Dublin, Gill & Macmiillan, 2007)

Wyrall, E., *The Die-Hards (Middlesex Regiment) in the Great War* (London, Harrison, 1926-30)

Printed in Dunstable, United Kingdom

91343669R00275